"Dr. George Giuliani has written the best book I have ever read in the area of special education law. Practical, concise, and user-friendly, this book represents an exciting and up-to-date approach to addressing the legal issues faced by children with special needs. Dr. Giuliani explains the complexity of the special education process incredibly well, making it easy to understand. As a college professor and professional in the area of special education for the past 40 years, I believe that this book will become an authority in the field. This is a phenomenal book and I give it my highest recommendation."

—*Roger Pierangelo, PhD, Associate Professor in the Department of Special Education and Literacy at Long Island University and Executive Director of the National Association of Special Education Teachers, USA*

"As a former colleague and beneficiary of Dr. Giuliani's clear and succinct writing, presented in textbooks that I have employed in several of my graduate courses, I must commend him, once again, for providing another lucid 'gem' in *The Comprehensive Guide to Special Education Law*. The distinctive conversational style employed provides the reader with a 'user-friendly' approach to a subject that can be difficult to comprehend and, consequently, to navigate and use effectively. I believe that this book will serve as an invaluable resource for parents, teachers, and related service providers. My congratulations, then, to Dr. Giuliani for authoring such a lucid and comprehensible guide to what can seem, at times, an enigmatic and complex subject. To my knowledge, no similar exposition exists and, thus, Dr. Giuliani's guide addresses a critical need."

—*Vance L. Austin, PhD, Associate Professor and Chair of the Special Education Department, Manhattanville College, New York*

"This is a thorough, easy-to-understand book which is perfect not only for educators and administrators in the field, but also for parents who are newly navigating the often difficult world of special education. As a practicing school psychologist, these are answers to the questions I get asked on an almost daily basis. A wonderful resource!"

—*Kelly McCabe-Fitch, PhD, School Psychologist and Adjunct Professor of Psychology, Long Island, New York*

"Dr. George Giuliani has written a tremendously insightful and comprehensive book on special education law. It is very easy to read and user-friendly. It is clear that he did a great deal of research in putting this book together. It is well thought out and written in an easy-to-read format. Dr. Giuliani makes understanding the special education process—which can be overwhelming—simple and easy to grasp and he does a great job laying things out in a step-by-step fashion. As a Child and Adolescent Psychiatrist who often works with parents of children with special needs, it is my professional and personal opinion that Dr. Giuliani's book really clarifies the legal issues and rights of exceptional children. This is an excellent guide for anyone interested in special education law. I highly recommend it!"

—*Robert D. Colucci, DO, Child and Adolescent Psychiatrist, New York*

"Knowledge is power! *The Comprehensive Guide to Special Education Law* empowers professionals and parents. It levels the playing field for anyone who needs to be aware of the legal issues facing children with disabilities. Making informed educational decisions for a child when confronted with the reality that he or she has special needs can be overwhelming. Dr. Giuliani has dissected an extremely complex set of laws and procedures and consolidated them into a practical and simple straight-forward book. *The Comprehensive Guide to Special Education Law* is a must-have resource."

—*Michael E. Bergman, Esq., Partner, Bergman, Bergman, Goldberg, & Lamonsoff, LLP, New York*

"Finally! A comprehensive yet practical, to-the-point, legal reference book for all special education stakeholders: parents, special educators, school administrators, advocates, lawyers, students, and academics. Dr. Giuliani has thoughtfully compiled the essential questions about special education law—regarding its substance, process, and practice— that are raised in schools and homes every day, and provided the answers to those questions in a direct and eminently understandable way. The Q&A format keeps this book fresh. I will use it in my practice and in my classroom."

—*Matthew J. Delforte, Special Education Attorney, Shebitz Berman Cohen & Delforte, P.C., and Adjunct Professor of Law at Hofstra University School of Law, New York*

"Dr. Giuliani's book is packed with useful information about education law. The book explains complex legal topics in a way that is easy to understand and informative. The FAQ format enables the reader to quickly locate the information they are looking for. This book is a must-have for parents and professionals alike."

—*Nicholas J. Agro, Esq., Education Attorney, New York*

The Comprehensive Guide to **Special Education Law**

of related interest

A Guide to Special Education Advocacy
What Parents, Clinicians and Advocates Need to Know
Matthew Cohen
ISBN 978 1 84310 893 1
eISBN 978 1 84642 921 7

Challenges to the Human Rights of People with Intellectual Disabilities
Edited by Frances Owen and Dorothy Griffiths
Foreword by Orville Endicott
ISBN 978 1 84310 590 9
eISBN 978 1 84642 886 9

Kids in the Syndrome Mix of ADHD, LD, Asperger's,
Tourette's, Bipolar, and More!
The One Stop Guide for Parents, Teachers, and Other Professionals
Martin L. Kutscher MD
ISBN 978 1 84310 810 8 (hardback)
ISBN 978 1 84310 811 5 (paperback)
eISBN 978 1 84642 241 6

Alphabet Kids: From ADD to Zellweger Syndrome
A Guide to Developmental, Neurobiological and Psychological
Disorders for Parents and Professionals
Robbie Woliver
ISBN 978 1 84310 880 1 (hardback)
ISBN 978 1 84905 822 3 (paperback)
eISBN 978 1 84642 887 6

Common SENse for the Inclusive Classroom
How Teachers Can Maximise Existing Skills to Support Special Educational Needs
Richard Hanks
ISBN 978 1 84905 057 9
eISBN 978 0 85700 247 1

The Comprehensive Guide to **Special Education Law**

Over 400 Frequently Asked Questions and Answers Every Educator Needs to Know about the Legal Rights of Exceptional Children and their Parents

George A. Giuliani

Jessica Kingsley *Publishers*
London and Philadelphia

First published in 2012
by Jessica Kingsley Publishers
116 Pentonville Road
London N1 9JB, UK
and
400 Market Street, Suite 400
Philadelphia, PA 19106, USA

www.jkp.com

Library of Congress Cataloging in Publication Data
Giuliani, George A., 1938-
  The comprehensive guide to special education law : answering over 400 frequently asked questions about the legal rights of exceptional children and their parents / George A. Giuliani.
     p. cm.
  Includes bibliographical references and index.
  ISBN 978-1-84905-882-7 (alk. paper)
  1. Children with disabilities--Education--Law and legislation--United States--Miscellanea. 2. Special education--Law and legislation--United States--Miscellanea. I. Title.
  KF4210.G58 2012
  344.73'0791--dc23
                    2011049441

British Library Cataloguing in Publication Data
A CIP catalogue record for this book is available from the British Library

ISBN 978 1 84905 882 7
eISBN 978 0 85700 585 4

Printed and bound in the United States

This book is dedicated to my wife, Anita, and two children, Collin and Brittany, who give me the greatest life imaginable. The long hours and many months it took to finish this book would never have been possible without the support of my loving wife. Anita's constant encouragement, understanding, and love provide me with the strength I need to accomplish my goals. I thank her with all my heart.

Contents

a "reasonable effort" to obtain parental consent? 75; When is parental consent not required? 76; What if parents don't give their consent? 76; Can parental consent be revoked? 77; Is revocation of consent retroactive? 77; Does the requirement that a public agency obtain parental consent for the initial provision of special education and related services mean that parents must consent to each service included in the initial IEP developed for their child? 78; What recourse is available to parents who consent to the initial provision of special education and related services but who disagree with a particular service or services in their child's IEP? 78; May a foster parent provide consent for an initial evaluation even if the biological parent refuses to provide such consent? 79

5 Identification, Evaluations, and Independent Educational Evaluations of Children with Suspected Disabilities　　　80

he/she objects to the public evaluation, is the parent required to give a reason? 93; Whenever an IEE is made at public expense, must the school district criteria for evaluations be met? 93; If parents disagree with the school district's evaluation, in what ways can they proceed to obtain the IEE? 93; How many publicly funded IEEs are parents entitled to for each time an LEA evaluation is conducted over which there is disagreement? 94; Can parents get an IEE at their own expense? 94; If an IEE is paid for by the parent, must it be considered by the school district in determining the child's educational needs? 94; Who is responsible for payment of an IEE when it is requested by a hearing officer? 94

8 Individualized Education Programs (IEPs)   142

9 The Least Restrictive Environment (LRE) 167

that meets the requirements? 201; What is the SEA's obligation when it receives a state complaint? 201; What are the timelines for filing a state complaint? 201; How soon must the SEA resolve a state complaint? 202; Can the public agency attempt to resolve the complaint before an investigation occurs? 203; Must a state complaint be investigated if it is resolved through mediation? 203; What happens if a state complaint and a due process complaint are filed to resolve the same issue? 203; Can the SEA's decision be appealed? 204

V. Resolution meeting 204

What is a resolution meeting? 204; Does the resolution process apply when a public agency (e.g. school district) files a due process complaint? 205; What are the benefits of participating in a resolution meeting? 205; What are the concerns about the resolution meeting? 205; Is there a required agenda for a resolution meeting? 206; Who pays for the resolution meeting? 206; Can parents and/or the school district withdraw from an agreement reached at a resolution meeting? 207; What happens if parents do not reach an agreement in the resolution meeting? 207; Who can attend the resolution meeting? 207; Are resolution meetings confidential? 207; Are facilitators available for the resolution meeting? 207; Can the resolution meeting be waived? 208; What is the timeline for a resolution meeting? 208; Is there an expedited resolution meeting timeline? 209; Can attorney fees be awarded at a resolution meeting? 209; What happens when a resolution of a dispute is reached? 209; Is information discussed at a resolution meeting allowed to be introduced at a due process hearing? 210; In the event that an agreement is not reached during the resolution meeting, must mediation continue to be available? 210; Does the 30-day resolution period apply if the parties elect to use mediation rather than convene a resolution meeting? 210; Must the LEA continue its attempts to convince a parent to participate in a resolution meeting throughout the 30-day resolution period? 210; If a party fails to participate in the resolution meeting, must the other party seek the hearing officer's intervention? 211

VI. Due process complaint 211

What is a due process complaint? 211; Who may file a due process complaint? 211; What is the subject matter of a due process complaint? 211; Is there a timeframe as to when the due process complaint must be filed? 211; Does the school district need to provide the parents with information about legal services if they file a due process complaint? 212; Do all states have to have due process procedures? 212; Can a party have a hearing on a due process complaint until the party, or the attorney representing the party, files a due process complaint? 212; What is a "sufficient" due process complaint? 212; Does the complaint have to be sufficient? 213; What steps are available to the complaining party if a hearing officer rules that the due process complaint is "insufficient"? 213; When can a party amend a due process complaint? 214; Is the local education agency required to respond to a parent's due process complaint? 214; How would parents know how to draft a due process complaint? 214; When the local education agency is notified of a parent's due process complaint, what must it do? 215; What are the timelines for the due process hearing to occur? 215; Must each party disclose to the other parties all of the evaluations completed by the date of the due process hearing? 216; What are the requirements to be a hearing officer presiding over a due process hearing? 216; What are the rights of parties at a due process hearing? 217; Can the party requesting the due process hearing raise issues at the due process hearing that were not raised in the due process complaint? 217; Who has the burden of proof in an IDEIA due process hearing? 218; How is a decision about whether a child received a FAPE determined by a hearing officer? 218; Are decisions at due process hearings final? 219; How does the appeal process work? 219; What are the timelines and convenience of hearings and reviews? 219; Can parties bring a civil action with respect to the due process complaint notice requesting a due process hearing? 220; What is the child's status during the pendency of any administrative or judicial proceeding regarding a due process complaint notice requesting a due process hearing? 220; Can the hearing officer award attorney fees? 221

11 Discipline of Students with Disabilities 222

When did the federal law add explicit new provisions regarding the discipline of students with disabilities? 222; Why did the federal law add explicit new provisions regarding the discipline of students with disabilities? 222; How are discipline cases handled for children with disabilities? 223; Are the disciplinary measures available to the school the same for students with disabilities as for students without disabilities? 223; What are short-term disciplinary actions? 223; What is a change of placement? 224; Is parent notification required during disciplinary procedures involving a change of placement? 224; If specific concerns arise that a child may need special education and related services due to his/her pattern of behavior, must such concerns be submitted in writing to school officials in order for the public agency to be deemed to have knowledge that the child is a child with a disability? 225; What is a manifestation determination hearing? 225; What questions must be answered at a manifestation determination hearing? 226; What is the timeframe for a manifestation determination hearing to occur? 226; What is the scope of review at a manifestation determination hearing? 226; At the manifestation determination hearing, is it recommended for parents to engage the services of an educational legal advocate or a special education lawyer? 227; What happens if a student's behavior is *not* a manifestation of the disability? 227; What happens if a student's behavior is a manifestation of the disability? 228; Under what circumstances must an IEP team use a functional behavioral assessment (FBA) and behavior intervention plan (BIP)? 229; Is consent required to do an FBA for a child? 230; If a parent disagrees with the results of an FBA, can the parent obtain an independent educational evaluation (IEE) at public expense? 230; What recourse does a parent have if he/she disagrees with the determination that his/her child's behavior was not a manifestation of the child's disability? 231; Are there any "special circumstances" in which the school is authorized to take disciplinary action whether the student's behavior is a manifestation of the disability or not? 231; What are the consequences involving special circumstances? 232; Can parents challenge manifestation determination or any decision regarding placement with a right to have an expedited due process hearing? 233; If a parent appeals the decision of the manifestation determination hearing, what options does the hearing officer of the appeal have? 233; What is the appropriate placement of a student with a disability during an appeal of a manifestation determination decision? 233; What are the protections for a child who has not been determined to be eligible for special education and related services who has engaged in behavior that violated a code of student conduct? 234; Do IDEIA's discipline procedures allow school systems to report crimes that are committed by children with disabilities? 235

Disclaimer

The information in this book is intended for use as educational material to assist parents and professionals in understanding basic principles of special education law. The author has taken great care to provide in this book the most current and accurate information available concerning special education law on a wide variety of subjects. However, the information found herein is not intended in any way as legal advice and is not a substitute for individual consultation with an attorney. The book is not intended, and should not be used, as a substitute or replacement for individual legal advice. There is no substitute for individual consultation with a special education law expert. Reasonable efforts have been made to ensure the accuracy of the information contained in this book; however, the content and interpretation of laws and regulations are subject to change. The effect of future legislative, administrative, and judicial developments cannot be predicted. For these reasons, the utilization of these materials by any person represents an agreement to hold harmless the author and publisher for any liability, claims, damages, or expenses that may be incurred by any person as a result of reference to or reliance on the information contained in the book.

About the Author

Dr. George Giuliani is a full-time Associate Professor and former Director of the Graduate School Programs in Special Education at Hofstra University's School of Education, Health, and Human Services. He is also an Adjunct Professor at the Maurice A. Deane School of Law at Hofstra University, where he teaches the Special Education Law course.

Having earned his B.A. from the College of the Holy Cross, M.S. from St. John's University, J.D. from City University of New York School of Law, and M.A. and Psy.D. from Rutgers University, he earned Board Certification as a Diplomate Fellow in Advanced Child and Adolescent Psychology, Board Certification as a Diplomate Fellow in Forensic Sciences from the International College of Professional Psychology, and Board Certification in Special Education from the American Academy of Special Education Professionals.

Dr. Giuliani is a member of the American Psychological Association, New York State Psychological Association, American Bar Association, Council of Parent Attorneys and Advocates, Education Law Association, Suffolk County Psychological Association, Psi Chi, American Association of University Professors, and the Council for Exceptional Children.

In addition to being the Executive Director of the National Association of Special Education Teachers, Executive Director of the American Academy of Special Education Professionals, and President of the National Association of Parents with Children in Special Education, he has been a consultant for school districts and early childhood agencies, and has provided numerous workshops for parents, teachers, and other professionals on a variety of special education and psychological topics.

Dr. Giuliani is the co-author of various articles in the *New York State Family Law Review* of the New York State Bar Association. He is the co-author of *The Educator's Diagnostic Manual of Disabilities and Disorders (EDM)*, *The Special Educator's Comprehensive Guide to 301 Diagnostic Tests*, and *The Special Educator's Complete Guide to 109 Diagnostic Tests*, all published by Jossey Bass; the co-author of college textbooks titled *Assessment in Special Education: A Practical Approach (Third Edition)*, *Transition Services in Special Education: A Practical Approach*, and *Learning Disabilities: A Practical Approach to Foundations, Diagnosis, Assessment, and Teaching*, all published by Allyn and Bacon; co-author of *Why Your Students Do What They Do—and What to Do When They Do It—Grades K–5*, *Why Your Students Do What They Do—and What to Do When They Do It—Grades 6–12*, *Creating Confident Children in the Classroom: The Use of Positive Restructuring*, and *What Every Teacher Should Know about Students with Special Needs*, all published by Research Press; co-author of *The Big Book of Special Education Resources*,

Classroom Management for Students with Emotional and Behavioral Disorders, Classroom Management Techniques for Students with ADHD, Frequently Asked Questions about Response to Intervention, Teaching in a Special Education Classroom, Teaching Students with Autism Spectrum Disorders, Teaching Students with Learning Disabilities, Understanding Assessment in the Special Education Process, 100 Frequently Asked Questions about the Special Education Process, Special Education Eligibility, and *Understanding, Developing, and Writing Effective IEPs,* all published by Corwin Press.

Acknowledgements

In the course of writing this book, I have encountered many professional and outstanding websites. It has been my experience that those resources have contributed and continue to contribute enormous information, support, guidance, and education to parents, students, and professionals in the area of special education. Although I have accessed many worthwhile websites, I especially thank and acknowledge the National Dissemination Center for Children with Disabilities, the U.S. Department of Education, and the National Association of Special Education Teachers (NASET).

This book would not have been possible without the support of so many people.

Let me first thank my parents, Dr. George Giuliani and Mrs. Carol Giuliani, who have given me support and guidance throughout my life. Their words of encouragement and guidance have made my professional journey a rewarding and successful experience.

I thank my co-author on so many books, Dr. Roger Pierangelo, who has been such a guiding and exceptional mentor to me. I cannot express how appreciative I am to work with him on so many projects.

I also owe a great deal of thanks to Mr. Richard Scott, Chief Operating Officer of the National Association of Special Education Teachers. Without Rich's incredible ability to run NASET, there is no way that I could have done all that I needed to do to have this book written in such a timely fashion.

Thank you to my graduate assistant from Hofstra University, Diana Bilello, for her hard work, wonderful edits, and suggestions that she made.

Finally, I owe so many thanks to my wonderful colleagues at Hofstra University's Graduate School of Education, Health, and Human Services (SOEHHS) and the School of Law. In particular, I thank Provost Herman Berliner, Nora Demleitner (Dean of the School of Law), Maureen Murphy (former Dean of SOEHHS), and Nancy Halliday (current Dean of SOEHHS). I owe tremendous thanks to Jennifer Gundlach and Amy Stein at the Law School, as well, for their support. I also need to thank my incredible colleagues in the Special Education program, Diane Schwartz, Darra Pace, Gloria Wilson, Mary McDonald, Elfreda Blue, and Stephen Hernandez. The Special Education program is such a phenomenal one, and it is such a privilege to work with you on a daily basis. There's no way that this book would ever have been written if not for all of the above-mentioned support in allowing me to create and teach the course, Special Education Law, at the Law School. I thank all of you again for giving me the opportunity to teach Special Education Law, which has led me down the path of writing this book on the areas I cover when teaching the course. It wouldn't have happened without your confidence in me, as well as believing that the course was a worthy elective for students to take.

Preface

Introduction

On November 29, 1975, Congress enacted the Education for All Handicapped Children Act (Public Law (P.L.) 94-142). The purpose of the Education for All Handicapped Children Act was:

1. "To assure that all children with disabilities have available to them a free appropriate public education."

2. "To assure that the rights of children with disabilities and their parents are protected."

Prior to the enactment of the Education for All Handicapped Children Act, millions of children with disabilities were denied access to education and opportunities to learn. For example, according to the U.S. Department of Education, in 1970, U.S. schools educated only 20 percent of children with disabilities, and many states had laws excluding certain students, including children who were deaf, blind, had emotional disturbances, or were diagnosed with mental retardation, from its schools.

In 1990, the Education for All Handicapped Children Act was reauthorized, and its name was changed to the Individuals with Disabilities Education Act (IDEA). It was again reauthorized in 1997 and 2004, when the name was changed to the Individuals with Disabilities Education Improvement Act (IDEIA).

IDEIA is the federal law in the United States that governs how states must provide special education to children with disabilities.

Today, thanks to IDEIA, the U.S. Department of Education reports that early intervention programs and services are provided to more than 200,000 eligible infants and toddlers and their families, and about 6.5 million children and youths receive special education and related services to meet their individual needs. Furthermore, more students with disabilities than ever before are attending schools in their own neighborhoods—schools that may not have been open to them previously. And fewer students with disabilities are in separate buildings or separate classrooms on school campuses, and are instead learning in classes with their peers.

The protection of the rights of students with disabilities and their parents is only possible due to a federal law that mandates due process. It is therefore essential that, in order to truly understand the intricacies and complexities of special education, one must have a strong awareness of the legal issues involved in the field.

Why this book was written

Let me give you some background as to how I came to write this book.

After being graduated from the College of the Holy Cross as a Psychology major, I went to St. John's University and enrolled in the Graduate School Program in School Psychology. I always had a deep passion for psychology, as both of my parents were in the field (my father as a clinical psychologist and my mother as a psychiatric nurse). However, while I was at St. John's, I became fascinated with the area of special education and, in particular, special education law. I wanted to know all about how the laws for children with special needs were enacted and why they were designed in the way that they were, and often had numerous questions of my faculty. After about six months of this, one of the professors said to me, "Giuliani, why don't you just go to law school and learn everything about the law?" I think it was his nice way of trying to shut me up or pass the buck to another school. But not a bad idea. So, after careful thought, I did just that. I went to City University of New York Law School during the day and then continued my graduate education in school psychology in the evening.

For the next three years, I learned to love the law, but still had my passion for psychology. In the spring of 1992, I was graduated from both law school and graduate school and then had a decision to make. Which path to pursue? I decided that my love of psychology was still where my passion lay, so I went to Rutgers University and got my doctorate (Psy.D.) in School Psychology and also became licensed as a psychologist in the State of New York.

My interest in law and special education never wavered. I wrote many books in the field of special education and even became board-certified in forensic psychology, where my law degree was especially helpful. But I never had the chance to truly tie in law, psychology, and special education. Not until 2008.

I was hired as a full-time faculty member at Hofstra University on Long Island, New York, in 2003. As a professor of numerous courses in the Graduate School Program in Special Education, I had a chance to discuss legal issues in special education throughout the variety of topics I taught. In the spring of 2008, the Dean of the School of Education, Health, and Human Services, Dr. Maureen Murphy, told me that the Dean of Hofstra University's School of Law, Nora Demleitner, J.D., wanted to speak with me. I was called into the School of Law to discuss the possibility of teaching a few weeks of classes on special education law in the Family Law program. I informed the Dean and her colleagues that this was a great idea but would not be practical, as special education law is a complex and detailed area of study, requiring more than just a few weeks of training. Upon further discussion of what was entailed in the field of special education law, Dean Demleitner was very receptive to what I was explaining. She asked if I would be interested in teaching a new course at the law school—Special Education Law. The course had not yet been created, and I was asked to build the course from scratch, have it presented to the faculty of the Law School, and, if approved, teach the course. That spring, I researched other universities throughout the country that offered this course, their requirements, and their formal methods of assessment. Later that spring, I submitted the proposal to the Hofstra University School of Law for its consideration. With the support of the Law School faculty and the Provost of Hofstra University, Dr. Herman Berliner, the course was immediately approved, and I went through the appropriate process at the School of Law to be accepted as a Special Professor of Law to teach this course—Special Education Law.

The description of the course reads as follows:

This course examines the historical development of special education through landmark legislation and litigation, parent advocacy, and national economic and social needs. It reviews U.S. public policies pertaining to children and youth with disabilities. Focus on past and current federal and state policies and their impact on educational, social, and vocational services for individuals with disabilities will be examined. The role of law in forming and shaping special education practices, the ethical dilemmas and debates that drive much of special education, and the opportunity that exists to develop cooperative, collaborative, and effective partnerships between parents, districts, and service providers that result in quality education programs for students with disabilities will be analyzed.

When I first started to research and review textbooks to use for this new course—Special Education Law (LAW 2950)—I was very disappointed by my options. First, there were very few books that were comprehensive enough to meet the needs of my course. And, second, those that were comprehensive were very difficult to read and understand. One of the challenges facing the course is that most law school students have absolutely no background in the field of special education, let alone special education law. Therefore, I had to teach them not only the provisions of law but also the basics of the special education process. Unfortunately, no textbooks that I reviewed were able to cover completely what I needed for this course. Ultimately, I found a textbook to use that met some of my needs, but still lacked many of the qualities that I thought would be more beneficial for this course.

Flash forward three years later. Teaching the Special Education Law course has been a wonderful experience. The students are thoroughly engaged and seem really to enjoy learning about this field of study. My reviews from students at the Law School have been very high, and course feedback has been overwhelmingly positive from students. However, over the past three years, I have found that I am increasingly moving away from having students read just materials in the textbook assigned and, instead, giving them more and more outside readings to do. The longer I teach the course, the more I realize that the need for a more concise, practical, and understandable book on special education law needs to be written.

Because of my experiences with reading book after book on special education law (I think I may own every one ever written at this point), I decided that I wanted to write one that I felt could be understood by anyone, even if he or she had no knowledge of the field whatsoever. I contemplated back and forth about whether to write a textbook on special education law for students or a practical guide for anyone interested in the field (administrators, educators, parents, etc.). The style of the book would be different but ultimately, in my opinion, it would cover the same important areas of study.

When I researched books for administrators, educators, and parents on special education law, I was amazed to find that very few were user-friendly. States have brochures or guides to provide educators, but I found a limited number of books that were written in a comprehensive yet easy-to-read manner on this critical area of study.

I decided that it was important for me to put together my knowledge in the field to write a question-and-answer type of book that would address the issues often faced by individuals working with children with special needs. As the Executive Director of the National Association of Special Education Teachers (NASET) and graduate school professor at Hofstra University in the Special Education program, I felt it important to write a book on the topic of special education law so that people can understand the fundamental principles of the rights of children with disabilities and their parents, as well as schools. My road to doing this wasn't the typical one, for sure, but I believe that the format of the book and way it is now written are the result of my experiences in getting here.

Objectives of the book

The Comprehensive Guide to Special Education Law represents a new and unique direction of books in this field. The format is based on what I believe is the need to have a practical, user-friendly, comprehensive, and clearly understood book that also can be used as a reference guide.

My primary objective for *The Comprehensive Guide to Special Education Law* is to provide individuals with a book that has real meaning for them. Many books that I have reviewed on special education law have ten or more chapters that are not connected, but rather offer separate pieces that never clearly show the overall process in a straight line. In this book, my objective is to provide educators with the information necessary to understand special education law and to learn how to "put it all together."

Ultimately, the goals of this book are many. These include:

- providing knowledge of the requirements, history, and evolution of laws impacting the field

- guiding readers on how to help parents obtain better services for their children with disabilities

- providing educators with the most up-to-date and accurate information on the laws impacting the field of special education today

- enabling readers to understand the evolving nature of special education legislation and how it is interpreted by case law

- helping readers understand what the law requires so that when they advocate for children with disabilities, they can potentially help in the development of policies and aid in making decisions that comply with these laws.

Understanding citations in the book

You will notice in the book that all questions have references citing the source where the information was found. Many of the references will have a citation of U.S.C. or C.F.R. The abbreviation U.S.C. stands for the United States Code. C.F.R. stands for the Code of Federal Regulations. Each of these is briefly explained below.

United States Code (U.S.C.)

The United States Code (U.S.C.) has 50 subject classifications called "Titles." For example, Title 17 is Copyright, Title 26 is the Internal Revenue Code, Title 42 is about Public Health and Welfare. Title 20 represents the laws in Education. When you see "20 U.S.C.," you know it's an education law.

In each Title, laws are indexed and assigned section numbers. IDEIA is cited as 20 U.S.C. 1400-1482. So, any time you see 20 U.S.C. with index numbers that follow that are between 1400 and 1482, you know it's a special education law (IDEIA). For example, the definition of special education in the United States Code is 20 U.S.C. 1401(29).

Code of Federal Regulations (C.F.R.)

You can also find IDEIA in the Code of Federal Regulations (C.F.R.). Volume 34 of the C.F.R. is the section on Education. Part 300 is the information on IDEIA. The special education regulations are published in Volume 34, Part 300 of the Code of Federal Regulations. The legal citation is 34 C.F.R. 300. For example, the definition of special education in the C.F.R can be found in 34 C.F.R. 300.39(b)(3).

Overview of **Special Education Law**

What is the legal definition of special education?

Under the federal law that protects students in special education and their parents and guardians, the Individuals with Disabilities Education Improvement Act (IDEIA), special education is:

Specially designed instruction, at no cost to the parents, to meet the unique needs of a child with a disability, including:

- instruction conducted in the classroom, in the home, in hospitals and institutions, and in other settings

- instruction in physical education.

Special education includes each of the following:

- speech-language pathology services, or any other related service, if the service is considered special education rather than a related service under state standards

- travel training

- vocational education.

[34 C.F.R. 300.39(b)(3); 20 U.S.C. 1401(29)]

Given the importance of understanding the definition, let's take a look at each of the terms and what they mean.

Specially designed instruction

"Specially designed instruction" means adapting, as appropriate to the needs of an eligible child, the content, methodology, or delivery of instruction to address the unique needs of the child that result from the child's disability; and to ensure access of the child to the general curriculum, so that the child can meet the educational standards within the jurisdiction of the public agency that apply to all children.

Thus, as part of designing the instruction to fit the needs of a specific child, adaptations may be made in the content, methodology, or delivery of instruction.

This is a strong point of pride within the special education field and a considerable accomplishment that has come from almost 40 years of practice: the individualization of instruction.

At no cost

"At no cost" means that all specially designed instruction is provided without charge. This concept of a "free" education will be addressed in Chapter 3: Free Appropriate Public Education (FAPE).

Parents

See the next question for a definition of "parent," as well as Chapter 2: Requirements for Being a "Parent."

To meet the unique needs of a child

Each individual receiving special education is different and has different needs. As will be discussed later, each child will have an individualized education program (IEP) because of his/her unique needs and abilities (see Chapter 8: Individualized Education Program).

Disability

A student with a disability is a student who may have one or more of the 13 disabling conditions as set forth under IDEIA (see the question in this chapter: "What disabilities are covered under IDEIA?" for a list and description of each of the disabling conditions).

Physical education

Physical education is the development of physical and motor fitness, fundamental motor skills and patterns, and skills in aquatics, dance, and individual and group games and sports (including intramural and lifetime sports), and includes special physical education, adapted physical education, movement education, and motor development.

Travel training

Travel training means providing instruction, as appropriate, to children with significant cognitive disabilities, and any other children with disabilities who require this instruction, to enable them to develop an awareness of the environment in which they live and learn the skills necessary to move effectively and safely from place to place within that environment (e.g. in school, in the home, at work, and in the community).

Vocational education

Vocational education means organized educational programs that are directly related to the preparation of individuals for paid or unpaid employment, or for additional preparation for a career not requiring a baccalaureate or advanced degree.

To summarize, special education is instruction that is specially designed to meet the unique needs of a child with a disability. It is education that is individually developed to address a *specific* child's needs that result from his/her disability. Since each child is unique, it is difficult to give an overall example of special education. It is individualized for each child.

Some students may be working at the pre-kindergarten-grade level, others at the first-, second-, or third-grade level. There may be students whose special education focuses primarily on speech and language development, cognitive development, or needs related to a physical or learning disability. Special education for any student can consist of:

- an individualized curriculum that is *different* from that of same-age, nondisabled peers (e.g. teaching a blind student to read and write using Braille)

- the *same* (general) curriculum as that for nondisabled peers, with adaptations or modifications made for the student (e.g. teaching third-grade math but including the use of counting tools and assistive technology for the student)

- a combination of these elements.

(National Dissemination Center for Children with Disabilities, 2010)

In the definition of special education, who is considered a "parent"?

A parent or guardian of a student with a disability can include [34 C.F.R. 300.320; 20 U.S.C. 1401(23)]:

- a natural (biological) or adoptive parent or guardian of a student

- a foster parent or guardian, unless state law, regulations, or contractual obligations with a state or local entity prohibit a foster parent or guardian from acting as a parent or guardian

- a guardian (but not the state if the student is a ward of the state)

- an individual acting in the place of a natural or adoptive parent or guardian (including a grandparent-guardian, stepparent-guardian, or other relative) with whom the student lives, or an individual who is legally responsible for the student's welfare

- a surrogate parent or guardian who has been appointed in accordance with IDEIA regulations.

Note: If a judicial decree or order identifies a specific person or persons to act as the parent or guardian of a student or to make educational decisions on behalf of a student, then such person or persons is considered to be the parent or guardian. For more information on this topic, see Chapter 2: Requirements for Being a Parent.

In the definition of special education, who is a "child with a disability"?

A disability can be thought of as an inability or a reduced capacity to perform as other children do because of some impairment in sensory, physical, cognitive, or other areas of functioning. It is very important to understand that all children in special education have disabilities, but not all children with disabilities need special education.

Under IDEIA, a child with a disability is defined as:

> a student evaluated as having mental retardation, a hearing impairment (including deafness), a speech or language impairment, a visual impairment (including blindness), a serious emotional disturbance (referred to in this part as emotional disturbance), an orthopedic impairment, autism, traumatic brain injury, another health impairment, a specific learning disability, deaf-blindness, or multiple disabilities, and who, by reason thereof, needs special education and related services. [34 C.F.R. 300.8]

For students aged three through nine, a "student with a disability," and who needs, for that reason, special education and related services, may include, at the discretion of the state and the local education agency (LEA), a student who is experiencing developmental delays, as defined by the state and as measured by appropriate diagnostic instruments and procedures, in one or more of the following areas:

- physical development
- cognitive development
- communication development
- social or emotional development
- adaptive development.

From birth through age two, children may be eligible for services through the Infants and Toddlers with Disabilities Program (Part C) of the IDEIA. For more information on this topic, see Chapter 13: Early Intervention for Infants and Toddlers with Disabilities.

What is the Individuals with Disabilities Education Improvement Act (IDEIA)?

IDEIA is an acronym for the Individuals with Disabilities Education Improvement Act, our nation's special education law. Originally passed in 1975 under the title Education for All Handicapped Children's Act (Public Law 94-142), IDEIA is the United States federal law that governs how states must provide special education to children with disabilities. IDEIA requires school districts to provide a "free appropriate public education" (FAPE) to eligible children with disabilities [34 C.F.R. 300.8; 20 U.S.C. 1401(3); 1401(30)]. A FAPE means that special education and related services are to be provided as described in an individualized education program (IEP) and under public supervision to a child at no cost to the parents [34 C.F.R. 300.17; 20 U.S.C. 1401(9)].

The law has been amended and renewed several times, a process called reauthorization. Today, IDEIA is Public Law 108-446 and is often referred to as IDEA 2004 or simply IDEA. Throughout this book, we will be using "IDEIA" to represent the Individuals with Disabilities Education Improvement Act.

What are the purposes of IDEIA?

IDEIA states that its purposes are:

- to ensure that all students with disabilities have available to them a free appropriate public education that emphasizes special education and related services designed to meet their unique needs and prepare them for further education, employment, and independent living

- to ensure that the rights of students with disabilities and their parents or guardians are protected

- to assist states, localities, educational service agencies, and federal agencies to provide for the education of all students with disabilities

- to assess and ensure the effectiveness of efforts to educate students with disabilities.

[34 C.F.R. 300.1; 20 U.S.C. 1400(d)]

Is IDEIA made of separate parts?

Yes. When reviewing IDEIA, you will see that is it divided into four distinct parts. These are referred to as Parts A through D, as outlined below (for further information see LDonline, 2012; Pulsifer, 2010).

Part A: General Provisions

Part A provides:

- an overview of the purposes and goals that IDIEA was expected to meet

- definitions of the terms used throughout the document

- an explanation of who is considered a child with a disability

- clarification as to whom the public school system is required to serve and to what extent.

Part B: Assistance for Education of All Children with Disabilities

Part B gives money to states to provide services for eligible children and youth with disabilities, and details the rules and regulations that states and school systems must follow to receive funds from the federal government. Part B includes, but is not limited to:

- definitions of the laws and procedures governing how students with disabilities will be identified and provided services

- explanations of prior written notice

- identification procedures for how students will be evaluated

- steps for discipline

- explanations of grant money for preschool programs

- working with parents to write IEPs

- providing services

- resolving conflicts between parents and the school system

- providing accessible text to students.

Part C: Early Intervention Program for Infants and Toddlers with Disabilities

This section defines an "at-risk infant or toddler" as a child under age three who appears likely to have a significant developmental delay if no intervention is given. It also describes requirements for how school systems find and identify these children and explains individualized family service plans (IFSPs), which are similar to individualized education plans (IEPs) in grade school. Services that may be included in this program are family training, counseling, home visits, speech-language services, occupational therapy and physical therapy.

Part D: National Activities to Improve Education with Disabilities

This section of the IDEIA is divided into two parts:

1. State Program Improvement Grants for Children with Disabilities.

2. Coordinated Research, Personnel Preparation, Technical Assistance, Support, and Dissemination of Information.

Part D provides for research and the application of its findings on how best to educate students with disabilities. It helps state education departments and other agencies improve how they work with children and youth with disabilities. This section provides information and research that informs professional practitioners and families, including:

*   teacher education

*   operation of parent training and information (PTI) centers

*   identification of best practices and promising practices

*   development of technologies

*   public dissemination of information.

Where can you find IDEIA?

If you wanted to read IDEIA, you could find it in one of two places, the United States Code (U.S.C) or the Code of Federal Regulations (C.F.R.):

1. The United States Code (U.S.C.) has 50 subject classifications called "Titles." For example, Title 17 is Copyright, Title 26 is the Internal Revenue Code, and Title 42 is about Public Health and Welfare. Title 20 represents the laws in Education. When you see "20 U.S.C.," you know it's an education law. In each Title, laws are indexed and assigned Section Numbers. IDEIA is cited as 20 U.S.C. 1400-1482. So, any time you see 20 U.S.C. with index numbers that follow that are between 1400 and 1482, you know it's a special education law (IDEIA). For example, the definition of special education in the United States Code is 20 U.S.C. 1401(29).

2. You can also find IDEIA in the Code of Federal Regulations (C.F.R.). Volume 34 of the C.F.R. is the section on Education. Part 300 is the information on IDEIA. The special education regulations are published in Volume 34, Part 300 of the Code of Federal Regulations. The legal citation is 34 C.F.R. 300. For example, the definition of special education in the C.F.R can be found in 34 C.F.R. 300.39(b)(3).

What disabilities are covered under IDEIA?

Under IDEIA, there are 13 categories of disability. A "child with a disability" may have one or more of the following disabling conditions [34 C.F.R. 300.8; 20 U.S.C. 1401(3) and 1401(30)].

Autism

Autism means a developmental disability significantly affecting verbal and nonverbal communication and social interaction, generally evident before age three, that adversely affects a student's educational performance. Other characteristics often associated with autism are engagement in repetitive activities and stereotyped movements, resistance to environmental change or change in daily routines, and unusual responses to sensory experiences. Autism does not apply to a student whose educational performance is adversely affected primarily because the student has an emotional disturbance.

Deaf-blindness

Deaf-blindness means concomitant hearing and visual impairments, the combination of which causes such severe communication and other developmental and educational needs that the affected person cannot be accommodated in special education programs for students solely with deafness or solely with blindness.

Developmental delay

A student with a developmental delay is one who, in physical development, cognitive development, communication development, social or emotional development, adaptive development, or any combination thereof:

- is so defined by the state and as measured by appropriate diagnostic instruments and procedures, and

- by reason thereof, needs special education and related services.

Emotional disturbance

Emotional disturbance means a condition exhibiting one or more of the following characteristics over a long period of time and to a marked degree that adversely affects a student's educational performance:

- an inability to learn that cannot be explained by intellectual, sensory, or health factors

- an inability to build or maintain satisfactory interpersonal relationships with peers and teachers

- inappropriate behavior or feelings under normal circumstances

- a general pervasive mood of unhappiness or depression
- a tendency to develop physical symptoms or fears associated with personal or school problems.

Emotional disturbance includes schizophrenia. The term does not apply to students who are socially maladjusted.

Hearing impairment

Hearing impairment means a level of sensitivity in hearing, whether permanent or fluctuating, that adversely affects a student's educational performance but that does not meet the definition of deafness. Deafness means a hearing impairment that is so severe that the student is impaired in processing linguistic information through hearing, with or without amplification, and that adversely affects a student's educational performance.

Mental retardation

Mental retardation means significantly subaverage general intellectual functioning, existing concurrently with deficits in adaptive behavior and manifested during the developmental period, that adversely affects a student's educational performance.

Multiple disabilities

Multiple disabilities means concomitant impairments (such as mental retardation and blindness or mental retardation and orthopedic impairment), the combination of which causes such severe educational needs that they cannot be accommodated in special education programs solely for one of the impairments. Multiple disabilities does not include deaf-blindness.

Orthopedic impairment

Orthopedic impairment means a severe physical condition that adversely affects a student's educational performance. The term includes impairments caused by a congenital anomaly, impairments caused by disease (e.g. poliomyelitis, bone tuberculosis), and impairments from other causes (e.g. cerebral palsy, amputations, and fractures or burns that cause contractures).

Other health impairment

Other health impairment means having limited strength, vitality, or alertness, including a heightened alertness to environmental stimuli, that results in limited alertness with respect to the educational environment, and that:

- is due to chronic or acute health problems such as asthma, attention deficit disorder or attention deficit/hyperactivity disorder, diabetes, epilepsy, a heart condition, hemophilia, lead poisoning, leukemia, nephritis, rheumatic fever, and sickle cell anemia

- adversely affects a student's educational performance.

Specific learning disability

Specific learning disability means a disorder in one or more of the basic psychological processes involved in understanding or in using language, spoken or written, that may manifest itself in the imperfect ability to listen, think, speak, read, write, spell, or to do mathematical calculations, including conditions such as perceptual disabilities, brain injury, minimal brain dysfunction, dyslexia, and developmental aphasia.

Specific learning disability does not include learning problems that are primarily the result of visual, hearing, or motor disabilities, of mental retardation, of emotional disturbance, or of environmental, cultural, or economic disadvantage.

Speech and language impairments

Speech and language impairments means a communication disorder, such as stuttering, impaired articulation, a language impairment, or a voice impairment, that adversely affects a student's educational performance.

Traumatic brain injury

Traumatic brain injury means an acquired injury to the brain caused by an external physical force, resulting in total or partial functional disability or psychosocial impairment, or both, that adversely affects a student's educational performance. Traumatic brain injury applies to open or closed head injuries resulting in impairments in one or more areas, such as cognition, language, memory, attention, reasoning, abstract thinking, judgment, problem solving, psychosocial behavior, physical functions, information processing, speech, and sensory, perceptual, and motor abilities. Traumatic brain injury does not apply to brain injuries that are congenital or degenerative or to brain injuries induced by birth trauma.

Visual impairment

Visual impairment means a level of acuity in vision that, even with correction, adversely affects a student's educational performance. The term includes both partial sight and blindness.

Why is "gifted and talented" not a classification under IDEIA?

Under the federal definition, in order for a child to receive special education services, he/she must be a child "with a disability." Being a gifted child does not represent having a "disability." Yes, the child is "exceptional," but he/she does not have a disability as defined under the law.

Note: If the gifted child has a specific learning disability (LD) or any other disability as defined under IDEIA, then he/she can receive special education services, not for the "giftedness" but for the LD (Pierangelo and Giuliani, 2008).

How many children currently receive special education services?

According to the U.S. Department of Education's latest data on prevalence of students in special education, more than 6 million (6,606,000) U.S. children between 6 and 21 years of age receive special education services (U.S. Department of Education, 2011). Broken down by classification (in alphabetical order):

- Autism 4.5%

- Deaf-blindness 0.1%

- Developmental delay 5.4%

- Emotional disturbance 6.7%

- Hearing impairments 1.2%

- Learning disabilities 39.0%

- Mental retardation 7.6%

- Multiple disabilities 2.1%

- Orthopedic impairments 1.0%

- Other health impairments 9.7%

- Speech and language impairments 22%

- Traumatic brain injury 0.4%

- Visual impairment 0.4%.

Children with disabilities in special education represent approximately what percentage of all children in school?

Children with disabilities in special education represent approximately 12 percent of all children in school (U.S. Department of Education, 2011).

Does IDEIA address the needs of infants and toddlers?

Yes. IDEIA addresses their needs in a separate section of the law. In the general population, about 300,000 or about 2 percent of U.S. infants and toddlers (birth to 36 months) receive early intervention services (U.S. Department of Education, 2011).

Where is special education instruction provided?

Special education instruction must be provided to students with disabilities in the least restrictive environment (LRE) [34 C.F.R. 300.117; 20 U.S.C. 1412(a)(5)(B)].

IDEIA has specific provisions to ensure that students with disabilities are educated with students without disabilities to the maximum extent appropriate. This concept, known as the "least restrictive environment" or LRE, will be addressed in detail in Chapter 9. Special education instruction can be provided in a number of settings across a continuum of placements (from least severe to most severe), including:

- general education classroom
- resource room
- special education classroom
- special education school
- residential facility
- hospital
- homebound instruction.

Under the federal law, unless a student's individualized education program (IEP) requires some other arrangement, the student must be educated in the school he/she would attend if he/she did not have a disability.

All states are required to be sure that special classes, separate schooling, or other removal of students with disabilities from the general educational environment happen only if the nature or severity of the disability is such that education in regular classes with the use of supplementary aids and services cannot be achieved satisfactorily.

Why was a federal law in special education enacted?

Generally, over the years, special education has been restructured and transformed by legislation. If we examine the history of special education and services for children with disabilities after World War II in the United States, the picture becomes clear as to why our nation needed a federal special education law (Pierangelo and Giuliani, 2008).

Children with disabilities were, for the most part, unprotected and not given much of a chance in education. In 1948, only 12 percent of all children with disabilities received some form of special education—which means that 88 percent of children with disabilities were receiving virtually nothing in terms of an appropriate education.

By the early 1950s, things were not much better for students with disabilities. During this time, state law either permitted or explicitly required the exclusion of the "weak minded" or individuals with physical disabilities. Many states that did educate such children provided separate facilities that isolated them from their peers. Special education services and programs were available in some school districts, but often undesirable results occurred. For example, students in special classes were very often considered unable to perform academic tasks. Consequently, students with disabilities went to special schools or classes that focused on learning manual skills such as weaving and bead stringing. Although programs existed, it was clear that discrimination was still as strong as ever for those with disabilities in schools.

Legislation and court cases to prevent discrimination in education first came to notice in 1954 with the famous case *Brown v. Board of Education of Topeka, Kansas. Brown* was not a special education case, but it played a significant role in the development of special education laws to come.

For much of the 90 years preceding the *Brown* case, race relations in the U.S. had been dominated by racial segregation. This policy had been endorsed in 1896 by the United States Supreme Court case of *Plessy v. Ferguson*. In *Plessy*, the court held that that as long as the separate facilities for the separate races were "equal," the segregation did not violate the Fourteenth Amendment of the U.S. Constitution ("no state shall…deny to any person…the equal protection of the laws"). The concept of "separate but equal" was challenged in *Brown* as being unconstitutional.

On May 17, 1954, Chief Justice Earl Warren read the decision of the unanimous court:

> We come then to the question presented: Does segregation of children in public schools solely on the basis of race, even though the physical facilities and other "tangible" factors may be equal, deprive the children of the minority group of equal educational opportunities? We believe that it does… We conclude that in the field of public education the doctrine of "separate but equal" has no place. Separate educational facilities are inherently unequal. Therefore, we hold that the plaintiffs and others similarly situated for whom the actions have been brought are, by reason of the segregation complained of, deprived of the equal protection of the laws guaranteed by the Fourteenth Amendment. (*Brown v. Board of Education of Topeka*, 347 U.S. 483, 1954)

The Supreme Court struck down the "separate but equal" doctrine of *Plessy* for public education, ruled in favor of the plaintiffs, and required the desegregation of schools across America.

The court in *Brown* stated that segregation based on unalterable characteristics with the result being inequitable opportunities could not be upheld in the United States and demanded that such segregation end with "all deliberate speed."

Brown set the precedent for future discrimination cases in education. People with disabilities were recognized as another group whose rights had been violated because of arbitrary discrimination. For children, the discrimination occurred because they were denied access to schools because of their disabilities.

Using *Brown* as their legal precedent, parents of students with disabilities claimed that their children's segregation and exclusion from school violated their opportunity for an equal education under the Fourteenth Amendment of the U.S. Constitution—the Equal Protection Clause. If *Brown* could not segregate by race, then schools should not be able to segregate or otherwise discriminate by ability and disability.

During the early 1960s, there was a pervasive national concern with the rights of the individual, especially the rights of persons who had previously been discriminated against by the government. In fact, the rights of people with disabilities became a significant part of the larger social issue at the time. In the 1960s, parents began to become advocates for better educational opportunities for their children with disabilities. Parents started to speak out more about how segregated special schools and classes were not the most appropriate educational setting for many students with disabilities. Consequently, some parents began to take legal action against their respective school districts when they felt their children's rights were being violated.

President John F. Kennedy also raised public awareness of individuals with mental and physical disabilities. President Kennedy, whose sister Rosemary was born with a cognitive disability, was a major champion of education for children with disabilities. In 1961, he initiated a Presidential Panel on Mental Retardation. President Kennedy expressed his concern about the issues:

> The manner in which our Nation cares for its citizens and conserves its manpower resources is more than an index to its concern for the less fortunate. It is a key to its future. Both wisdom and humanity dictate a deep interest in the physically handicapped, the mentally ill, and the mentally retarded. Yet, although we have made considerable progress in the treatment of physical handicaps, although we have attacked on a broad front the problems of mental illness, although we have made great strides in the battle against disease, we as a nation have for too long postponed an intensive search for solutions to the problems of the mentally retarded. That failure should be corrected. (President's Panel on Mental Retardation, 1962)

In the early 1970s, two significant court cases paved the way towards future federal legislation protecting the rights of children with disabilities and their parents:

- *PARC v. Commonwealth of Pennsylvania*
- *Mills v. Board of Education of District of Columbia.*

In *PARC*, the court ruled that schools may not exclude students who have been classified with mental retardation. Also, the court mandated that all students must be provided with a free appropriate public education (*PARC v. Commonwealth of Pennsylvania*, 343 F. Supp. 279, E.D. PA, 1972). Both of these holdings would play a fundamental role in the enactment of future federal special education laws.

Mills involved the practice of suspending, expelling, and excluding "exceptional children" from the D.C. public schools. In *Mills*, the court held that:

> No child eligible for a publicly supported education in the District of Columbia public schools shall be excluded from a regular public school assignment… The District of Columbia shall provide to each child of school age a free and suitable publicly supported education regardless of the degree of the child's mental, physical or emotional disability or impairment. (*Mills v. Board of Education of District of Columbia*, 348 Supp. 866, C.D. DC, 1972)

Mills set forth future guidelines for federal legislation by rejecting the District's argument that funds were insufficient to educate students with disabilities. The court in Mills mandated that students with disabilities receive special education services regardless of the school district's financial capability, stating that "Insufficient resources may not be the basis for exclusion" (*Mills v. Board of Education of District of Columbia*, 348 Supp. 866, C.D. DC, 1972).

PARC and *Mills* set the stage for enactment of federal laws to protect the rights of children with disabilities and their parents. As a result of these cases and other historical court cases at the time, federal legislation for all individuals with disabilities began to develop in the early 1970s.

The Rehabilitation Act of 1973, 29 U.S.C. 701 *et seq.*, is a civil rights law that made discrimination against individuals unlawful by those who receive funds by federal subsidies or grants. All public elementary and secondary schools and most postsecondary institutions receive federal subsidies and grants and therefore must comply with the Rehabilitation Act of 1973. Section 504 of the Rehabilitation Act of 1973 ensures students have equal opportunity to all school activities. The law prohibits discrimination against students with disabilities in federally funded programs: "Individuals with disabilities cannot be excluded from participation in, denied benefits of, or subjected to discrimination under any program or activity receiving federal financial assistance."

Because of the victories that were being won for students with disabilities in the 1960s and early 1970s, as well as the enactment of the Rehabilitation Act of 1973, parents and student advocates began to lobby Congress for federal laws and money that would ensure students with disabilities got an education that would meet their needs. Years of exclusion, segregation, and denial of basic educational opportunities to students with disabilities and their families set an imperative for a civil rights law guaranteeing these students access to the education system.

In 1975, a Congressional investigation revealed that (Pierangelo and Giuliani, 2008):

- over four million children with disabilities in the United States were not receiving appropriate educational services

- because of the lack of adequate services in the public school system, families were often forced to find services outside the public school system, often at a great distance from their homes at their own expense.

Congress determined that it is in the national interest that the federal government assist state and local efforts to provide programs to meet the educational needs of children with disabilities. Congress recognized the necessity of special education for children with disabilities and was concerned about the widespread discrimination.

On November 29, 1975, President Gerald Ford signed into law the Education for All Handicapped Children Act (EHA), Public Law 94-142.

The passage of Public Law 94-142 was the end result of many years of litigation and state legislation to protect and promote the civil rights of all students with disabilities. This federal law required states to provide a free appropriate public education (FAPE) for students with disabilities no matter how serious the disability. P.L. 94-142 was the first law to clearly define the rights of students with disabilities. Some of the key provisions of P.L. 94-142 were:

- Clearly defined for the first time in law the rights of students with disabilities to free appropriate public education (FAPE).

- Required the school systems to include the parents and guardians when meeting about the student or making decisions about his/her education.

- Mandated an individualized education program (IEP) for every student with a disability. (The IEP must include short- and long-term goals for the student, as well as ensure that the necessary services and products are available to the student.)

- Required that students be placed in the least restrictive environment (LRE).

- Ensured that students with disabilities be given nondiscriminatory tests (tests that take into consideration the native language of the student and the effects of the disability).

- Required due process procedures to be in place (to protect families and students).

In 1986, the Education for All Handicapped Children Act was amended by Public Law 99-457, the Education of the Handicapped Act Amendments. These amendments, which are also known as the Early Intervention Amendments to Public Law 94-142, extended FAPE to all students aged three to five by October 1991 in all states that wanted to participate (all 50 wanted to and did, even states that do not have public schooling for students at those ages). Provisions were also included to help states develop early intervention programs for infants and toddlers with disabilities; this part of the legislation became known as the Part H Program. (Note: In 1997, the section of the law that applies to infants and toddlers changed to Part C.)

In 1990, the Education for All Handicapped Children Act was once again reauthorized by Public Law 101-476. Most obvious was the legislation's change of name to IDEA—the Individuals with Disabilities Education Act. IDEA continued to uphold the provisions set forth in P.L. 94-142. Notice that IDEA changed the terms in the previous law as follows:

- from "children" to "individuals"

- from "handicapped" to "with disabilities."

IDEA reaffirmed P.L. 94-142's requirements of a free appropriate public education (FAPE) through an individualized education program (IEP) with related services and due process procedures. This act also supported the amendments to P.L. 94-142 that expanded the entitlement in all states to ages 3 to 21, designated assistive technology as a related service in IEPs, strengthened the law's commitment to greater inclusion in community schools (least restrictive placement), provided funding for infant and toddler early intervention programs, and required that by age 16 every student have explicitly written in the IEP a plan for transition to employment or postsecondary education.

The newest amendments of IDEA were the Individuals with Disabilities Education Act Amendments of 1997 (P.L. 105-17). These amendments restructured IDEA into four parts: Part A addressed general provisions; Part B covered assistance for education of all students with disabilities; Part C covered infants and toddlers with disabilities; and Part D addressed national activities to improve the education of students with disabilities.

On December 3, 2004, the Individuals with Disabilities Education Improvement Act was enacted into law as Public Law 108-446. The statute, as passed by Congress and signed by President George W. Bush, reauthorized and made significant changes to the Individuals with Disabilities Education Act. It is now Public Law 108-446 and can be found in 20 U.S.C 1400-1482.

Is there a law to protect students with disabilities who are deemed not eligible for special education?

Yes. Section 504 of the Rehabilitation Act protects students with disabilities who are not deemed eligible for special education under IDEIA. Section 504 of the Rehabilitation Act of 1973 is a federal civil rights law that prohibits discrimination against individuals with disabilities:

> no other qualified handicapped individual in the United States…shall solely by reason of his handicap, be excluded from participation in, be denied benefits of, or be subjected to discrimination under any program or activity receiving federal financial assistance.

Senator Hubert Humphrey introduced the bill to the United States Senate in 1972, stating:

> The time has come when we can no longer tolerate the invisibility of the handicapped in America…children who are excluded from school… These people have the right to live, to work to the best of their ability, to know the dignity to which every human being is entitled. But too often we keep children whom we regard as "different" or a "disturbing influence" out of school and community activities altogether, rather that help them develop their abilities… Every child, gifted, normal and handicapped, has a fundamental right to educational opportunity. Justice delayed is justice denied. (117 Cong. Rec. 45, 974)

A student with a disability who does not need special education but who needs a related service may be eligible for that service under Section 504 of the Rehabilitation Act of 1973 (Diagnostic Center of Northern California, 2010).

Section 504 and special education are not the same. Do not confuse the two. Section 504 is a civil rights law that protects a broad range of students with disabilities from discrimination on the basis on their handicapping conditions.

The major differences between IDEIA and Section 504 are in the flexibility of the procedures. For a child to be identified as eligible for services under Section 504, there are less specific procedural criteria that govern the requirements of the school personnel. Schools may offer a student less assistance and monitoring with Section 504 because there are fewer regulations by the federal government to instruct them, especially in terms of compliance (Council for Exceptional Children, 2002).

To be protected under Section 504, a student must be determined to (1) have a physical or mental impairment that substantially limits one or more major life activities, (2) have a record of such an impairment, or (3) be regarded as having such an impairment. Section 504 requires that school districts provide a free and appropriate public education to qualified students in their jurisdictions who have a physical or mental impairment that substantially limits one or more major life activities.

The determination of whether a student has a physical or mental impairment that substantially limits a major life activity must be made on the basis of an individual inquiry. Section 504 regulation defines a physical or mental impairment as:

> any physiological disorder or condition, cosmetic disfigurement, or anatomical loss affecting one or more of the following body systems: neurological; musculoskeletal; special sense organs; respiratory, including speech organs; cardiovascular; reproductive; digestive; genito-urinary; hemic and lymphatic; skin; and endocrine; or any mental or psychological disorder, such as mental retardation, organic brain syndrome, emotional or mental illness, and specific learning disabilities.

The regulation does not set forth an exhaustive list of specific diseases and conditions that may constitute physical or mental impairments because of the difficulty of ensuring the comprehensiveness of such a list.

Major life activities include functions such as caring for one's self, performing manual tasks, walking, seeing, hearing, speaking, breathing, learning, and working. This list is not exhaustive. Other functions can be major life activities for the purposes of Section 504.

To learn more about Section 504, go to Chapter 14: Section 504 and the Education of Children with Disabilities.

What are the legal steps required in the special education process under IDEIA?

The process of identifying, evaluating, determining eligibility, and educational placement of children in special education is a step-by step process. IDEIA mandates that certain procedural steps occur to ensure that students with disabilities are afforded the right to a free appropriate public education (FAPE), as well as have substantive and procedural due process rights. All of these steps will be addressed in much more detail in the upcoming chapters.

Step 1: Identification of children

Generally, the two ways in which children are identified as possibly needing special education and related services are *Child Find* (which operates in each state) and by referral of a parent or school personnel.

CHILD FIND

IDEIA mandates that all states identify, locate, and evaluate all children with disabilities in the state who need special education and related services. To do so, states conduct what are known as Child Find activities. When a child is identified by Child Find as possibly having a disability and as needing special education, parents may be asked for permission to evaluate their child. Parents can also call the Child Find office and ask that their child be evaluated.

REFERRAL OR REQUEST FOR EVALUATION

A school professional may ask that a child be evaluated to see if he/she has a disability. A parent may also contact the child's teacher or other school professional to ask that their child be evaluated. Parental consent is needed before a child may be evaluated. Under the federal IDEIA regulations, evaluation needs to be completed within 60 days after the parent gives consent. However, if a state's IDEIA regulations give a different timeline for completion of the evaluation, the state's timeline is applied.

Step 2: Full and individual evaluation of the child by a multidisciplinary team

A comprehensive evaluation done by a multidisciplinary team is an essential early step in the special education process for a child. It is intended to answer these questions:

- Does the child have a disability that requires the provision of special education and related services?

- What are the child's specific educational needs?

- What special education services and related services, then, are appropriate for addressing those needs?

By law, the initial evaluation of the child must be "full and individual"—which is to say, focused on that child and that child alone. The evaluation must assess the child in all areas related to the child's suspected disability.

The evaluation results will be used to decide the child's eligibility for special education and related services and to make decisions about an appropriate educational program for the child.

If the parents disagree with the evaluation, they have the right to take their child for an Independent Educational Evaluation (IEE) and can ask that the school system pay for this IEE.

Step 3: Determination of eligibility for special education

Once the comprehensive assessment of the child is completed, a committee meeting is formed (in some states referred to as the Committee on Special Education or CSE) where professionals and the parents look at the child's evaluation results. Together, a determination is made as to whether the child meets the criteria for a "child with a disability," as defined by IDEIA. If the parents do not agree with the eligibility decision, they may ask for a hearing to challenge the decision.

If the child is found to be a child with a disability (as defined by IDEIA), he/she is eligible for special education and related services.

Step 4: Scheduling an IEP meeting

A team of school professionals and the parents must meet to write an individualized education program (IEP) for the child within 30 calendar days after a child is determined eligible. The school system schedules and conducts the IEP meeting. School staff must:

- contact the participants, including the parents

- notify parents early enough to make sure they have an opportunity to attend

- schedule the meeting at a time and place agreeable to parents and the school

- tell the parents the purpose, time, and location of the meeting

- tell the parents who will be attending

- tell the parents that they may invite people to the meeting who have knowledge or special expertise about the child.

Step 5: Holding the IEP meeting and then writing the IEP

The IEP team gathers to talk about the child's needs and write the student's IEP. Parents and the student (when appropriate) are full participating members of the team. If the child's placement (meaning, where the child will receive his/her special education and related services) is decided by a different group, the parents must be part of that group as well.

Before the school system may provide special education and related services to the child for the first time, the parents must give consent. The child begins to receive services as soon as possible after the IEP is written and this consent is given.

If the parents do not agree with the IEP and placement, they may discuss their concerns with other members of the IEP team and try to work out an agreement. If they still disagree, parents can ask for mediation, or the school may offer mediation. Parents may file a state complaint with the state education agency or a due process complaint, which is the first step in requesting a due process hearing, at which time mediation must be available.

Step 6: Providing special education and related services to the student

The school makes sure that the child's IEP is carried out as it was written. Parents are given a copy of the IEP. Each of the child's teachers and service providers has access to the IEP and knows his/her specific responsibilities for carrying out the IEP. This includes the accommodations, modifications, and supports that must be provided to the child, in keeping with the IEP.

Step 7: Progress monitoring

The child's progress toward the annual goals is measured, as stated in the IEP. His/ her parents are regularly informed of their child's progress and whether that progress is enough for the child to achieve the goals by the end of the year. These progress reports must be given to parents at least as often as parents are informed of their nondisabled children's progress.

Step 8: IEP is reviewed

The child's IEP is reviewed first by the IEP team at least once a year, or more often if the parents or school ask for a review. If necessary, the IEP is revised. Parents, as team members, must be invited to participate in these meetings. Parents can make suggestions for changes, can agree or disagree with the IEP, and agree or disagree with the placement.

If parents do not agree with the IEP and placement, they may discuss their concerns with other members of the IEP team and try to work out an agreement. There are several options, including additional testing, an independent evaluation, or asking for mediation or a due process hearing. They may also file a complaint with the state education agency.

Step 9: Child is reevaluated

At least every three years the child must be reevaluated. This evaluation is often referred to as a "triennial review." Its purpose is to find out if the child continues to be a child with a disability, as defined by IDEIA, and to determine the child's educational needs. However, the child must be reevaluated more often if conditions warrant or if the child's parent or teacher asks for a new evaluation (Office of Special Education and Rehabilitative Services, 2000).

Requirements for
Being a "Parent"

Who is a "parent" as defined under IDEIA?

Perhaps the most important element afforded under IDEIA is the right to parental participation at almost all stages of the special education process. To increase the odds that each child has a parent in the special education process, IDEIA does define the term "parent" but does so in a broad way.

Under IDEIA, a "parent" means:

1. A biological (natural) or adoptive parent of a child

2. A foster parent, unless State law, regulations, or contractual obligations with a State or local entity prohibit a foster parent from acting as a parent

3. A guardian generally authorized to act as the child's parent, or authorized to make educational decisions for the child (but not the State if the child is a ward of the State)

4. An individual acting in the place of a biological or adoptive parent (including a grandparent, stepparent, or other relative) with whom the child lives, or an individual who is legally responsible for the child's welfare, or

5. A surrogate parent who has been appointed in accordance with 34 C.F.R. 300.519.

[34 C.F.R. 300.30; 20 U.S.C. 1401(23)]

Note: The biological or adoptive parent, when attempting to act as the parent under this part and when more than one party is qualified to act as a parent, must be presumed to be the parent unless the biological or adoptive parent does not have legal authority to make educational decisions for the child.

If a judicial decree or order identifies a specific person or persons to act as the "parent" of a child or to make educational decisions on behalf of a child, then such person or persons shall be determined to be the "parent."

Why is there such a broad definition of a parent under IDEIA?

IDEIA defines a "parent" broadly so as to include a wide variety of different caregivers, with many possible individuals in a caregiving role able therefore to qualify as a parent [34 C.F.R. 300.20].

Who is considered an adoptive parent?

An adoptive parent is a person who legally adopts a child of other parents as his/her own child. Adoption is the official transfer through the court system of all of the parental rights that a biological parent has to a child, along with an assumption by the adopting parent of all of the parental rights of the biological parents that are being terminated and are assumed in their entirety by the adoptive parents, including the responsibility for the care and supervision of the child, his/her nurturing and training, physical and emotional health, and financial support (Adoption Media LLC, 2011a).

Are biological or adoptive parents always presumed to be authorized to make educational decisions for the child even if other individuals also meet the definition of parent?

Yes. The biological or adoptive parents are always presumed to be authorized to make educational decisions for the child even if other individuals also meet the definition of parent, unless a judicial order states that specific individuals are to make the child's educational decisions.

If there is more than one "parent," then the biological or adoptive parent who attempts to act as parent for educational decisions is presumed to be the parent, unless he/she does not have legal authority to make educational decisions [34 C.F.R. 300.30(b)(1)].

Under IDEIA, whenever a birth or adoptive parent is "attempting to act" on behalf of the child in the special education system, the school must treat that parent as the decision maker. This means that if the school proposes an IEP for the child and the birth or adoptive parent disapproves of the plan, the school cannot go around the parent by getting the agreement of a foster parent, kinship parent, or other relative. The school can only accept the decision of another person when the birth or adoptive parent is not "attempting to act" on behalf of the child, unless a judge has appointed an alternative decision maker for the child. In that case, the school must treat the person appointed by the judge as the only person authorized to make special education decisions for the child (Education Law Center, 2007).

Who is considered a foster parent?

A foster parent is a person who acts as parent and guardian for a child in place of the child's natural parents but without legally adopting the child.

Although this term has a wide variety of possible definitions, it is generally used to refer to adults who are licensed by the state or county to provide a temporary home for children whose birth parents are unable to care for them. These services may be provided with or without compensation, and can often continue for several months or even years, depending on the circumstances of the child and the foster parents (Adoption Media LLC, 2011b).

Under IDEIA, a foster parent can act as a parent unless state law prohibits the foster parent from acting as a parent [34 C.F.R. 300.30].

What rights do foster parents have in the educational decision making for a child in special education?

This is an issue for the states. Some states have separate provisions for the appointment of a foster parent as the educational decision maker. Check your state regulations as to the specific rights of foster parents in your school district. In the past, foster parents were only allowed to advocate for special education students in a limited number of circumstances. Those restrictions were eliminated under the Individuals with Disabilities Education Improvement Act of 2004 (Legal Services of Missouri, 2006).

Who is considered a guardian?

A guardian is a non-parent to whom the court gives authority to take responsibility for the care of a child. In special education, a guardian is a person who has the legal responsibility for providing the care and management of a child with a disability. An appointment of guardianship may be permanent or temporary. Guardians are often appointed for children when the parents are deceased (Judicial Council of California, 1995).

Who is considered a surrogate parent?

IDEIA requires each state to have specific procedures to protect the rights of the child whenever:

1. the parents of the child are not known, or

2. the [school district] cannot, after reasonable efforts, locate the parents

3. the child is a ward of the State under the laws of that State (e.g. in the custody of a public child welfare agency), or

4. the child is an unaccompanied homeless youth as defined in section 725(6) of the McKinney-Vento Homeless Assistance Act.

[42 U.S.C. 11434(a)(6)]

A surrogate parent is appointed by the local education agency (LEA; the school district) or other responsible state agency to assume parental rights under the special education regulations in order to protect the student's rights [34 C.F.R. 300.519; 20 U.S.C. 1415(b)(2)]. A surrogate parent acts in the place of a child's natural parent to make decisions about the child's education when the child's natural parent is unavailable to make decisions. A parent is unavailable when he/she cannot be located or when he/she chooses not to act as a parent for the child. A parent is also unavailable if he/she has lost the ability to act as parent by court order. The surrogate parent makes decisions for a child with a disability in all matters relating to the identification, evaluation, and educational placement of the child and the provision of a free appropriate public education to the child.

Are surrogate parents required to have knowledge and skills that ensure adequate representation of the student?

Yes. Unlike other "parents," surrogate parents are required to have knowledge and skills that ensure adequate representation of the student [34 C.F.R. 300.519(d)(2)(iii)].

What rights does a surrogate parent have under IDEIA?

When a surrogate is appointed, he/she has all the rights and responsibilities under IDEIA [34 C.F.R. 300.519; 20 U.S.C. 1415(b)(2)]. The surrogate parent may represent the child in all matters relating to [34 C.F.R. 300.519(g)]:

1. the identification, evaluation, and educational placement of the child, and

2. the provision of a free appropriate public education (FAPE) to the child.

What are the guidelines for being a surrogate parent for a student?

Public agencies shall ensure that a person selected as a surrogate parent [34 C.F.R. 300.519(h)]:

1. is not an employee of the state educational agency (SEA), the LEA, or any other agency that is involved in the education or care of the child

2. has no interest that conflicts with the interest of the child represented

3. has knowledge and skills that ensure adequate representation of the child, and

4. is assigned not more than 30 days after there is a determination by the agency that the child needs a surrogate parent.

Can the state be considered a surrogate parent?

No, the state cannot be considered a surrogate parent even if the child is a ward of the state. Someone who is an employee of a state, local, or any other public agency that is involved in the education or care of the child cannot be a surrogate. This is because that person could have a conflict of interest with the child. For example, a teacher could not be a surrogate because he/she may be required to advocate for services for a child, but be hesitant to do so because it would create a financial burden for his/her employer. If a child is in the custody of children's services, a children's services worker could not be a surrogate for similar reasons (Ohio Legal Rights Service, 2005).

Someone who is an employee of a nonpublic agency that provides only non-educational care for the child can be a surrogate if he/she has the knowledge and skills, no conflict of interest and otherwise meets the criteria for being a surrogate parent, including surrogate training requirements [34 C.F.R. 300.519(h)].

Can a foster parent serve as a surrogate parent?

Yes, provided certain conditions are met. A foster parent may serve as a surrogate parent if the following four conditions are met [34 C.F.R. 300.30]:

- the natural parents' rights have been terminated

- the foster parent has a long-term relationship with the child

- the foster parent is willing to participate in the role of "parent," and

- no conflict of interest occurs with the foster parent assuming that role.

Note: A foster parent may also be appointed as surrogate parent for a foster child if the foster parent does not meet the qualifications to be a "parent" and meets the qualifications for being a surrogate.

How long can a surrogate parent act as surrogate parent?

A surrogate parent may continue to serve as long as he/she continues to meet the surrogate parent requirements of federal and state law. Every year, the school district is required to review the appointment of each parent surrogate to ensure that the rights of the child are protected. Similarly, the appointment of a surrogate for a child in early intervention must be reviewed at least annually. When a student with a disability turns the age of majority, all of the rights of the surrogate parent transfer to the student, unless the student has been determined to be incompetent under state law, in which case educational decisions would be made by the student's court appointed guardian (Ohio Legal Rights Service, 2005).

Is there a timeframe for assignment of a surrogate parent?

To ensure that children receive a speedy surrogate parent appointment, IDEIA now requires that schools make reasonable efforts to assign a surrogate parent within 30 days after determining that a child needs a surrogate [34 C.F.R. 300.519(h)].

When parents divorce, who exercises the rights under IDEIA?

Where parents are divorced, the question of which parent exercises rights under IDEIA is a question of state law and the judicial order in the divorce (*Taylor v. Vermont Department of Education*, 2002).

Who is considered a ward of the state?

Under IDEIA, [34 C.F.R 300.45], a ward of the state means a child who, as determined by the state where the child resides, is:

1. a foster child

2. a ward of the state, or

3. in the custody of a public child welfare agency.

There is an exception. A ward of the state does not include a foster child who has a foster parent who meets the definition of a parent under IDEIA.

If the student is a ward of the state, the identification and location of the parent, as well as the status of residual parent rights, should be known. If these factors are not known, then the agency with which wardship resides is the agency that is responsible for the general care of the individual. That agency shall identify a surrogate parent.

Note: IDEIA allows for the appointment of a surrogate parent by a judge overseeing the case of a child who is a ward of the state, provided that the surrogate parent meets the requirements at 34 C.F.R. 300.519(c).

Is there a transfer of parental rights at the age of majority in special education?

Yes. Age of majority is the legal age established under state law at which an individual is no longer a minor and, as a young adult, has the right and responsibility to make certain legal choices that adults make (National Center on Secondary Education and Transition, 2002). Thus, when people use the term "age of majority," they are generally referring to when a young person reaches the age at which one is considered to be an adult. Depending upon state law, this usually happens at some point between 18 and 21 (National Center on Secondary Education and Transition, 2002).

Beginning not later than one year before the child reaches the age of majority under state law, the IEP must include a statement that the child has been informed of the child's rights under Part B of the Act, if any, that will transfer to the child on reaching the age of majority under 34 C.F.R. 300.520 [34 C.F.R. 300.320(c)].

How are children informed of the transfer of rights?

IDEIA does not specify the manner in which schools must inform children of any rights that will transfer to them upon reaching the age of majority. This is a matter best left to states, districts, and IEP teams to decide, based on their knowledge of the child and any unique local or state requirements.

Free Appropriate Public Education (FAPE)

What is a FAPE?

FAPE is an acronym for "free appropriate public education." When P.L. 94-142 was enacted in 1975 (see Chapter 1), it required that states submit plans that assured all students with disabilities the right to a free appropriate public education.

IDEIA defines FAPE as special education and related services that [34 C.F.R. 300.17; 20 U.S.C. 1401(9)]:

- are provided at public expense, under public supervision and direction, and without charge

- meet state standards

- include preschool, elementary school, or secondary school education in the state

- are provided in conformity with the individualized education program.

Today, IDEIA requires that all states demonstrate that they have in effect "a policy that assures all children with disabilities the right to a free appropriate education" [34 C.F.R. 300.101(a)].

A free appropriate public education must be available to all children residing in the state between the ages of 3 and 21 inclusive, including children with disabilities who have been suspended or expelled from school.

What does "free" actually mean?

The word "free" is not defined in IDEIA. When looking at the legislative history in the creation of P.L. 94-142, Congress stated:

> The Committee rejects the argument that the Federal Government should only mandate services to handicapped children if, in fact, funds are appropriated in sufficient amounts to cover the full cost of this education. (Sen. Rep. No. 168, 94th Congress, 1st Session, 1975)

Although the definition of "free" is not explicitly laid out, the concept is clear that special education and related services should be "provided at public expense...and without charge" [20 U.S.C. 1401(a)(18)].

According to the U.S. Department of Education (2010), a "free" education is defined as follows:

> Recipients operating federally funded programs must provide education and related services free of charge to students with disabilities and their parents or guardians. Provision of a free education is the provision of education and related services without cost to the person with a disability or his or her parents or guardians, except for fees equally imposed on nondisabled persons or their parents or guardians. If a recipient is unable to provide a free appropriate public education itself, the recipient may place a person with a disability in, or refer such person to, a program other than the one it operates.
>
> However, the recipient remains responsible for ensuring that the education offered is an appropriate education, as defined in the law, and for coverage of financial obligations associated with the placement. The cost of the program may include tuition and other related services, such as room and board, psychological and medical services necessary for diagnostic and evaluative purposes, and adequate transportation. Funds available from any public or private source, including insurers, may be used by the recipient to meet the requirements of FAPE. If a student is placed in a private school because a school district cannot provide an appropriate program, the financial obligations for this placement are the responsibility of the school district. However, if a school district makes available a free appropriate public education and the student's parents or guardian choose to place the child in a private school, the school district is not required to pay for the student's education in the private school. If a recipient school district places a student with a disability in a program that requires the student to be away from home, the recipient is responsible for the cost of room and board and nonmedical care. To meet the requirements of FAPE, a recipient may place a student with a disability in, or refer such student to, a program not operated by the recipient. When this occurs, the recipient must ensure that adequate transportation is provided to and from the program at no greater personal or family cost than would be incurred if the student with a disability were placed in the recipient's program.

Is lack of funds a sufficient defense for not providing a student with a disability an appropriate education?

No. Lack of funds may not limit the availability of "appropriate" educational services to children with disabilities. Regardless of the funding available, a school district cannot refuse to provide an appropriate education due to insufficient funding (Guersney and Klare, 2008).

Is "cost of services" a defense for not providing a student with a disability an appropriate education?

No. Cost of services is insufficient as a defense under IDEIA. Cost considerations are only relevant when choosing between several options, all of which offer an appropriate education. When only one is appropriate, then there is no choice.

The U.S. Department of Education has emphasized that it is important that school personnel do not make FAPE decisions solely on the basis of cost of services, but rather that the decisions be based on the individual needs of a student (Letter to Greer, 1992).

Is there ever an instance where students with disabilities may be charged for services?

Yes, there is one instance. Uniformly assessed fees are permissible. A fee for a service may be charged only if this is a fee on all students in the school. The term "at no cost" does not preclude incidental fees that are normally charged to students without disabilities or their parents as part of the regular education program [34 C.F.R. 300.39(b)(1)].

What are third-party payments?

School districts work with public assistance programs, such as Medicaid, to pay for some IEP service costs. In addition, IDEIA outlines how schools can bill the parents' private health insurance if they consent. Payments for IEP services received by the school system from these sources are third-party payments. Examples of third-party payors include Medicaid and the parents' private insurance company (PACER Center: Families and Advocates Partnership for Education, 2011).

What types of services are billed to third parties?

Related services (see Chapter 7), such as physical therapy, occupational therapy, speech and language therapy, and rehabilitation counseling, are often billed to third parties. Usually, third parties cover health-related therapies but not educational services. A parent's public or private insurer may pay for some of the services (PACER Center: Families and Advocates Partnership for Education, 2011).

Will third-party payments cost parents anything?

IDEIA requires that a school's use of third-party payments won't cost parents any out-of-pocket expenses now or in the future. The regulations allow a school district to bill third parties only if [34 C.F.R. 300.154(d)(2)]:

- it does not cost the parents anything (schools can offer to pay out-of-pocket expenses, such as co-pays or deductibles, in order to meet this requirement— parents can still say no)

- it does not reduce parental coverage

- it does not cause the child to lose services needed elsewhere

- it does not put parents at risk of losing eligibility in other programs.

Can Medicaid funds be used to pay for health-related services provided under IDEIA?

With limited federal funding for education and growth in eligible populations, states have been under pressure to seek out sources of special education financing beyond state and local tax bases; one such source is Medicaid. An amendment to IDEIA, included in the Medicare Catastrophic Coverage Act of 1988, clarified that Medicaid funds could be used to pay for health-related services provided under IDEIA.

For health-related services provided under IDEIA to be reimbursed by Medicaid, they must be (MedStat, n.d.):

- provided by a participating Medicaid provider

- medically necessary

- included in the state's Medicaid plan

- provided to an individual eligible for Medicaid, and

- screened for any other third party payment that may be available for reimbursement.

Can a school district bill Medicaid without the parent's permission to do so?

No. In order to access Medicaid, the parent's signed consent to release the personal identifiable information listed in the student's education record is required. Submitting information to Medicaid or any private insurance company without the parent's permission violates the Family Educational Rights and Privacy Act (FERPA) (Arkansas Department of Education, 2011).

If a student has private health insurance and Medicaid, can the school district still bill Medicaid for the related services offered to these students?

Yes, but the district must first bill the private insurance company to determine the extent of the insurer's payment liability. The private insurance will notify the district when the benefits have been expended (or if they deny payment for school-related services). It is at this time that Medicaid can be billed (Arkansas Department of Education, 2011).

Note: Federal and state requirements indicate that Medicaid is the "payer of last resort." This means that third-party payments must be pursued before billing Medicaid for IDEIA-related services.

Will a child receive more services if the school can bill a third party?

No. A child's IEP reflects his/her individual needs and the services to meet those needs. No matter who pays for them, the services, as written into the IEP, remain the same and must be delivered in a timely manner. A child won't receive more services if a third party can be billed or less if it can't (PACER Center: Families and Advocates Partnership for Education, 2011).

Does a school need parental consent to use private health insurance?

Under IDEIA, the school needs parental consent to use private health insurance. Each time a school wants to bill the parents' private insurance it must:

- get parental written consent and

- remind parents that their child will receive all the services in his/her IEP even if they refuse to consent to the use of their private insurance.

Parents are not required to allow the school to bill their private insurance. They can refuse to consent to this type of third-party billing for any reason [34 C.F.R. 300.154(e)].

What does "appropriate" mean?

IDEIA does not have a specific definition for the meaning of "appropriate." The interpretation of this term has a detailed history (one which will be addressed in later questions in this chapter). The lack of a specific definition of an "appropriate" education in IDEIA has led to frequent disagreements between parents and schools regarding what constitutes an appropriate education for a particular student.

According to the U.S. Department of Education (2010), an appropriate education:

> …may comprise education in regular classes, education in regular classes with the use of related aids and services, or special education and related services in separate classrooms for all or portions of the school day. Special education may include specially designed instruction in classrooms, at home, or in private or public institutions, and may be accompanied by related services such as speech

therapy, occupational and physical therapy, psychological counseling, and medical diagnostic services necessary to the child's education.

An appropriate education will include:

- education services designed to meet the individual education needs of students with disabilities as adequately as the needs of nondisabled students are met

- the education of each student with a disability with nondisabled students, to the maximum extent appropriate to the needs of the student with a disability

- evaluation and placement procedures established to guard against misclassification or inappropriate placement of students, and a periodic reevaluation of students who have been provided special education or related services, and

- establishment of due process procedures that enable parents and guardians to: receive required notices; review their child's records; and challenge identification, evaluation and placement decisions.

Due process procedures must also provide for an impartial hearing with the opportunity for participation by parents and representation by counsel, and a review procedure. (U.S. Department of Education 2010)

Has an "appropriate" education been challenged in the U.S. Supreme Court?

Yes. Given the absence of a clear definition of the term "appropriate" in the federal law, the meaning of the term was first addressed by the U.S. Supreme Court in *Hendrick Hudson District Board of Education v. Rowley* (1982). An analysis of whether a school system is meeting its statutory obligation under IDEIA must begin with a consideration of *Rowley*.

The facts presented to the court in *Rowley* were rather straightforward. The case concerned a first-grade girl with a hearing impairment named Amy Rowley, who was a student at the Furnace Woods School in Hendrick Hudson Central School District, Peekskill, N.Y. Amy had minimal hearing but was an excellent lip reader. When she was only in first grade, a dispute arose between parents and school officials.

Although no one challenged Amy's eligibility for special education and related services under the P.L. 94-142, the school and parents disagreed about what services were necessary for Amy. Amy's parents, also deaf, argued that the school district should provide Amy a sign language interpreter in order to allow her to understand her teachers and classmates.

School officials contended that the services she was already receiving were sufficient. Amy received speech and language therapy and the services of a teacher of the deaf in addition to the program available in the first-grade classroom. The school also outfitted her with an FM amplification system. School officials argued that Amy was achieving passing marks with the programming provided and therefore did not need additional services to succeed.

The parents maintained that Amy's impairment was such that only a fraction of information was available to her through audition or speech reading, and thus an interpreter was necessary to provide her learning opportunities comparable to those of nondisabled peers. The parents filed an administrative complaint to contest the denial of the interpreter services. The hearing officer ruled in favor of the school district and the parents appealed. The federal district court ruled in the parents' favor and the second Circuit Court of Appeals affirmed that ruling. The school district appealed to the United States Supreme Court.

In *Rowley*, the U.S. Supreme Court identified two areas of inquiry in determining whether a State has met its requirements of a FAPE:

1. Did the state comply with the procedures set forth under IDEIA (e.g. parental consent, nondiscriminatory evaluation, parental involvement in decision making, etc.)? (See Chapters 4 and 5 and the next question below for a more detailed explanation.)

2. Was the individualized educational program developed to enable the child to receive "educational benefits"?

"If these requirements are met, the state has complied with the obligations imposed by Congress and the courts can require no more." (Judge Rehnquist)

The U.S. Supreme Court overturned the Court of Appeals' decision. It held that that the federal law (P.L. 94-142) did not require schools to proportionally "maximize the potential" of handicapped children.

The Supreme Court found that the standard for FAPE required educational instruction specially designed to meet the unique needs of the handicapped child, supported by such services as are necessary to permit the child "to benefit" from the instruction.

> We hold that the state satisfies the FAPE requirement by providing personalized instruction with sufficient support services to permit the child to benefit educationally from that instruction. (*Hendrick Hudson District Board of Education v. Rowley*, 1982)

What are examples of procedural violations under IDEIA?

According to St Cyr (2011), the four broad categories that most rules fall into are the following.

Timeliness

Whenever a school is making a special education decision (evaluation, placement, IEP changes, etc.), it must occur within a specified time frame. The reason that Congress, through IDEA, put so much emphasis on timeliness is because, historically, schools tended to severely prolong decision making. This deprived special education students of precious instructional time.

Parent participation

Special education rules heavily emphasize a parent's right to participate meaningfully in the decision-making process. In the pre-regulation era, many school districts discounted parental insight and knowledge. Congress recognized that this is critical to understanding a student's learning needs.

Notice

Congress recognized that parents have an inherent right to make decisions about their child's best interests. The purpose of notice procedures is to ensure that parents are the ultimate decider of important educational decisions and that they understand what they are agreeing to.

Arbitrary decisions

The fourth category pertains to rules that prohibit arbitrary decisions when considering a student's special education needs. In the pre-regulation era, schools tended to make important special education decisions which weren't based on data, facts, or "good reasons."

What are examples of a student not receiving educational benefit?

The second take-away from *Rowley* is that a mere procedural violation, in itself, does not mean a student is deprived of a FAPE. *Rowley* held that special education procedures were merely mechanisms to protect one's substantive rights: an education (St Cyr, 2011). This means that one must tie the procedural violation to an educational impact (substantive right). When a court or hearing officer is trying to determine whether a substantive educational violation occurred, they look at whether the current educational services were "reasonably calculated to provide an educational benefit" [*Hendrick Hudson District Board of Education v. Rowley*, 458 U.S. 176, 203 (1982)]. The analysis tends to be qualitative, but often considers whether the education was likely to produce progression versus regression. Other questions include whether the student made meaningful progress and whether the current services provided only a minimal benefit to the learner. The take-away is that while the strictly academic impact is telling, the overall analysis varies from student to student.

The bottom line is that there is no typical depiction of a learner whose educational needs aren't being met. The following is a non-exclusive list of substantive educational deficits:

- the student had an educational impairment that the school failed to identify

- grade retention

- using the regular school discipline system to punish behavior that is attributed to an educational impairment, which excludes the student from special education services

- failure to evaluate a high incidence of behavior problems that may be attributed to an already identified educational impairment

- below-level performance in an academic area (reading, reading fluency, math, writing, etc.)

- failure to make progress on an individualized education plan (IEP)

- student drop-out

- education occurs outside of the least restrictive environment (LRE)

- failure to perform in the proficient range on high-stakes tests

- poor grades

- child is so discouraged with school that he/she skips classes frequently.

What does the *Rowley* decision mean to children with disabilities today?

Subsequent court decisions interpreted *Rowley* to mean that IDEIA does not require schools to provide students with the best or optimal education, nor to ensure that students with disabilities receive services to enable them to maximize their potential.

Since IDEIA is silent as to what constitutes educational benefit, the standard is often defined by ongoing case law. Most courts have found that in order to show a FAPE is being provided, the child must make some educational progress. A number of courts have struggled with the question of how much progress is sufficient, as the standards are still somewhat vague (Guersney and Klare, 2008).

Does a FAPE require a child with a disability to receive the "best" education available?

No. Essentially, FAPE requires that every child with a disability receive an education that is individually tailored to meet his/her needs and includes all related services necessary to benefit from the special education instruction.

It is important to note that FAPE does *not* require that children with disabilities receive the "best" educational program available; FAPE requires only that children with disabilities receive an "appropriate" educational program, uniquely suited to their needs.

Courts sometimes refer to this as the Cadillac versus Chevrolet argument, with the student entitled to a serviceable Chevrolet, not a brand-new Cadillac (Johnson, 2003).

Does a FAPE require a child with a disability to maximize his/her potential?

No. The U.S. Supreme Court, in *Rowley*, ruled that a FAPE does not require schools to maximize the potential of students with disabilities. Rather, a FAPE is a specially designed program that meets the individual needs of students and allows them to receive "educational benefit" (*Hendrick Hudson District Board of Education v. Rowley*, 1982).

The lack of a specific definition of an "appropriate" education in IDEIA has led to frequent disagreements between parents and schools regarding what constitutes an appropriate education for a particular student.

How do we know if an education is providing educational benefit to a student?

Perhaps the clearest evidence that the educational program is not providing educational benefit is that the child is not progressing educationally, or is even actually regressing in the present educational placement. Under IDEIA, an "appropriate" education enables the child to make progress in the general curriculum as well as advance towards IEP goals [34 C.F.R. 300.101; 20 U.S.C. 1412(a)(1)(A)].

No generic formula can be applied, nor can the progress of a child with a disability be compared to children without disabilities.

Essentially, FAPE requires that every child with a disability receive an education that is individually tailored to meet his/her needs and includes all related services necessary to benefit from the special education instruction.

Is a student with a disability required to receive a FAPE upon graduation with a regular high school diploma?

No. A student with a disability who graduates does not have the right to educational services beyond graduation [34 C.F.R. 300.102(a)(3)(i)]. There is no duty to provide a FAPE to any students with disabilities who graduate with a regular high school diploma [34 C.F.R. 300.102]. Under IDEIA, the school system is only obligated to provide post-graduation educational services "to the extent and in the same proportion that it does for non-handicapped students."

Notice of **Procedural Safeguards, Prior Written Notice, and Consent**

What are parental rights of participation?

A primary principle of IDEIA is the right of parents of children with disabilities to participate in all aspects of their child's educational decision making [34 C.F.R. 300.121]. Briefly summarized, some of the most important parental rights of participation under IDEIA are (Pierangelo and Giuliani, 2012):

- The right to participate in meetings related to the evaluation, identification, and educational placement of their child.

- The right to participate in meetings related to the provision of a free appropriate public education (FAPE) to their child.

- The right to be members of any group that decides whether their child is a "child with a disability" and meets eligibility criteria for special education and related services.

- The right to be members of the team that develops, reviews, and revises the individualized education program (IEP) for their child.

- The right to be members of any group that makes placement decisions for their child. If neither parent can attend the meeting where placement is decided, the school must use other methods to ensure their participation, including individual or conference calls, or video conferencing.

Must parents participate in every aspect of the special education process?

No. There is no federal requirement that parents *must* participate. Participation is a voluntary choice on the part of parents. IDEIA ensures that parents are afforded every chance to participate; however, the amount of participation and the extent of involvement on the part of the parent is at the discretion of each parent. As you can imagine, parents differ in the extent and ways in which they become involved in their child's education. However, research suggests that collaborative working partnerships between schools and families develop over time when there is a feeling of mutual respect and consideration, and where there is a strong common focus working towards providing an appropriate education for the child (National Association of Special Education Teachers, 2011).

What is the Notice of Procedural Safeguards?

School districts are required to provide parents of a child with a disability with a notice containing a full explanation of the procedural safeguards available under IDEIA and U.S. Department of Education regulations. This is known as the Notice of Procedural Safeguards (sometimes referred to as the PSN or Procedural Safeguards Notice). The 13 specific safeguards that must be described in the Notice of Procedural Safeguards are ([34 C.F.R. 300.504(c)]; Pierangelo and Giuliani, 2012):

- prior written notice

- independent educational evaluations

- parental consent

- access to education records

- the opportunity to present and resolve complaints through the due process complaint and state complaint procedures, including the timeline for filing a complaint, the opportunity to resolve the complaint, and the differences between the two procedures (such as their jurisdiction or authority, issues covered, filing and decisional timelines, and relevant procedures)

- the availability of mediation

- the child's placement while any due process complaint is pending procedures for students who are subject to placement in an interim alternative educational setting

- requirements for parents who unilaterally place their child in a private school at public expense

- hearings on due process complaints, including requirements that evaluation results and recommendations be disclosed

- state-level appeals (if applicable in the state)

- civil actions, including the time period in which to file those actions

- attorneys' fees

- procedures for students who are subject to placement in an interim alternative educational setting.

How often does the Notice of Procedural Safeguards have to be given to parents?

The Notice of Procedural Safeguards must be given to parents at least once a year [34 C.F.R. 300.504(a)].

When does the Notice of Procedural Safeguards have to be given to parents?

The Notice of Procedural Safeguards must be given to parents:

- the first time their child is referred for a special education evaluation or if they request an evaluation [34 C.F.R. 300.504(a)(1)]

- the first time the parents file a complaint with the Department of Education in a school year [34 C.F.R. 300.504(a)(2)]

- the first time the parents or the district requests a due process hearing in a school year [34 C.F.R. 300.504(a)(2)]

- on the date the district decides to change the placement of their child by removing him/her from school for a violation of the district discipline policy [34 C.F.R. 300.504(a)(3)], or

- upon parental request [34 C.F.R. 300.504(a)(4)].

A public agency also may place a current copy of the procedural safeguards notice on its internet website, if a website exists [34 C.F.R. 300.504(a) and (b); 20 U.S.C. 1415(d)(1)].

Is the Notice of Procedural Safeguards automatically sent to parents or do they have to ask for it?

The Notice of Procedural Safeguards will be automatically sent to the parents by the school system. It is the responsibility of the school system to provide parents with their rights under IDEIA [34 C.F.R. 300.504(a)].

What is prior written notice (PWN)?

Prior written notice (PWN) is written notification from the school telling parents that it is considering making certain decisions or taking certain actions regarding the child's education. The purpose is to provide parents with information so that they will be able to participate in the decision-making process (Texas Education Agency, Division of IDEA Coordination, 2006).

Prior written notice must:

- describe what the school district proposes or refuses to do

- explain why the school district is proposing or refusing to take the action

- describe how the school district decided to propose or refuse to take the action, including telling the parent about each evaluation procedure, assessment, record, or report that the school district used to make its decision, and

- describe any other options that the student's IEP team considered and the reasons why those options were rejected.

Simply stated, prior written notice is notification that parents will receive from the school system at specific times. It must describe what the school is proposing to do or refusing to do and it must explain why the action is proposed or refused (Arkansas Department of Education, 2011).

Prior written notice includes informing parents of future meetings well enough in advance to guarantee that they have the chance to attend and scheduling those meetings at a mutually agreed time and place.

When must a school district provide the parent(s) with prior written notice?

A school district must provide parents with prior written notice each time it proposes to initiate or change, or refuses to initiate or change:

- the identification of a child

- the evaluation and educational placement of a child, or

- the provision of a free appropriate public education (FAPE) to a child.

The school district must give the parent(s) the prior written notice a reasonable time before the district proposes to or refuses to initiate or change the identification, evaluation, educational placement of the student, or the provision of FAPE to the student. If a proposed action by the school district requires parental consent, the district must give prior notice at the same time it requests parental consent.

What is required in the written notice?

IDEIA requires that specific information be included in the written notice. The written notice must include:

- a description of the action proposed or refused by the district [34 C.F.R. 300.503(b)(1)]

- an explanation of why the district proposes or refuses to take the action [34 C.F.R. 300.503(b)(2)]

- a description of each evaluation procedure, assessment, record, or report the district used as a basis for its proposal or refusal [34 C.F.R. 300.503(b)(3)]

- a statement that the parents of a child with a disability have protection under these procedural safeguards and information about how they can get a copy of the brochure describing the procedural safeguards [34 C.F.R. 300.503(b)(4)]

- sources for parents to contact as to where they can obtain assistance in understanding these procedural safeguards [34 C.F.R. 300.503(b)(5)]

- a description of other options the IEP team considered and the reasons why those options were rejected [34 C.F.R. 300.503(b)(6)], and

- a description of other factors relevant to the district's proposal or refusal [34 C.F.R. 300.503(b)(7)].

What are the language requirements of written notice?

Notice must be written in language understandable to the general public and provided in the native language of the parent(s) or other mode of communication used by the parent(s), unless it is clearly not feasible to do so (Hamilton County Educational Service Center, 2011). If the native language or other mode of communication of the parent(s) is not a written language, the school district must take steps to ensure that [34 C.F.R. 300.503(c)]:

- the notice is translated orally or by other means to the parent(s) in his/her native language or other mode of communication

- the parent(s) understands the content of the notice, and

- there is written evidence that the above requirements have been met.

Can notice be provided by an electronic mail communication?

Yes. A parent of a child with a disability may elect to receive notices by an electronic mail communication, if the public agency makes that option available [34 C.F.R. 300.505; 20 U.S.C. 1415(n)].

Is a school district required to inform parents about upcoming meetings?

Yes. Notice regarding upcoming meetings that the school provides to parents will (Pierangelo and Giuliani, 2012):

- include the purpose, time, and location of the meeting

- indicate who will attend the meeting, and

- let parents know that they may invite individuals with knowledge or special expertise about their child.

If a child is moving from early intervention services to school-age services, is prior written notice required?

Yes. If a child is moving from early intervention services (known as Part C of IDEIA) to school-aged services, including preschool (funded under Part B of IDEIA), the notice the school sends the parents will also let them know that they, as parents, may ask that the Part C service coordinator or other representatives of the Part C system be invited to the initial IEP meeting. The purpose of inviting Part C staff to the meeting is to help the parents' child make a smooth transition from one set of services to another (National Dissemination for Children with Disabilities, 2009).

Does everything in the special education process require prior written notice?

No. Some gatherings are not considered "meetings" that require schools to give parents prior written notice (National Dissemination for Children with Disabilities, 2009). Meetings that do not require that parents be given notice are:

- informal or unscheduled conversations between school system staff

- conversations on issues such as teaching methodology, lesson plans, or coordination of services

- the preparations and activities of school staff developing a proposal (or a response to a parent proposal) that will be discussed at a later meeting.

Are meetings the only time the school will provide parents with prior written notice?

No, there are other times when school systems will need to provide parents with prior written notice. As previously mentioned, these include whenever the school system:

- proposes to initiate or change the identification, evaluation, or educational placement of a child or the provision of FAPE to a child, or

- refuses to initiate or change the identification, evaluation, or educational placement of a child or the provision of FAPE to a child.

This means that the school system must give parents prior written notice before it may take action or refuse to take action with regard to identifying their child as a "child with a disability," evaluating their child, determining their child's placement, or changing it. Notice is also required regarding providing FAPE to their child—in other words, the school system must provide prior written notice a reasonable time before it begins providing FAPE to a child, refuses to provide FAPE, or changes (or refuses to change) what that free appropriate public education involves (e.g. the services and supports that a child receives). Parents may choose to receive prior written notice by email communication, if the school makes that option available (National Dissemination for Children with Disabilities, 2009).

What are the IDEIA criteria for obtaining parental consent?

There are three criteria for parental consent. Parental consent is defined as the following [34 C.F.R. 300.9; 20 U.S.C. 1414(a)(1)(D)]:

1. The parent has been fully informed of all information relevant to the activity for which consent is sought, in his/her native language, or other mode of communication.

    Native language: When used with reference to a person of limited English-speaking ability, means the language normally used by the individual, or in the case of a child, the language normally used by the parents of the child [20 U.S.C. 1401(20)].

    Mode of communication: The means of communication normally used by individuals who are deaf, blind, or have no written language, and may include Braille, sign language, oral communication, or some form of technologically enhanced communication [34 C.F.R. 300.12].

2. The parent understands and agrees in writing to the carrying out of the activity for which his/her consent is sought, and the consent describes that activity and lists the records (if any) which will be released and to whom.

3. The parent understands that the gaining of consent is voluntary and may be revoked at any time.

What is the difference between consent and agreement?

It's important to recognize that there is a difference between "consent" and "agreement." In the school life of a child, there are many occasions when the parents and the school system can agree to take certain actions for the benefit of their child. Usually, this is done orally, and that's sufficient. But an oral agreement is *not* sufficient when parental consent is required. *Consent must be in writing.*

When will a school district ask for parental consent?

There are specific times the school system must make reasonable efforts to obtain parental consent before it may proceed on a proposed action [34 C.F.R. 300.300]. The most prominent of these times are:

*   before it may conduct an initial evaluation of a child

*   before it may begin providing special education and related services to a child for the first time, and

- before it may reevaluate a child

- excusal of members of the IEP team

- transition services.

Each of these is explained below.

Initial evaluation

The school must make reasonable efforts to obtain parental informed consent to determine whether their child is a child with a disability. Without parental consent, the school cannot conduct an initial evaluation of the child to determine if the child qualifies as a child with a disability [34 C.F.R. 300.300(a)(1)(i)].

Parental consent is not consent for initial provision of special education [34 C.F.R. 300.300(a)(1)(ii)].

If parents do not respond to a request for consent or if they refuse to provide consent for an initial evaluation, the district cannot override their refusal to provide consent [34 C.F.R. 300.300(a)(3)(i)].

Note: If a child is enrolled in the public school and the parent refuses to give consent for an initial evaluation or reevaluation, the school may request a due process hearing (see Chapter 10). A hearing officer may order the school to proceed without parental consent. A hearing officer may not order that the child be placed in special education without parental consent.

A district will not be found in violation of meeting its Child Find obligation or its obligations to conduct evaluations and reevaluations if parents refuse to consent to or fail to respond to a request for consent for an initial evaluation [34 C.F.R. 300.300(a) (3)(ii)].

For initial evaluations only, if the child is a ward of the state and is not residing with the child's parent, the public agency is not required to obtain informed consent from the parent for an initial evaluation to determine whether the child is a child with a disability if [34 C.F.R. 300.300(a)(2); 20 U.S.C. 1414(a)(1)(D)(iii)]:

- despite reasonable efforts to do so, the public agency cannot discover the whereabouts of the parent of the child

- the rights of the parents of the child have been terminated in accordance with state law, or

- the rights of the parent to make educational decisions have been subrogated by a judge in accordance with state law and consent for an initial evaluation has been given by an individual appointed by the judge to represent the child.

Initial placement and provision of special education services and related services

The district must obtain parental written consent before proceeding with the initial placement of a child in a special education program and the initial provision of special education services and related services to the child determined to be a child with a disability [34 C.F.R. 300.300(b)(1)].

If parents refuse to provide consent for the initial provision of special education and related services, or they fail to respond to a request to provide consent for the initial provision of special education and related services, the district will not be considered in violation for failure to provide the child with special education and related services for which the district requested consent [34 C.F.R. 300.300(b)(4)(i)].

Reevaluation

Parental consent is required before a district conducts a reevaluation of a child [34 C.F.R. 300.300(c)]. If parents refuse consent to a reevaluation, the district may not override their written refusal [34 C.F.R. 300.300(c)(1)(ii)].

Note: The school needs parental consent to reevaluate a child after the child begins to receive special education services. However, if the school can demonstrate that it took reasonable measures to obtain parental consent and the parents failed to respond, then the school can proceed without parental consent.

Excusal of members of the IEP team from attending a team meeting

Members of the IEP team may be excused from attending a team meeting if parents agree in writing in advance of the meeting. If the team will be discussing the excused team member's area, then the excused member must provide his/her input in writing before the team meeting. If parents do not agree to excuse the team member, then he/she must attend the IEP team meeting.

Transition services

Parental consent is required before personally identifiable information is released to officials of participating agencies providing or paying for transition services [34 C.F.R. 300.622(a)(2) and 300.321(b)(3)].

What is considered a "reasonable effort" to obtain parental consent?

IDEIA does not specifically define how much effort to obtain parental consent is "reasonable." However, school systems must maintain documentation of reasonable efforts to obtain parental consent for initial evaluations, to provide special education and related services for the first time, to reevaluation, and to locate parents of wards of the state for initial evaluations. The documentation must include a record of the school district's attempts in these areas, such as [34 C.F.R. 300.300(d)(5)]:

- detailed records of telephone calls made or attempted and the results of those calls

- copies of correspondence sent to the parents and any responses received

- detailed records of visits made to the parent's home or place of employment and the results of those visits.

When is parental consent not required?

Parental consent is not required before the school district (Indiana Department of Education, 2011):

- reviews existing data or information as part of an initial evaluation or a reevaluation

- administers a test or other assessment that is given to all children unless consent is required of all parents, or

- changes a child's placement for disciplinary reasons and certain other decisions relating to discipline (see Chapter 11 for more specific detail regarding the discipline of students with disabilities).

What if parents don't give their consent?

There are two ways in which a school system would not obtain parental consent for a proposed action:

- Parents explicitly refuse to provide consent.

- Parents don't respond to a request to provide consent.

When school systems cannot obtain a parent's consent for either of these reasons, their choices about what to do next are limited. IDEIA includes what are called "consent override" procedures, which permit schools to use IDEIA's procedural safeguards (such as mediation or due process) to try to obtain parental agreement or a ruling that overrides the parent's lack of consent—but only for certain proposed activities. Consent override is only an option for schools when the child is enrolled in a public school (or seeking to be enrolled there) and parents have not given consent for:

- an initial evaluation of their child, or

- their child's reevaluation.

Further, school systems may only exercise their consent override options to the extent that doing so does not violate the state's law regarding parental consent.

Schools may not attempt to override a parent's lack of consent (Pierangelo and Giuliani, 2012):

- for a child's initial evaluation or reevaluation, if parents are home-schooling the child or have placed the child in a private school at their own expense, or

- for the initial provision of special education and related services to the child (regardless of where that child is being schooled—at home, in a public school, or in a private school at parents' expense).

Can parental consent be revoked?

Yes. Consent is voluntary and may be revoked (taken back) in writing at any time [34 C.F.R. 300.9(c)(1) and 300.300(b)(4)].

If parents inform the school district in writing that they revoke their consent for their school district to provide special education and related services to their child, the school district:

- may not continue to provide special education and related services to the child

- must provide the parents with timely prior written notice of their proposal to discontinue special education and related services based on receipt of the written revocation of consent

- may not use due process procedures (i.e. mediation, resolution meeting, or an impartial due process hearing) in order to obtain agreement or a ruling that the services may be provided to their child

- is not in violation of the requirement to make FAPE available to the child for its failure to provide further special education and related services to their child

- is not required to have an IEP meeting or develop an IEP for their child for the further provision of special education and related services, and

- is not required to amend the child's education records to remove any reference to the child's receipt of special education and related services because of the revocation of consent.

Is revocation of consent retroactive?

No, revocation of consent is not retroactive; meaning revocation of consent does not negate an action that has occurred after the consent was given and before the consent was revoked [34 C.F.R. 300.9(c)(2)].

Does the requirement that a public agency obtain parental consent for the initial provision of special education and related services mean that parents must consent to each service included in the initial IEP developed for their child?

No. A public agency that is responsible for making FAPE available to a child with a disability must obtain consent from the parent of the child before the initial provision of special education and related services [34 C.F.R. 300.300(b)(1)]. However, this consent requirement only applies to the initial provision of special education and related services generally, and not to the particular special education and related services to be included in the child's initial IEP. In order to give consent to the initial provision of special education and related services, parents must be fully informed of what special education and related services are and the types of services their child might need, but not the exact program of services that would be included in an IEP to be developed for their child.

Once the public agency has obtained parental consent and before the initial provision of special education and related services, the IEP team would convene a meeting to develop an IEP for the child. Decisions about the program of special education and related services to be provided to the child are left to the child's IEP team, which must include the child's parents, a public agency representative, and other individuals. Although IDEIA does not require public agencies to obtain parental consent for particular services in a child's IEP, under the regulations, states are free to create additional parental consent rights, such as requiring parental consent for particular services. In cases where a state creates additional parental consent rights, the state must ensure that each public agency in the state has effective procedures to ensure that the parent's exercise of these rights does not result in a failure to provide FAPE to the child [34 C.F.R. 300.300(d)(2)].

What recourse is available to parents who consent to the initial provision of special education and related services but who disagree with a particular service or services in their child's IEP?

In situations where parents agree with the majority of services in their child's IEP, but disagree with the provision of a particular service or services, such as physical therapy or occupational therapy, the public agency should work with the parents informally to achieve agreement. While the parents and public agency are attempting to resolve their differences, the agency should provide the service or services that are not in dispute.

In situations where parents disagree with the provision of a particular special education or related service, and the parents and public agency later agree that the child would be provided with FAPE if the child did not receive that service, the public agency could decide not to provide the service with which the parents disagree. If, however, the parents and the public agency disagree about whether the child would be provided with FAPE if the child did not receive a particular special education or related service with which the parent disagrees, and the parents and public agency cannot resolve their differences informally, the parent may use dispute resolution options such as mediation or due process procedures to pursue the issue of whether the service with which the parent disagrees is not appropriate for their child (U.S. Department of Education, 2010).

May a foster parent provide consent for an initial evaluation even if the biological parent refuses to provide such consent?

No. If the biological parent of the child refuses consent for an initial evaluation of the child, and the parental rights of the biological parent have not been terminated in accordance with state law, or a court has not designated a foster parent to make educational decisions for the child in accordance with state law, a foster parent may not provide consent for an initial evaluation [34 C.F.R. 300.30(b)(1)].

Identification, Evaluations, and Independent Educational Evaluations
of Children with Suspected Disabilities

What are "Child Find" efforts?

Under IDEIA, each local education agency (LEA) must establish procedures by which children in need of special education and related services are identified. These are known as "Child Find" efforts. States are left to develop their own identification procedures, but IDEIA requires an active effort to identify children in need of special education services.

IDEIA defines "Child Find" as:

> The State must have in effect policies and procedures to ensure that all children with disabilities residing in the State, including children with disabilities who are homeless children or are wards of the State, and children with disabilities attending private schools, regardless of the severity of their disability, and who are in need of special education and related services, are identified, located, and evaluated; and a practical method is developed and implemented to determine which children are currently receiving needed special education and related services. [34 C.F.R. 300.111; 20 U.S.C. 1401(3); 1412(a)(3)]

What is annual public notice?

IDEIA mandates that it is the responsibility of the Department of Education in each state to ensure that all children with disabilities, regardless of the severity of the disability, residing there who are suspected to be in need of special education and related services are located, evaluated, and identified. According to state and federal special education regulations, annual public notice to parents of children who reside within a school district is required regarding Child Find responsibilities. This notice shall inform parents throughout the school district of the child identification activities and of the procedures followed to ensure confidentiality of information pertaining to students with disabilities or eligible young children.

Annual public notice must be given to inform the community about the right to, and availability of, educational services for children with disabilities. This includes highly mobile children, such as migrant and homeless children, and students in juvenile detention centers and adult correctional facilities. The notice must be calculated to reach all persons within the district and all persons responsible for children who are enrolled in the district's statewide correspondence program. It may include dissemination of information through public meetings, posters, district website, brochures, newspapers, radio, television, and presentations to community groups and agencies (Alaska State Department of Education, 2007).

The content of the annual public notice should include at least the following information:

1. the types of disabilities that qualify as a disabling condition

2. the educational needs of children with disabilities

3. the rights of children with disabilities (FAPE)

4. the services available to children with disabilities

5. confidentiality protections

6. whom to contact in the district (e.g. Child Find Coordinator) and how to get in touch with that person.

The public notice must be disseminated on an annual basis and be provided in each language for which a bilingual program is required in the district. Additionally, the district must maintain a yearly record of its techniques to ensure public awareness (e.g. clippings from newspapers, copies of brochures and letters).

What is an initial evaluation?

Under IDEIA, an evaluation means procedures used to determine whether a child has a disability and the nature and extent of the special education and related services that the child needs [34 C.F.R. 300.315; 20 U.S.C. 1414(a)(c)].

Each public agency must conduct a full and individual initial evaluation before the initial provision of special education and related services to a child with a disability [34 C.F.R. 300.301(a); 20 U.S.C. 1414(a)].

Either a parent of a child or a public agency may initiate a request for an initial evaluation to determine if the child is a child with a disability [34 C.F.R. 300.301(b); 20 U.S.C. 1414(a)].

Is an evaluation of a child for a suspected disability individualized?

Yes. The evaluation of a child for a suspected disability must be individualized, meaning that the procedures and methods of evaluation must address a student's unique needs, rather than be a general assessment that can be used interchangeably with all students [Pierangelo and Giuliani, 2012; 34 C.F.R. 300.301(a); 20 U.S.C. 1414(a)].

What are indicators of children who may have a suspected disability and need an evaluation?

- The child's rate of progress is not what is expected or the child is not meeting developmental milestones.

- The child's level of performance is significantly discrepant from that of his/ her peers.

- The child has a physical or health condition affecting educational performance.

- The child's behavior or interpersonal interactions are adversely affecting educational performance.

- The child's response to classroom accommodations and modifications has not been successful.

(Pierangelo and Giuliani, 2008)

Does IDEIA require screening of children?

Yes. A school district must establish and implement written procedures for screening all children in the district ages 3 through 21. Screening programs are intended to efficiently collect objective information in a few critical areas to complement any existing subjective information.

The screening of a student by a teacher or specialist to determine appropriate instructional strategies for curriculum implementation shall not be considered to be an evaluation for eligibility for special education and related services [34 C.F.R. 300.302(d); 20 U.S.C. 1414(a)(1)(E)].

Is parental consent required for an evaluation of a student with a suspected disability?

Yes. Before any evaluations, testing, and placement can be done, there must be parental consent [34 C.F.R. 300.300].

If the parent does not provide consent or fails to respond to a request for consent, the school may, but is not required to, use mediation or due process procedures to initiate an evaluation (Pierangelo and Giuliani, 2012).

For more detailed information on requirements for parental consent under IDEIA, see Chapter 4.

What evaluation procedures are required when assessing whether a child has a suspected disability?

A school must use a variety of evaluation tools and strategies when it conducts a full and individual evaluation of a child. The evaluation must assess the child in all areas related to the suspected disability. It must be sufficiently comprehensive to identify all of the child's needs for special education and related services, even if the needs are not commonly related to the child's particular category of disability.

The school must use technically sound instruments and procedures that are not biased against the child because of race, culture, language, or disability. These materials and procedures must be provided and administered in the language and form most likely to provide accurate information on what the child knows and can do [34 C.F.R. 300.304].

Once parental consent is obtained, when must the initial evaluation be conducted?

The initial evaluation must be conducted within 60 days of receiving parental consent [34 C.F.R. 300.301(c)(i)(ii)]. The IDEIA 60-day timeline applies only to the initial evaluation. Public agencies are not required to make the eligibility determination, obtain parental consent for the initial provision of special education and related services, conduct the initial meeting of the IEP team to develop the child's IEP, or initially provide special education and related services to a child with a disability during the IDEIA 60-day initial evaluation timeline.

The initial evaluation:

- must be conducted within 60 days of receiving parental consent for the evaluation, or

- if the state establishes a timeframe within which the evaluation must be conducted, within that timeframe.

The timeframe does not apply to a public agency if [34 C.F.R. 300.301(d); 20 U.S.C. 1414(a)]:

- the parent of a child repeatedly fails or refuses to produce the child for the evaluation, or

- a child enrolls in a school of another public agency after the relevant timeframe has begun, and prior to a determination by the child's previous public agency as to whether the child is a child with a disability. This applies only if the subsequent public agency is making sufficient progress to ensure a prompt completion of the evaluation, and the parent and subsequent public agency agree to a specific time when the evaluation will be completed.

Does the evaluation of a child for a suspected disability have to be performed before any action is taken with regard to an initial special education placement?

Yes. The evaluation of a child for a suspected disability must be performed before any action is taken with regard to an initial special education placement [34 C.F.R. 300.301; 20 U.S.C. 1414(a)].

When considering eligibility for special education, who must perform the evaluation?

When considering eligibility for special education, the evaluation must be done by trained and knowledgeable personnel, also referred to as a multidisciplinary team (MDT) [34 C.F.R. 300.304(c)(iv)]. The MDT performs the evaluation of the child for a suspected disability and then makes a recommendation to a committee on special education (states have different names for this committee) as to the child's eligibility for special education services (Pierangelo and Giuliani, 2008).

The MDT must use a variety of assessment tools and strategies to gather relevant functional and developmental information, including information provided by the parent that will assist in determining whether a child has a disability as defined under federal law.

Who are the members of the multidisciplinary team?

Members of the multidisciplinary team include:

- general education teacher
- school psychologist
- educational evaluator
- special education teacher
- speech and language pathologist
- medical personnel (when appropriate)
- social worker

- school/guidance counselor

- parents

- school nurse

- occupational and physical therapists (when appropriate).

Note: Under IDEIA, there has always been the general requirement of parental consent and notice. However, only recently have parents been mandated under IDEIA to be a part of the multidisciplinary team. The parents are part of the team that reviews existing evaluation data for both the initial and subsequent reevaluations of the child (Pierangelo and Giuliani, 2012).

Does IDEIA address concerns regarding testing bias?

Yes. All testing materials and procedures used for the purposes of evaluation and placement of children with disabilities must be selected and administered so as not to be racially or culturally discriminatory [34 C.F.R. 300.304(c)(1)(i)].

Does IDEIA address concerns pertaining to validation of tests?

Yes. All testing materials and procedures used for the purposes of evaluation and placement of children with disabilities must be validated for the specific purpose for which they are used [34 C.F.R. 300.304(c)(1)(iii)].

Can a single procedure be used as the sole criterion for determining an appropriate educational program for a child?

No. IDEIA is very explicit that no single procedure can be used as the sole criterion for determining an appropriate educational program for a child [34 C.F.R. 300.304(b)(2); 20 U.S.C. 1412(a)(6)(B)]. The assessment must be sufficiently comprehensive and use a variety of tools and strategies to gather relevant information on the child [34 C.F.R. 300.304(b)(2) and (6)].

What are the goals of a comprehensive assessment?

The goals of a comprehensive assessment vary for each child with a suspected disability. However, in general, the objectives to be attained are (Pierangelo and Giuliani, 2012):

- to measure a student's current levels of academic performance/learning characteristics, social/emotional performance, health, and physical development

- to identify a student's strengths and weaknesses in each of these areas in order to formulate realistic expectations for achievement

- to identify a student's strengths and weaknesses in each of these areas in order to facilitate enhanced student outcomes through effective teaching

- to identify the language needed for instruction and special education services, and

- to collect and organize information that the IEP team can use to determine a student's need and eligibility for special education services.

Must all areas related to a suspected disability be assessed?

Yes. The extent of the evaluation performed is dependent on the suspected disability of the child. All areas related to a suspected disability must be assessed, including, if appropriate, health, vision, hearing, social and emotional status, general intelligence, academic performance, communicative status, and motor abilities [34 C.F.R. 300.304(c)(4); 20 U.S.C. 1412(a)(6)(B)].

What evaluation procedures are required under IDEIA?

In conducting the evaluation, the public agency must meet the following three conditions:

1. Use a variety of assessment tools and strategies to gather relevant functional, developmental, and academic information about the child, including information provided by the parent, that may assist in determining—

   a. Whether the child is a child with a disability under IDEIA, and

   b. The content of the child's IEP, including information related to enabling the child to be involved in and progress in the general education curriculum (or for a preschool child, to participate in appropriate activities).

2. Not use any single measure or assessment as the sole criterion for determining whether a child is a child with a disability and for determining an appropriate educational program for the child, and

3. Use technically sound instruments that may assess the relative contribution of cognitive and behavioral factors, in addition to physical or developmental factors.

   [34 C.F.R. 300.304(b); 20 U.S.C. 1414(b)(1)–(3), 1412(a)(6)(B)]

Each public agency must also ensure that:

1. Assessments and other evaluation materials used to assess a child—

   a. Are selected and administered so as not to be discriminatory on a racial or cultural basis

b. Are provided and administered in the child's native language or other mode of communication and in the form most likely to yield accurate information on what the child knows and can do academically, developmentally, and functionally, unless it is clearly not feasible to so provide or administer

c. Are used for the purposes for which the assessments or measures are valid and reliable

d. Are administered by trained and knowledgeable personnel, and

e. Are administered in accordance with any instructions provided by the producer of the assessments.

2. Assessments and other evaluation materials include those tailored to assess specific areas of educational need and not merely those that are designed to provide a single general intelligence quotient.

3. Assessments are selected and administered so as best to ensure that if an assessment is administered to a child with impaired sensory, manual, or speaking skills, the assessment results accurately reflect the child's aptitude or achievement level or whatever other factors the test purports to measure, rather than reflecting the child's impaired sensory, manual, or speaking skills (unless those skills are the factors that the test purports to measure).

4. The child is assessed in all areas related to the suspected disability, including, if appropriate, health, vision, hearing, social and emotional status, general intelligence, academic performance, communicative status, and motor abilities.

5. Assessments of children with disabilities who transfer from one public agency to another public agency in the same school year are coordinated with those children's prior and subsequent schools, as necessary and as expeditiously as possible to ensure prompt completion of full evaluations.

6. In evaluating each child with a disability, the evaluation is sufficiently comprehensive to identify all of the child's special education and related services needs, whether or not commonly linked to the disability category in which the child has been classified.

7. Assessment tools and strategies that provide relevant information that directly assists persons in determining the educational needs of the child are provided.

[34 C.F.R. 300.304(c); 20 U.S.C. 1414(b)(1)–(3), 1412(a)(6)(B)]

Must the assessments and other evaluation measures used to determine eligibility for special education and related services include a doctor's medical diagnosis, particularly for children suspected of having autism or attention deficit disorder/attention deficit hyperactivity disorder?

No. There is no explicit requirement in IDEIA to include a medical diagnosis as part of the eligibility determination for any of the disability categories. The purpose of the evaluation is to determine whether the child qualifies as a child with a disability and the nature and extent of the educational needs of the child. Under the law [34 C.F.R. 300.304(b)(1)], in conducting the evaluation, the public agency must use a variety of assessment tools and strategies to gather relevant functional, developmental, and academic information about the child that may assist in determining whether the child is a child with a disability and the educational needs of the child. That information could include information from a physician, if determined appropriate, to assess the effect of the child's medical condition on the child's eligibility and educational needs. However, no single measure or assessment may be used as the sole criterion for determining whether the child is a child with a disability and for determining an appropriate educational program for the child [34 C.F.R. 300.304(b)(2)].

In interpreting evaluation data for the purpose of determining whether the child is a child with a disability under IDEIA and the educational needs of the child, the group of qualified professionals and the parent must draw upon information from a variety of sources, including aptitude and achievement tests, parent input, and teacher recommendations, as well as information about the child's physical condition, social or cultural background, and adaptive behavior [34 C.F.R. 300.306(c)(1)(i)]. The public agency must ensure that information obtained from all of these sources is documented and carefully considered [34 C.F.R. 300.306(c)(1)(ii)]. There is nothing in IDEIA that would prevent a public agency from obtaining a medical diagnosis prior to determining whether the child has a particular disability and the educational needs of the child. Also, there is nothing in IDEIA that would prohibit a state from requiring that a medical diagnosis be obtained for purposes of determining whether a child has a particular disability, such as attention deficit disorder/attention deficit hyperactivity disorder or autism, provided the medical diagnosis is obtained at public expense and at no cost to the parents and is not used as the sole criterion for determining an appropriate educational program for the child. Further, if a state requires a medical diagnosis consistent with the above criteria, such a requirement exceeds the requirements of IDEIA.

When doing the evaluation, must all tests be given in the child's native language?

Yes. When doing the evaluation, all tests must be given in the child's native language [34 C.F.R. 300.304(c)(1)(ii–v)].

When doing the evaluation, must all reports be written in the parent's native language?

Yes. When doing the evaluation, all reports must be written in the parent's native language [34 C.F.R. 300.304(c)(1)(ii–v)].

If a student is identified for special education services, do the parents meet again with the school to discuss how their child is doing?

Yes. If a student is identified for special education services, there must be a meeting at the end of each year to discuss the progress made toward the student's goals. This is known as the annual review (Pierangelo and Giuliani, 2008).

Are reevaluations required if a child is receiving special education services?

Yes. A public agency must ensure that a reevaluation of each child with a disability is conducted:

- If the public agency determines that the educational or related services needs, including improved academic achievement and functional performance, of the child warrant a reevaluation, or

- If the child's parent or teacher requests a reevaluation.

[34 C.F.R. 300.303]

A reevaluation:

- May occur not more than once a year, unless the parent and the public agency agree otherwise, and

- Must occur at least once every 3 years, unless the parent and the public agency agree that a reevaluation is unnecessary. This is called a "triennial review."

[34 C.F.R. 300.303]

What does IDEIA require regarding reevaluations?

As part of any reevaluation, the IEP team and other qualified professionals, as appropriate, must:

1. Review existing evaluation data on the child, including—

   a. Evaluations and information provided by the parents of the child

   b. Current classroom-based, local, or State assessments, and classroom-based observations, and

   c. Observations by teachers and related services providers, and

2. On the basis of that review, and input from the child's parents, identify what additional data, if any, are needed to determine—

   a. Whether the child is a child who continues to meet the criteria as a child with a disability

   b. The present levels of academic achievement and related developmental needs of the child

   c. Whether the child continues to need special education and related services, and

   d. Whether any additions or modifications to the special education and related services are needed to enable the child to meet the measurable annual goals set out in the IEP of the child and to participate, as appropriate, in the general education curriculum.

[34 C.F.R. 300.305(a)]

If the IEP team and other qualified professionals, as appropriate, determine that no additional data are needed to determine whether the child continues to be a child with a disability, and to determine the child's educational needs, the public agency must notify the child's parents of:

- that determination and the reasons for the determination, and

- the right of the parents to request an assessment to determine whether the child continues to be a child with a disability, and to determine the child's educational needs.

The evaluation is not required before the termination of a child's eligibility due to graduation from secondary school with a regular diploma, or due to exceeding the age eligibility for FAPE under state law [34 C.F.R. 300.305(e)(2); 20 U.S.C. 1414(c)]. For a child whose eligibility terminates, a public agency must provide the child with a summary of the child's academic achievement and functional performance, which shall include recommendations on how to assist the child in meeting the child's postsecondary goals [34 C.F.R. 300.305(e)(3); 20 U.S.C. 1414(c)].

What if a parent refuses to consent to the three-year reevaluation?

The three-year evaluation is also referred to as the triennial review. If a parent refuses to consent to a three-year reevaluation [34 C.F.R. 300.303(b)(2)], but requests that the public agency continue the provision of special education and related services to their child, the public agency has the following options:

1. The public agency and the parent may agree that the reevaluation is unnecessary [34 C.F.R. 300.303(b)(2)]. If such an agreement is reached, the three-year reevaluation need not be conducted. However, the public agency must continue to provide FAPE to the child.

2. If the public agency believes that the reevaluation is necessary, and the parent refuses to consent to the reevaluation, the public agency may, but is not required to, pursue the reevaluation by using the IDEIA's consent override procedures [34 C.F.R. 300.300(a)(3)], as long as overriding a parental refusal to consent to a reevaluation is permissible under state law.

3. If the public agency chooses not to pursue the reevaluation by using the consent override procedures, and the public agency believes, based on a review of existing evaluation data on the child, that the child does not continue to have a disability or does not continue to need special education and related services, the public agency may determine that it will not continue the provision of special education and related services to the child. If the public agency determines that it will not continue the provision of special education and related services to the child, the public agency must provide the parent with prior written notice of its proposal to discontinue the provision of FAPE to the child, including the right of the parent to use mediation or due process procedures if the parent disagrees with the public agency's decision to discontinue the provision of FAPE to the child.

What is an independent educational evaluation (IEE)?

Under certain circumstances, the local education agency (LEA) is required to provide, at public expense, an independent educational evaluation (IEE). An IEE is defined as an evaluation conducted by a qualified examiner who is not employed by the agency responsible for the child's education [34 C.F.R. 300.502(a)(3)(i)].

Why would a parent wish to obtain an IEE?

According to Imber and Cortiella (2010), there are several reasons that parents often seek to obtain an IEE. These include:

- a belief that their child has an undiagnosed disability or, conversely, that their child does not have a disability

- a belief that the school's evaluation was inadequate (lacks thoroughness)

- disagreement about such issues as:

  ○ whether a child should continue to receive special education services

  ○ the specific nature of the disability (such as other health-impaired v. emotional disturbance)

  ○ the type of services offered (such as inclusion v. self-contained)

  ○ the qualifications of the school's evaluators (such as experience with evaluating a particular disability such as Asperger's syndrome)

  ○ a child's present level of performance and/or annual goals

  ○ the relative progress accomplished toward the goals.

When can parents request an independent educational evaluation at public expense?

Parents have the right to an IEE of their child at public expense if they disagree with an evaluation of their child obtained by their school district, subject to the following conditions:

1. If parents request an IEE of their child at public expense, their school district must, without unnecessary delay, either: (a) provide an IEE at public expense, or (b) file a due process hearing request to show that its evaluation of their child is appropriate; unless the school district demonstrates in a hearing that the evaluation of their child that they obtained did not meet the school district's criteria.

2. If the parents' school district requests a hearing and the final decision is that their school district's evaluation of their child is appropriate, they still have the right to an IEE, but not at public expense.

3. If parents request an IEE of their child, the school district may ask why they object to the evaluation of their child obtained by their school district. However, the school district may not require an explanation and may not unreasonably delay either providing the IEE of the child at public expense or filing a due process complaint to request a due process hearing to defend the school district's evaluation of the child.

Note: Parents are entitled to only one IEE of their child at public expense each time their school district conducts an evaluation of their child with which they disagree [34 C.F.R. 300.502(b)].

Must school districts provide parents with information concerning where an IEE may be obtained?

Yes. IDEIA regulations require that, at the request of the parent, school districts provide parents with information concerning where an IEE may be obtained, including a list of qualified examiners [34 C.F.R. 300.502(a)(2)].

Can the school district limit the parents in their choice of an examiner for an IEE?

No. Although a school district may provide parents with a list of qualified examiners, it cannot limit the parents in their choice of an examiner listed [34 C.F.R. 300.502].

If a parent requests an IEE, does the school district have the right to ask the parent for the reasons he/she objects to the public evaluation?

Yes. If a parent requests an IEE, the school district may ask the parent for the reasons he/she objects to the public evaluation [34 C.F.R. 300.502(b)(4)].

If a parent requests an IEE, and the school district asks the parents for the reasons he/she objects to the public evaluation, is the parent required to give a reason?

No. The parent is not required to give reasons for disagreement [34 C.F.R. 300.502(b)(4)].

Whenever an IEE is made at public expense, must the school district criteria for evaluations be met?

Yes. If an IEE is at public expense, the criteria under which the evaluation is obtained, including the qualifications of the examiner, must be the same as the criteria that the school district uses when it initiates an evaluation (to the extent those criteria are consistent with the right to an independent educational evaluation) [34 C.F.R. 300.502(e)].

If parents disagree with the school district's evaluation, in what ways can they proceed to obtain the IEE?

If parents disagree with the school district's evaluation, they have three ways to proceed to obtain the IEE:

- First, they may seek agreement of the school district to pay for the IEE.

- Second, they may unilaterally seek an evaluation and subsequently seek reimbursement from the school district. No approval from or notice to the school district is required by parents in order to permit later reimbursement for the IEE.

- Third, rather than seeking an IEE and risking success in seeking reimbursement, a parent may opt to request a due process hearing. At the hearing, the parents request that an IEE is ordered by the hearing officer (Guersney and Klare, 2008).

How many publicly funded IEEs are parents entitled to for each time an LEA evaluation is conducted over which there is disagreement?

Parents are entitled to only one publicly funded IEE for each time a school district evaluation is conducted over which there is disagreement [34 C.F.R. 300.502(a)(5)].

Can parents get an IEE at their own expense?

Yes. Parents always have the right to get an IEE at their own expense, even if a due process hearing holds that the school district's evaluation was appropriate [34 C.F.R. 300.502(c)].

If an IEE is paid for by the parent, must it be considered by the school district in determining the child's educational needs?

Yes. An IEE paid for by the parent must be considered by the school district in determining the child's educational needs and may be presented at any due process hearing [34 C.F.R. 300.502(c)].

Who is responsible for payment of an IEE when it is requested by a hearing officer?

If a hearing officer requests an independent educational evaluation as part of a hearing on a due process complaint, the cost of the evaluation must be at public expense [34 C.F.R. 300.502(d)]. Public expense means that the public agency either pays for the full cost of the evaluation or ensures that the evaluation is otherwise provided at no cost to the parent [34 C.F.R. 300.502(a)(3)(i)].

Eligibility for Special Education

Who determines whether a child is eligible for special education?

Upon completion of the administration of tests and other evaluation materials, a determination of whether the student is eligible for special education services shall be made by a group of qualified professionals and a parent of the child. This team is often referred to as the committee on special education, or pupil personnel team, or eligibility committee or IEP team. The names of this particular group vary from state to state [34 C.F.R. 300.306].

Note: We will use the term "eligibility committee" throughout the rest of this chapter.

When is a school-age student eligible for special education services?

A school-age student is eligible for special education services when (Pierangelo and Giuliani, 2007a):

- the student meets the criteria for one or more of the 13 IDEIA disability classifications indicated in this chapter, and

- the student requires special education services to benefit from instruction, and

- the determining factor in making the eligibility determination is not limited English proficiency or lack of instruction in reading or math.

When is a school-age student not eligible for special education services?

A school-age student is not eligible for special education services if [34 C.F.R. 300.306(b)]:

- the student does not meet the criteria for one or more of the 13 IDEIA disability classifications indicated in this chapter, or

- the student meets the criteria but does not require special education services to benefit from instruction, or

- the IEP team has concluded that limited English proficiency or the lack of instruction in reading or math is the determining factor in making the eligibility determination.

How many possible classifications are there in special education?

There are 13 IDEIA categories of disabilities. They include autism, deaf-blindness, developmental delay, hearing impairment, emotional disturbance, learning disability, mental retardation, multiple disabilities, orthopedic impairment, other health impairment, speech or language impairment, traumatic brain injury, and visual impairment including blindness. Each of these has a specific definition and criteria that the student must meet in order to be classified as having that disability. These disability classifications are defined in Chapter 1.

Eligibility for special education and related services is determined by documenting the existence of one or more of the disabilities listed above, its adverse effect on educational performance, and the consequent need for special education services. If the eligibility committee determines that one or more of these elements does not apply to a particular student, that student is not eligible for special education services (Pierangelo and Giuliani, 2007b).

What are the responsibilities of the eligibility committee?

Some of the responsibilities of the district's eligibility committee are to (Pierangelo and Giuliani, 2007a):

- review and evaluate all relevant information that may appear on each student with a disability

- determine the least restrictive educational setting for any student having been classified as having a disability

- follow appropriate procedures and take appropriate action on any student referred as having a suspected disability

- determine the suitable classification for a student with a suspected disability

- review, at least annually, the status of each student with a disability residing within the district

- evaluate the adequacy of programs, services, and facilities for students with disabilities in the district

- maintain ongoing communication in writing to parents/guardians in regards to planning, modifying, changing, reviewing, placing, or evaluating the program, classification, or educational plan for a student with a disability

- advise the Board of Education as to the status and recommendations for all students with disabilities in the district.

Who are the members of the eligibility committee?

Membership of the eligibility committee shall include school division personnel representing the disciplines providing assessments, the special education administrator or designee, and the parents/guardians. At least one representative in the group must have either assessed or observed the student (Pierangelo and Giuliani, 2012).

What are the procedures for determining eligibility?

In interpreting evaluation data for the purpose of determining if a child is a child with a disability, and the educational needs of the child, each public agency must:

- draw upon information from a variety of sources, including aptitude and achievement tests, parent input, and teacher recommendations, as well as information about the child's physical condition, social or cultural background, and adaptive behavior, and

- ensure that information obtained from all of these sources is documented and carefully considered.

If a determination is made that a child has a disability and needs special education and related services, an IEP must be developed for the child [34 C.F.R. 300.306; 20 U.S.C. 1414(b)(4) and (5)].

What are the eligibility criteria for a classification of autism?

To receive the classification of autism as student with a disability for special education services under IDEIA, the following criteria (1 through 7) should be met:

1. *The student exhibits impairments in communication:* The student is unable to use expressive and receptive language for social communication in a developmentally appropriate manner; lacks nonverbal communication skills or uses abnormal nonverbal communication; uses abnormal form or content when speaking and/or is unable to initiate or sustain conversation with others.

2. *The student exhibits difficulties in forming appropriate relationships:* The student exhibits deficits relating to people, marked lack of awareness of others' feelings, abnormal seeking of comfort at times of distress, absent or abnormal social play, and/or inability to make friends. The student does not relate to or use objects in an age-appropriate or functional manner.

3. *The student exhibits unusual responses to sensory information:* The student exhibits unusual, repetitive, non-meaningful responses to auditory, visual, olfactory, taste, tactile, and/or kinesthetic stimuli.

4. *The student exhibits impairments in cognitive development:* The student has difficulty with concrete versus abstract thinking, awareness, judgment, and/or the ability to generalize. The student may exhibit perseverative thinking or impaired ability to process symbolic information.

5. *The student exhibits an abnormal range of activities:* The student shows a restricted repertoire of activities, interests, and imaginative development evident through stereotyped body movements, persistent preoccupation with parts of objects, distress over trivial changes in the environment, unreasonable insistence on routines, restricted range of interests, or preoccupation with one narrow interest.

6. *The student has been previously diagnosed with autism by a qualified professional:* A licensed clinical psychologist, psychiatrist, clinical neuropsychologist, specially trained neurologist, developmental pediatrician, or other specific medical or mental health professional qualified to diagnose autism has previously diagnosed the student; accompanied by a report with recommendations for instruction.

7. *The disability (autism) is adversely affecting the student's educational performance:* The eligibility committee uses multiple sources of information to determine that educational performance is adversely affected and is not primarily due to an emotional disability.

What are the eligibility criteria for a classification of deaf-blindness?

NOTE_____

The eligibility criteria for deaf-blindness under IDEIA are not specifically stated under the law. The eligibility criteria for this particular disability may differ from state to state. Therefore, the information pertaining to "eligibility" for this classification is the author's professional interpretation based on reviewing the states' guidelines and criteria.

In order to identify and be determined as eligible for special education services as a student with deaf-blindness, the eligibility committee shall document that the following four standards have been met:

1. The eligibility committee has determined that:

    a. the student meets the eligibility criteria for special education as a student with vision impairment *and* as a student with a hearing impairment, or

    b. the student meets eligibility criteria for either a hearing or vision impairment, but demonstrates inconclusive or inconsistent responses in the other sensory area (a functional assessment in the other sensory area substantiates the presence of an impairment in that area), or

    c. the student meets the minimum criteria for either a hearing or vision impairment and has a degenerative disease or pathology that affects the acuity of the other sensory area.

2. The student's disability has an adverse impact on the student's educational performance when the student is at the age of eligibility for kindergarten through age 21, or has an adverse impact on the student's developmental progress when the student is age three through kindergarten.

3. The student needs special education services.

4. The eligibility committee has considered the student's special education eligibility and determined that the eligibility is not due to a lack of instruction in reading or math or due to limited English proficiency.

What are the eligibility criteria for a classification of developmental delay?

NOTE_____

The eligibility criteria for developmental delay under IDEIA are not specifically stated under the law. The eligibility criteria for this particular disability may differ from state to state. Therefore, the information pertaining to "eligibility" for this classification is the author's professional interpretation based on reviewing the states' guidelines and criteria.

An evaluation team may determine that a student is eligible for special education services as a student with a developmental delay when all of the following criteria are met:

1. An evaluation that meets the criteria has been conducted.

2. The student is at least three years of age but less than ten years of age.

3. The student has developmental and/or learning problems that are not primarily the result of limited English proficiency, cultural difference, environmental disadvantage, or economic disadvantage.

4. The student meets either of the following two criteria (a or b):

   a. The student functions at least **#** standard deviations below the mean; or has a **#** percent delay in age equivalency; or functions at less than the **#** percentile in one or more of the following five developmental areas:

      • cognitive

      • fine motor or gross motor

      • speech-language (that includes articulation, fluency, voice, and receptive/expressive language)

      • social/emotional

      • self-help/adaptive.

   b. The student functions at least **#** standard deviations below the mean; or has a **#** percent delay in age equivalency; or functions at less than the **#** percentile in two or more of the five developmental areas listed in "a" above.

   Note: For the information above, see your specific state requirements for what number is represented by **#**.

5. The student's condition adversely affects educational performance.

6. The student needs special education.

What are the eligibility criteria for a classification of emotional disturbance?

NOTE_____

The eligibility criteria for emotional disturbance under IDEIA are not specifically stated under the law. The eligibility criteria for this particular disability may differ from state to state. Therefore, the information pertaining to "eligibility" for this classification is the author's professional interpretation based on reviewing the states' guidelines and criteria.

In order to be eligible for a classification as a student with an emotional disturbance under IDEIA, the following standards should be met:

1. Determine whether the student exhibits one or more of the following:

    a. *An inability to learn at a rate commensurate with the student's intellectual, sensory motor, and physical development:* This characteristic requires documentation that a student is not able to learn, despite appropriate instructional strategies and/or support services. A comprehensive and differential assessment is performed to establish an "inability to learn." The assessment should rule out any other primary reasons for the suspected disability, such as mental retardation, speech and language disorders, autism, learning disability, hearing/vision impairment, multi-handicapping conditions, traumatic brain injury, neurological impairment, or other medical conditions. If any of these other conditions is the primary cause, then the student may be deemed eligible for special education under that category of disability.

    b. *An inability to build or maintain satisfactory interpersonal relationships with peers and teachers:* This characteristic requires documentation that the student is unable to initiate or to maintain satisfactory interpersonal relationships with peers and teachers. Satisfactory interpersonal relationships include the ability to demonstrate sympathy, warmth, and empathy toward others; establish and maintain friendships; be constructively assertive; and work and play independently. These abilities should be considered when observing the student's interactions with both peers and teachers. This characteristic does not refer to the student who has conflict with only one teacher or with certain peers. Rather it is a pervasive inability to develop relationships with others across settings and situations.

    c. *Inappropriate types of behavior or feelings under normal circumstances:* This characteristic requires documentation that the student's inappropriate behavior or feelings deviate significantly from expectations for the student's age, gender, and culture across different environments. The eligibility committee must determine whether the student's inappropriate responses are occurring "under normal circumstances." When considering "normal circumstances," the eligibility committee should take into account whether a student's home or school situation is disrupted by stress, recent changes, or unexpected events.

d. *A general pervasive mood of unhappiness or depression:* This characteristic requires documentation that the student's unhappiness or depression is occurring across most, if not all, of the student's life situations. The student must demonstrate a consistent pattern of depression or unhappiness in keeping with the criterion, "long period of time" (i.e. several months). In other words, this pattern is not a temporary response to situational factors or to a medical condition.

The characteristics should not be a secondary manifestation attributable to substance abuse, medication, or a general medical condition (e.g. hypothyroidism). The characteristics cannot be the effect of normal bereavement.

e. *Physical symptoms or fears associated with the student's personal or school life:* Physical symptoms that qualify under the emotional disturbance characteristic should adhere to the following four conditions:

- symptoms suggesting physical disorders are present with no demonstrable medical findings

- positive evidence or strong presumption exists that these symptoms are linked to psychological factors/conflict

- the person is not conscious of intentionally producing the symptoms, and

- the symptoms are not a culturally sanctioned response pattern.

2. Determine whether the student's educational performance is adversely affected. Indicators of educational performance include present and past grades, achievement test scores, and measures of ongoing classroom performance (e.g. curriculum-based assessment and work samples). Adverse effect on educational performance implies a marked difference between the student's academic performance and reasonable (not optimal) expectations of performance. The appropriateness of the school district's educational goals, as reflected in the curriculum and in the formal grading report, should be considered in determining whether the student's performance meets reasonable expectations.

3. Determine that the student does *not* meet the criteria for a "socially maladjusted" student. A social maladjustment is a persistent pattern of violating societal norms, such as multiple acts of truancy or substance or sex abuse, and is marked by struggle with authority, low frustration threshold, impulsivity,

or manipulative behaviors. A social maladjustment unaccompanied by an emotional disturbance is often indicated by some or all of the following:

- unhappiness or depression that is not pervasive

- problem behaviors that are goal-directed, self-serving, and manipulative

- actions that are based on perceived self-interest even though others may consider the behavior to be self-defeating

- general social conventions and behavioral standards are understood, but are not accepted

- negative counter-cultural standards or peers are accepted and followed

- problem behaviors have escalated during pre-adolescence or adolescence

- inappropriate behaviors are displayed in selected settings or situations (e.g. only at home, in school, or in selected classes), while other behavior is appropriately controlled

- problem behaviors are frequently the result of encouragement by a peer group, are intentional, and the student understands the consequences of such behaviors.

What are the eligibility criteria for a classification of hearing impairment?

NOTE

The eligibility criteria for a hearing impairment under IDEIA are not specifically stated under the law. The eligibility criteria for this particular disability may differ from state to state. Therefore, the information pertaining to "eligibility" for this classification is the author's professional interpretation based on reviewing the states' guidelines and criteria.

1. For a student suspected of having a hearing impairment, determine that the student shall meet one of the following minimum criteria:

    a. the student has a pure tone average loss of 25 dbHL or greater in the better ear for frequencies of 500 Hz, 1000 Hz, and 2000 Hz, or a pure tone average loss of 35 dbHL or greater in the better ear for frequencies of 3000 Hz, 4000 Hz, and 6000 Hz, or

    b. the student has a unilateral hearing impairment with a pure tone average loss of 50 dbHL or greater in the affected ear for the frequencies 500 Hz to 4000 Hz, or

  c. the loss is either sensorineural or conductive if the conductive loss has been determined to be currently untreatable by a physician.

 2. For a student to be eligible for special education services as a student with a hearing impairment, determine that the disability has an adverse impact on the student's:

  a. educational performance when the student is at the age of eligibility for kindergarten through age 21, or

  b. developmental progress when the student is age three through the age of eligibility for kindergarten.

 3. Determine that the student needs special education services as a result of the disability.

What are the eligibility criteria for a classification of specific learning disability?

NOTE_____

The eligibility criteria for a specific learning disability under IDEIA are not specifically stated under the law. The eligibility criteria for this particular disability may differ from state to state. Therefore, the information pertaining to "eligibility" for this classification is the author's professional interpretation based on reviewing the states' guidelines and criteria.

A state must adopt criteria for determining whether a child has a specific learning disability. In addition, the criteria adopted by the state:

- must not require the use of a severe discrepancy between intellectual ability and achievement for determining whether a child has a specific learning disability, as defined under IDEIA

- must permit the use of a process based on the child's response to scientific, research-based intervention, and

- may permit the use of other alternative research-based procedures for determining whether a child has a specific learning disability.

   [34 C.F.R. 300.307; 20 U.S.C. 1221e–3; 1401(30); 1414(b)(6)]

The determination of whether a child suspected of having a specific learning disability is a child with a disability must be made by the child's parents and a team of qualified professionals, which must include:

- the child's regular teacher, or

- if the child does not have a regular teacher, a regular classroom teacher qualified to teach a child of his/her age, or

- for a child of less than school age, an individual qualified by the SEA to teach a child of his/her age; and at least one person qualified to conduct individual diagnostic examinations of children, such as a school psychologist, speech-language pathologist, or remedial reading teacher.

[20 U.S.C. 1221e–3; 1401(30); 1414(b)(6)]

The group may determine that a child has a specific learning disability if the following three conditions are met:

1. The child does not achieve adequately for the child's age or to meet state-approved grade-level standards in one or more of the following areas, when provided with learning experiences and instruction appropriate for the child's age or state-approved grade-level standards:

   - oral expression

   - listening comprehension

   - written expression

   - basic reading skill

   - reading fluency skills

   - reading comprehension

   - mathematics calculation

   - mathematics problem solving.

2. The child does not make sufficient progress to meet age or state-approved grade-level standards in one or more of the areas identified above when using a process based on the child's response to scientific, research-based intervention; or the child exhibits a pattern of strengths and weaknesses in performance, achievement, or both, relative to age, state-approved grade-level standards, or intellectual development, that is determined by the group to be relevant to the identification of a specific learning disability, using appropriate assessments.

3. The group determines that its findings are not primarily the result of:

   - a visual, hearing, or motor disability

   - mental retardation

   - emotional disturbance

   - cultural factors

- environmental or economic disadvantage, or
- limited English proficiency.

To ensure that underachievement in a child suspected of having a specific learning disability is not due to lack of appropriate instruction in reading or math, the group must consider, as part of the evaluation:

- data that demonstrate that prior to, or as a part of, the referral process, the child was provided appropriate instruction in regular education settings, delivered by qualified personnel, and
- data-based documentation of repeated assessments of achievement at reasonable intervals, reflecting formal assessment of student progress during instruction, which was provided to the child's parents.

The public agency must promptly request parental consent to evaluate the child to determine if the child needs special education and related services.

The public agency must ensure that the child is observed in the child's learning environment (including the regular classroom setting) to document the child's academic performance and behavior in the areas of difficulty. The group must decide to:

- use information from an observation in routine classroom instruction and monitoring of the child's performance that was done before the child was referred for an evaluation, or
- have at least one member of the group conduct an observation of the child's academic performance in the regular classroom after the child has been referred for an evaluation and parental consent is obtained.

In the case of a child of less than school age or out of school, a group member must observe the child in an environment appropriate for a child of that age [34 C.F.R. 300.310; 20 U.S.C. 1221e–3; 1401(30); 1414(b)(6)].

For a child suspected of having a specific learning disability, the documentation of the determination of eligibility must contain a statement of:

1. Whether the child has a specific learning disability.

2. The basis for making the determination.

3. The relevant behavior, if any, noted during the observation of the child and the relationship of that behavior to the child's academic functioning.

4. The educationally relevant medical findings, if any.

5. Whether:

   - the child does not achieve adequately for the child's age or to meet state-approved grade-level standards, and

- the child does not make sufficient progress to meet age or state-approved grade-level standards, or

- the child exhibits a pattern of strengths and weaknesses in performance, achievement, or both, relative to age, state-approved grade level standards, or intellectual development.

6. The determination of the group concerning the effects of a visual, hearing, or motor disability; mental retardation; emotional disturbance; cultural factors; environmental or economic disadvantage; or limited English proficiency on the child's achievement level.

7. If the child has participated in a process that assesses the child's response to scientific, research-based intervention:

- the instructional strategies used and the student-centered data collected, and

- the documentation that the child's parents were notified about (a) the state's policies regarding the amount and nature of student performance data that would be collected and the general education services that would be provided; (b) strategies for increasing the child's rate of learning; and (c) the parents' right to request an evaluation.

Each group member must certify in writing whether the report reflects his/her conclusion. If it does not reflect his/her conclusion, the group member must submit a separate statement presenting his/her conclusions [34 C.F.R. 300.311; 20 U.S.C. 1221e–3; 1401(30); 1414(b)(6)].

What are the eligibility criteria for a classification of mental retardation?

NOTE_____

The eligibility criteria for mental retardation under IDEIA are not specifically stated under the law. The eligibility criteria for this particular disability may differ from state to state. Therefore, the information pertaining to "eligibility" for this classification is the author's professional interpretation based on reviewing the states' guidelines and criteria.

Based on the results of assessment, in order to meet eligibility standards for the classification of mental retardation, a student has to meet *all* of the following:

1. Determine whether the student exhibits "significantly impaired intellectual functioning."

   Significantly impaired intellectual functioning is normally indicated by IQ scores that are two or more standard deviations below the mean. Given the most IQ tests have a mean of 100 and a standard deviation of 15, an IQ score of less than 70 would be considered "significantly impaired intellectual functioning."

   Interpretation of evaluation results shall take into account factors that may affect test performance, including:

   a. limited English proficiency

   b. cultural background and differences

   c. medical conditions that impact school performance

   d. socioeconomic status, and

   e. communication, sensory, or motor disabilities.

   Difficulties in these areas cannot be the primary reason for significantly impaired scores on measures of intellectual functioning.

2. Determine whether the student exhibits "significantly impaired adaptive behavior in the home or community."

   Significantly impaired adaptive behavior can be determined by:

   a. a composite score on an individual standardized instrument to be completed with or by the student's principal caretaker which measures two standard deviations or more below the mean. Standard scores shall be used. A composite age equivalent score that represents a 50 percent delay based on chronological age can be used only if the instrument fails to provide a composite standard score. A composite score two or more standard deviations below the mean cannot be primarily the result of:

      • limited English proficiency

      • cultural background and differences

      • medical conditions that impact school performance

      • socioeconomic status, or

      • communication, sensory, or motor disabilities

   b. additional documentation which may be obtained from systematic documented observations, impressions, developmental history by an appropriate specialist in conjunction with the principal caretaker in the home, community, residential program or institutional setting.

3. Determine whether the student exhibits "significantly impaired adaptive behavior in the school, daycare center, residence, or program.

    This is normally determined by systematic documented observations by an appropriate specialist, which compare the student with other students of his/her chronological age group. Observations shall address age-appropriate adaptive behaviors. Adaptive behaviors to be observed in each age range are to include:

    •   birth to six years: communication, self-care, social skills, and physical development

    •   six to 13 years: communication, self-care, social skills, home living, community use, self-direction, health and safety, functional academics, and leisure

    •   14 to 21 years: communication, self-care, social skills, home living, community use, self-direction, health and safety, functional academics, leisure, and work.

4. Developmental history (birth to age 18) indicates delays in cognitive/intellectual abilities and a current demonstration of delays present in the student's' natural (home and school) environment.

5. The characteristics as defined above are present and cause an adverse affect on educational performance in the general education classroom or learning environment.

What are the eligibility criteria for a classification of multiple disabilities?

NOTE_____
The eligibility criteria for multiple disabilities under IDEIA are not specifically stated under the law. The eligibility criteria for this particular disability may differ from state to state. Therefore, the information pertaining to "eligibility" for this classification is the author's professional interpretation based on reviewing the states' guidelines and criteria.

In order to identify and be determined as eligible for special education services as a student with multiple disabilities, the eligibility committee shall document that the following standards have been met.

1. The eligibility committee must determine that the student shall have the following two characteristics:

    a. meet the standards for two or more identified disabilities, and

    b. be unable to benefit from services and supports designed for only one of the disabilities, as determined to be primary or secondary disabilities by the eligibility committee.

2. The Eligibility Committee must determine that:

    a. the student has a combination of two or more disabilities

    b. the nature of the combination of disabilities requires significant developmental and educational programming that cannot be accommodated with special education services that primarily serve one area of the disability.

3. The Eligibility Committee must determine that all exclusionary factors have been ruled out. An individual will not be considered eligible for services under multiple disabilities if one or more of the following exist:

- The adverse effects are from a lack of instruction in reading or math that is not related to the traumatic brain injury.

- The adverse effects are from environmental, cultural, or economic disadvantage as a result of such factors as second language, limited English proficiency, other cultural values and experiences, and experiential differences.

- The adverse effects are judged to result from absenteeism (unrelated to health) or change in residence or schools.

- The disability is more accurately described by another category of eligibility.

- The student does not meet the eligibility criteria for "deaf-blindness."

What are the eligibility criteria for a classification of an orthopedic impairment?

NOTE_____

The eligibility criteria for orthopedic impairment under IDEIA are not specifically stated under the law. The eligibility criteria for this particular disability may differ from state to state. Therefore, the information pertaining to "eligibility" for this classification is the author's professional interpretation based on reviewing the states' guidelines and criteria.

In general, states use two different methods to determine whether a student meets the eligibility criteria as a student with an orthopedic impairment under IDEIA. Below is a synopsis of these two options for an eligibility committee to consider.

Option 1

A student suspected of having an orthopedic impairment is eligible and in need of special education instruction and services if the student meets the criterion in item A and one of the three criteria in item B.

A. There must be documentation of a medically diagnosed physical impairment.

B. The student's:

1. need for special education instruction and service is supported by a lack of functional level in organizational or independent work skills as verified by a minimum of two or more documented, systematic observations in daily routine settings, one of which is completed by a physical and health disabilities teacher

2. need for special education instruction and service is supported by an inability to manage or complete motoric portions of classroom tasks within time constraints as verified by a minimum of two or more documented systematic observations in daily routine settings, one of which is completed by a physical and health disabilities teacher

3. physical impairment interferes with educational performance as shown by an achievement deficit of 1.0 standard deviation or more below the mean on an individually administered, nationally normed standardized evaluation of the pupil's academic achievement.

Option 2

One condition from each criterion below must be judged to have been met in order to be eligible for the category "orthopedic impairment."

A. Physical criteria for eligibility: The student has a classification from a medical doctor of one or more of the following orthopedic conditions which is temporary or permanent in nature and may require adaptations in the physical plant:

1. impairments caused by congenital anomaly (e.g. clubfoot, absence of some member)

2. impairments caused by disease (e.g. poliomyelitis, bone tuberculosis)

3. impairments from other causes (e.g. cerebral palsy, amputations, and fractures or burns that cause contractures).

B. Academic criteria for eligibility: An assessment of motor function in the educational environment (conducted by the physical and/or occupational therapist) must demonstrate the following adverse affects upon educational performance that requires specialized instruction because of:

1. a lack of meaningful and productive participation

2. reduced efficiency in school work, and

3. inability to access educational environment despite environmental modifications.

Exclusionary factors for an orthopedic impairment

An individual will not be considered eligible for services under orthopedic impairment if one or more of the following exist:

- The adverse effect is from a lack of instruction in reading or math that is not related to the health impairment.

- The adverse effect is from environmental, cultural, or economic disadvantage as a result of such factors as second language, limited English proficiency, other cultural values and experiences, and experiential differences.

- The adverse effect is judged to result from absenteeism (unrelated to health) or change in residence or schools.

- The disability is more accurately described by another category of eligibility.

- The adverse effect is primarily due to active substance abuse.

What are the eligibility criteria for a classification of other health impairment?

NOTE_____

The eligibility criteria for other health impairment under IDEIA are not specifically stated under the law. The eligibility criteria for this particular disability may differ from state to state. Therefore, the information pertaining to "eligibility" for this classification is the author's professional interpretation based on reviewing the states' guidelines and criteria.

In order to identify and be determined as eligible for special education services as a student with other health impairment, the eligibility committee shall document that the following standards have been met:

1. The eligibility committee has obtained a medical statement or a health assessment statement indicating a classification of health impairment or a description of the impairment, and that the student's condition is permanent or is expected to last for more than 60 days.

2. The student exhibits limited strength, vitality, or alertness, including a heightened alertness to environmental stimuli that results in limited alertness with respect to the educational environment.

3. The student's limited strength, vitality, or alertness is due to a chronic or acute health problem.

4. The student's condition is permanent or is expected to last for more than 60 calendar days.

5. The student's disability has an adverse impact on the student's educational performance when the student is at the age of eligibility for kindergarten through age 21, or has an adverse impact on the student's developmental progress when the student is age three through kindergarten.

6. The student needs special education services.

What are the eligibility criteria for a classification of speech and language impairment?

NOTE_____

The eligibility criteria for speech and language impairment under IDEIA are not specifically stated under the law. The eligibility criteria for this particular disability may differ from state to state. Therefore, the information pertaining to "eligibility" for this classification is the author's professional interpretation based on reviewing the states' guidelines and criteria.

Four types of speech or language impairments are generally recognized:

1. Fluency disorder means the intrusion or repetition of sounds, syllables, and words; prolongation's of sounds; avoidance of words; silent blocks; or inappropriate inhalation, exhalation, or phonation patterns. These patterns may also be accompanied by facial and body movements associated with the effort to speak.

2. Voice disorder means the absence of voice or presence of abnormal quality, pitch, resonance, loudness, or duration.

3. Articulation disorder means the absence of or incorrect production of speech sounds or phonological processes that are developmentally appropriate (e.g. lisp, difficulty articulating certain sounds, such as l or r).

4. Language disorder means a breakdown in communication as characterized by problems in expressing needs, ideas, or information that may be accompanied by problems in understanding.

There are two ways in which many states identify students with one of these four types of speech and language impairments. Both options are explained below.

Option 1

In order to identify and be determined as eligible for special education services as a student with a speech and language impairment, the eligibility committee shall document that the following standards have been met. Based on the results of the assessment:

1. Determine that the student meets one or more of the following criteria:

    a. For a voice impairment, determine whether:

        •   the student demonstrates chronic vocal characteristics that deviate in at least one of the areas of pitch, quality, intensity or resonance, and

        •   the student's voice disorder impairs communication or intelligibility, and

        •   the student's voice disorder is rated as moderate to severe on a voice assessment scale.

    b. For a fluency impairment, determine whether:

        •   the student demonstrates an interruption in the rhythm or rate of speech which is characterized by hesitations, repetitions, or prolongations of sounds, syllables, words, or phrases, and

        •   the student's fluency disorder interferes with communication and calls attention to itself across two or more settings, and

        •   the student demonstrates moderate to severe vocal dysfluencies or the student evidences associated secondary behaviors such as struggling or avoidance, as measured by a standardized measure.

    c. For a phonological or articulation impairment, determine whether:

        •   the student's phonology or articulation is rated significantly discrepant as measured by a standardized test, and

        •   the disorder is substantiated by a language sample or other evaluation(s).

    d. For a syntax, morphology, pragmatic, or semantic impairment, determine whether:

        •   the student's language in the area of syntax, morphology, pragmatics, or semantics is significantly discrepant as measured by standardized test(s), and

        •   the disorder is substantiated by a language sample or other evaluation(s), and

        •   the disorder is not the result of another disability.

2. Determine whether the student's disability has an adverse impact on educational performance. The student's disability must have an adverse impact on educational performance when the student is at the age of eligibility for kindergarten through age 21, or has an adverse impact on the student's developmental progress when the student is age three through kindergarten.

3. Determine that the eligibility is not due to a lack of instruction in reading, math or due to limited English proficiency.

4. Determine whether the student needs special education services.

Option 2

A speech or language impairment shall be demonstrated by significant deficits in listening comprehension or oral expression. The eligibility committee shall obtain an opinion from a licensed speech-language pathologist as to the existence of a speech or language impairment and its effect on the student's ability to function. The determination of a speech or language impairment shall be based on the following criteria:

1. Determine whether a deficit exists in listening comprehension. A significant deficit in listening comprehension exists when a student demonstrates a significant deficit from the test mean on one or more measures of auditory processing or comprehension of connected speech. Auditory processing or comprehension includes:

   - semantics

   - syntax

   - phonology

   - recalling information

   - following directions

   - pragmatics.

2. Determine whether a deficit exists in oral expression. For purposes of determination of a speech and language impairment, a significant deficit in oral expression exists when a student demonstrates one or more of the following conditions:

   a. *Voice:* A significant deficit in voice exists when both of the following are present:

      - documentation by an otolaryngologist that treatment is indicated for a vocal pathology or speech related medical condition

- abnormal vocal characteristics in pitch, quality, nasality, volume or breath support, which persist for at least one month.

b. *Fluency:* A significant deficit in fluency exists when the student exhibits one or more of the following behaviors:

- part word repetitions or sound prolongations occur on at least 5 percent of the words spoken in two or more speech samples

- sound or silent prolongations exceed one second in two or more speech samples

- secondary symptoms or signs of tension or struggle during speech which are so severe as to interfere with the flow of communication.

c. *Articulation:* A significant deficit in articulation attributed to an organic or functional disorder exists when a student is unable to articulate two or more of the unrelated phonemes in connected speech, and it is not attributed to dialect or second language difficulties.

d. *Oral discourse:* A significant deficit exists when a student demonstrates a deficit of at least two standard deviations from the test mean on one or more measures of oral discourse. Oral discourse includes:

- syntax

- semantics

- phonology

- pragmatics.

3. Determine whether the student's disability has an adverse impact on educational performance.

The student's disability must have an adverse impact on educational performance when the student is at the age of eligibility for kindergarten through age 21, or has an adverse impact on the student's developmental progress when the student is age three through kindergarten.

1. Determine that the eligibility is not due to a lack of instruction in reading, math or due to limited English proficiency.

2. Determine whether the student needs special education services.

What are the eligibility criteria for a classification of traumatic brain injury?

NOTE_____

The eligibility criteria for traumatic brain injury under IDEIA are not specifically stated under the law. The eligibility criteria for this particular disability may differ from state to state. Therefore, the information pertaining to "eligibility" for this classification is the author's professional interpretation based on reviewing the states' guidelines and criteria.

In order to identify and determine as eligible for special education services a student with a traumatic brain injury (TBI), the eligibility committee shall document that the following standards have been met.

1. The eligibility committee must first ensure that there is medical documentation of the traumatic brain injury completed by a physician, and kept in the student's school file. The team must then verify that there is a functional impairment attributable to the TBI that adversely affects the student's educational performance in one or more listed areas. This is determined through a comprehensive special education evaluation.

2. The team must have documentation by a physician or a health assessment statement that the student has an acquired injury to the brain caused by an external physical force. A key factor to consider when determining whether a student may be eligible for special education support under the category of TBI is the *type* of acquired brain injury. There must be medical documentation stating that the student's brain has been injured by an 'external force'. Students who have an acquired *non-traumatic* brain injury as a result of infection, cerebral vascular accidents, brain tumors, poisoning, or anoxic injury may have significant educational needs, but do not meet TBI criteria. In such situations, eligibility under other special education categories could be considered by the educational team, depending on the presenting problems (Minnesota Department of Education, 2004).

3. The team must have documentation by a physician or a health assessment statement of a medically verified traumatic brain injury in the student's school file.

4. The team should have some form of documentation by a physician or a health assessment statement that the student's condition is permanent or expected to last for a certain length of time (e.g. more than 60 calendar days).

5. The team must determine that there is a functional impairment attributable to the traumatic brain injury that adversely affects educational performance in one or more of the following areas:

- intellectual-cognitive

- academic

- communication

- motor

- sensory

- social-emotional-behavioral

- functional skills-adaptive behavior.

6. The team must determine that the functional impairments are *not* primarily the result of previously existing:

- vision, hearing, or motor impairments

- emotional-behavioral disorders

- mental retardation

- language or specific learning disabilities

- environmental or economic disadvantage

- cultural differences.

7. The team must determine that the student needs special education services as a result of the disability.

What are the eligibility criteria for a classification of a visual impairment?

NOTE_____

The eligibility criteria for a visual impairment under IDEIA are not specifically stated under the law. The eligibility criteria for this particular disability may differ from state to state. Therefore, the information pertaining to "eligibility" for this classification is the author's professional interpretation based on reviewing the states' guidelines and criteria.

In order to make a final determination whether a student meets the criteria as a student with a visual impairment, the following steps should be taken:

1. The team should review all existing information, including information from the parent/guardian(s), the student's cumulative records, and any previous individualized education programs (IEPs) or individualized family service plans (IFSPs). Evaluation documentation includes relevant information from these sources used in the eligibility determination.

2. The team should review all of the assessments done by the multidisciplinary team to determine the impact of the disability.

3. The team should then determine whether any additional assessments are necessary to identify the student's educational needs, including a functional assessment of the student's residual visual acuity or field of vision.

4. Upon successful completion of the above, the team must then show that the student meets *one* of the following criteria:

   • The student's residual acuity is 20/70 or less in the better eye with correction.

   • The student's visual field is restricted to 20 degrees or less in the better eye.

   • The student has an eye pathology or a progressive eye disease which is expected to reduce either residual acuity or visual field to either an acuity level of 20/70 in the better eye or a visual field of 20 degrees or less in the better eye.

   • The assessment results of a licensed ophthalmologist or optometrist are inconclusive, or the student demonstrates inadequate use of residual vision.

5. The team must also determine that the student's disability has an adverse impact on the student's educational performance when the student is at the age of eligibility for kindergarten through age 21, or has an adverse impact on the student's developmental progress when the student is age three through kindergarten.

6. The team must also determine that the student needs special education services.

7. The team must show that it has considered the student's special education eligibility, and determined that the eligibility is not due to:

   a. a lack of appropriate instruction in reading, including the essential components of reading instruction (phonemic awareness, phonics, vocabulary development; reading fluency/oral reading skills; and reading comprehension strategies)

   b. a lack of instruction in math; and is not due to limited English proficiency.

8. The team agrees that this student qualifies for special education.

Related Services

What are related services?

The Individuals with Disabilities Education Improvement Act (IDEIA) defines related services as:

> transportation and such developmental, corrective, and other supportive services as are required to assist a child with a disability to benefit from special education, and includes speech-language pathology and audiology services, interpreting services, psychological services, physical and occupational therapy, recreation, including therapeutic recreation, early identification and assessment of disabilities in children, counseling services, including rehabilitation counseling, orientation and mobility services, and medical services for diagnostic or evaluation purposes. Related services also include school health services and school nurse services, social work services in schools, and parent counseling and training. [34 C.F.R. 300.34]

IDEIA mandates that each child's IEP contain:

> A statement of the special education and related services and supplementary aids and services, based on peer-reviewed research to the extent practicable, to be provided to the child, or on behalf of the child, and a statement of the program modifications or supports for school personnel that will be provided to enable the child:
>
> 1. To advance appropriately toward attaining the annual goals
>
> 2. To be involved in and make progress in the general education curriculum in accordance with paragraph (a)(1) of this section, and to participate in extracurricular and other nonacademic activities, and
>
> 3. To be educated and participate with other children with disabilities and nondisabled children in the activities described in this section...
>
> [34 C.F.R. 300.320(a)(4)]

Are related services required under IDEIA?

Related services are part of FAPE that must be provided to all children with disabilities within the state in order for the state to be eligible for funding under IDEIA. The child must need the services to "benefit" from special education. Provision of FAPE requires "related services" as well as special education [34 C.F.R. 300.17; 20 U.S.C. 1401(9)].

Do schools have to provide related services to all children with disabilities?

No. A school district does not have to provide a service to a student with a disability. The service is only "related" if it is necessary to help the student obtain "educational benefit" from it. The related service must be "appropriate" for the child (*Hendrick Hudson District Board of Education v. Rowley*, 1982)

Is a student with a disability who needs only a related service but not special education eligible for related services?

No. A student with a disability who only needs a related service and not special education is not eligible under IDEIA, and hence is not eligible to receive related services (Pierangelo and Giuliani, 2012).

Are schools required to provide related services necessary to maximize a child's potential?

No. A school is not required to provide related services necessary to maximize a child's potential. Instead, schools are merely required to ensure that a student can "benefit" from special education (*Hendrick Hudson District Board of Education v. Rowley*, 1982).

What is the difference between direct services and indirect services?

Direct services usually refer to hands-on, face-to-face interactions between the related services professional and the student. These interactions can take place in a variety of settings, such as the classroom, gym, health office, resource room, counseling office, or playground. Typically, the related service professional analyzes student responses and uses specific techniques to develop or improve particular skills. The professional will also typically:

- monitor the student's performance within the educational setting so that adjustments can be made to improve student performance, as needed

- consult with teachers, administrators, and parents on an ongoing basis, so that relevant strategies can be carried out through indirect means (see below) at other times.

Indirect services may involve teaching, consulting with, and/or directly supervising other personnel (including paraprofessionals and parents) so that they can carry out therapeutically appropriate activities. For example, a school psychologist might train teachers and other educators how to implement a program included in a student's IEP to decrease the child's problem behaviors. Similarly, a physical therapist may serve as a consultant to a teacher and provide expertise to solve problems regarding a student's access to instruction (Texas Education Agency, Division of IDEA Coordination, 2008).

Must related services be provided if there are staff shortages or extended absences?

Yes. A school district must provide related services according to a child's IEP even during times of personnel shortages or extended absences. To do this, the school system can contract with qualified providers outside the school system through another public or private agency (Families and Advocates Partnership for Education, 2011).

Are related services available to a child who attends a private school?

It depends on the situation. If a child is placed in private school by the school district, then the district will arrange for the child to receive any related services in his/her IEP. IDEIA regulations for providing services to children with disabilities whose parents have taken them out of public school and enrolled them in private schools are different. These regulations allow policies to vary from state to state, and from school district to school district. Parents will need to contact their state department of education or local school district to find out if their child will get any special education or related services in this case (Guersney and Klare, 2008).

How must schools provide related services?

At all times, a school remains directly responsible for ensuring that the services are provided. Schools can provide services directly or can contract for their provision from other agencies. A school district must ensure that all of the related services specified in the student's IEP are provided, including the number of services specified. The district usually decides how the services listed in the IEP will be delivered to the student. For example, the district may provide the services through its own personnel resources, or it may contract with another public or private agency, which then provides the services. Contracted service providers must meet the same standards for credentialing and training as public agency service providers (Texas Education Agency, Division of IDEA Coordination, 2008).

Who decides which related services are right for the child?

The child's individualized education program (IEP) team (see Chapter 8) decides which related services to include in the child's IEP. The child's parents are an important member of this team. The IEP team gathers information from evaluations and members of the IEP team. This information is used to determine the child's individual needs. Related services are identified to meet these needs. No related service is automatically included or denied due to a child's disability (Families and Advocates Partnership for Education, 2011).

Who pays for related services?

Related services must be provided at no cost to parents. This is part of the state's responsibility to provide the child with a free appropriate public education (FAPE). The school may ask for parents' help in getting third-party payments for their child's related services. They can only do this if it won't cost the parents anything, out of pocket, either now or in the future. Third parties can be public programs, such as Medicaid, or the parents' private health insurance company. If Medicaid or other public insurance covers the child, the school can usually bill them for related services the child receives in school. The school does need parental permission to release personally identifiable information from the child's education record, including information about the kinds of services he/she receives in school. The school does need parental consent to bill a private health insurance for related services. Parents aren't required to give this consent. The child will receive the related services in his/her IEP whether or not parents agree to use their private health insurance (Families and Advocates Partnership for Education, 2011). See Chapter 3 for more details on third-party payments and FAPE.

Can related services be determined based on a particular disability category?

No. The IEP committee is responsible for determining appropriate educational services, including related services, based on the individual educational needs of a student. A policy of determining related services based on a disability category would be inconsistent with state and federal requirements that services be based on individual needs (Texas Education Agency, Division of IDEA Coordination, 2008).

What are the various types of related services?

IDEIA includes a long list of related services that schools must provide to students who need them to receive a meaningful education. It is important to note, however, that this list is not exhaustive and does not include all of the services that a school district may be required to provide. If the student requires a service that is not on the list, it must still be provided by the school as long as the service is necessary for the student to be able to obtain "educational benefit" from special education.

Related services help children with disabilities benefit from their special education by providing extra help and support in needed areas, such as speaking or moving. Related services can include, but are not limited to, any of the following (in alphabetical order) [34 C.F.R. 300.34]:

- audiology
- early identification and assessment of disabilities in children
- interpreting services
- medical services
- occupational therapy (OT)
- orientation and mobility services
- parent counseling and training
- physical therapy
- psychological and school counseling
- recreation
- rehabilitation counseling
- school health and school nurse services
- social work services in schools
- speech and language therapy
- transportation
- travel training.

The rest of this chapter describes some of the more common related services provided to children with disabilities.

What is audiology?

Audiology is the study of hearing and hearing-related disorders (Misericordia Community Hospital and Health Centre, 2011).

Under IDEIA, audiology includes:

- identification of children with hearing loss
- determination of the range, nature, and degree of hearing loss, including referral for medical or other professional attention for the habilitation of hearing

- provision of habilitative activities, such as language habilitation, auditory training, speech reading (lip-reading), hearing evaluation, and speech conservation

- creation and administration of programs for prevention of hearing loss

- counseling and guidance of children, parents, and teachers regarding hearing loss

- determination of children's needs for group and individual amplification, selecting and fitting an appropriate aid, and evaluating the effectiveness of amplification.

[34 C.F.R. 300.34(c)(1)]

Audiology as a related service is normally provided to support the needs of children with hearing loss and includes (but is not limited to) key services such as determining the range, nature, and degree of a child's hearing loss and both group and individual needs for amplification.

Audiologists are the primary health care professionals who evaluate, diagnose, treat, and manage hearing loss and balance disorders in children with special needs.

Some schools have hearing screening programs and staff trained to conduct audiology screenings of children. Others may participate in regional cooperatives or other arrangements that provide audiology services. Those school districts that do not have diagnostic facilities to evaluate children for hearing loss and related communication problems or central auditory processing disorders may refer children to a clinical setting, such as a hospital or audiology clinic, or make other contractual arrangements.

What is the related service of early identification and assessment of disabilities in children?

Early identification and assessment of disabilities in children means the implementation of a formal plan for identifying a disability as early as possible in a child's life [34 C.F.R. 300.34(c)(3)].

The disability and medical fields are full of information about early identification of disabilities in children as well as assessing the scope and impact of a child's disability. This literature is focused on system-level issues such as setting up screening programs for specific disabilities (e.g. autism, speech-language impairment, visual and hearing impairments) and establishing mechanisms within the educational system by which children who are at risk for learning problems are quickly identified and their learning issues addressed.

As a related service, however, early identification and assessment of disability in children represents an individual service for one child. If a child's IEP team determines that identifying and assessing the nature of a child's disability is necessary in order for the child to benefit from his/her special education, then this related service must be listed in the child's IEP and provided to the child by the public agency at no cost to the parents. A formal plan would be written to establish the process and procedures by which the child's disability will be identified.

What are interpreting services?

Interpreting services were added to IDEIA's list of related services in the 2004 reauthorization. Interpreting services include the following, when used with respect to children who are deaf or hard of hearing:

- oral transliteration services, cued language transliteration services, sign language transliteration and interpreting services, and transcription services, such as communication access real-time translation (CART), C-Print, and TypeWell

- special interpreting services for children who are deaf-blind.

[34 C.F.R. 300.34(c)(4)]

Interpreting services may be new to IDEIA's definition of related services, but they have been provided over the years to many children who are deaf or hard of hearing, as part of providing them with access to instruction. The definition of interpreting services indicates a range of possible such services (e.g. oral transliteration, cued language), all of which refer to specific communication systems used within the deaf and hard-of-hearing community (Classroom Interpreting.org, 2011).

IDEIA states that in the development, review, and revision of an IEP, the team *must* consider special factors as follows:

- Consider the communication needs of the child, and in the case of the child who is deaf or hard of hearing, consider the language and communication needs, opportunities for direct communication with peers and professionals in the child's language and communication mode, academic level, and full range of needs including opportunities for direct instruction in the child's language and communication mode.

- Consider whether the child requires assistive communication devices and services.

[34 C.F.R. 300.324(a)(2)]

This language underscores the significance of communication in school, and the unique, individual needs specific to each student who is deaf or hard of hearing. It is important to note that the federal statute does not proscribe the language or mode of communication of a child who is deaf or hard of hearing, but acknowledges the need to consider his/her individual communication needs, particularly as they relate to opportunities for direct communication with peers and direct instruction from professionals in whatever mode the child uses to communicate. This is extremely important as parents and IEP teams assign or hire educational interpreters, based on the child's mode of communication.

What are medical services?

Medical services are considered a related service only under specific conditions [34 C.F.R. 300.34(c)(5)]:

- when they are provided by a licensed physician, and for diagnostic or evaluation purposes only.

Medical services have a long history that has only become more interesting as medical science has advanced and children with diverse medical conditions are being educated in increasing numbers in general education classrooms. The support that many such children need in order to attend school, school districts have argued, is medical in nature, complex and continual, and is not the responsibility of public agencies because IDEIA clearly states that medical services are allowable related services only when provided for diagnostic or evaluation purposes (National Dissemination Center for Children with Disabilities, 2010).

The case of *Cedar Rapids Community School District v. Garret F.* (1999) turned the gray line about the provision of related services to children with complex medical needs into a "bright line." The U.S. Supreme Court found that if a related service is required to enable a qualified child with a disability to remain in school, it must be provided as long as it is not a purely "medical" service. Services considered "medical," as IDEIA's definition amply indicates, are those services that can only be provided by a licensed physician (and only for the purposes of diagnosis or evaluation). If a non-physician can deliver the services, then the service must be provided by public agencies, regardless of the staffing or fiscal burdens they may impose. Health care services that can be provided by a non-physician are not provided under the category of medical services, however. Today they would be considered as school health services and school nurse services. Examples of such services include bladder catheterization, tube suctioning, positioning, and monitoring of ventilator settings, to name a few.

What is occupational therapy (OT)?

Occupational therapy is a related service provided by a qualified occupational therapist and includes:

- improving, developing, or restoring functions impaired or lost through illness, injury, or deprivation

- improving ability to perform tasks for independent functioning if functions are impaired or lost, and

- preventing, through early intervention, initial or further impairment or loss of function.

[34 C.F.R. 300.34(c)(6)]

Occupational therapy emphasizes independence in activities of daily living (e.g. dressing, feeding, money management), skill acquisition (e.g. self-management skills, vocational skills), and school participation in various settings including the classroom, cafeteria, bathroom, and playground. Occupational therapy is designed to maintain, improve, or restore function of students in all educationally related activities including neuromusculoskeletal function (e.g. range of motion, muscle strength, endurance, postural control), motor function (e.g. fine motor skills, oral motor control, visual motor integration), sensory and perceptual function (e.g. integrating and processing of tactile, visual, auditory information), cognitive function (e.g. attention, memory), and psychosocial function (e.g. self-concept, interpersonal skills).

School-based occupational therapy addresses purposeful, goal-directed activities to improve student function within the educational environment, in the following areas (Los Angeles Unified School District, 2011a):

- postural stability
- fine motor skills
- visual perception and integration
- activities of daily living
- motor planning
- coordination
- sensory processing
- self-help activities
- social and play abilities
- environmental adaptations
- use of assistive devices.

Occupational therapy maintains and promotes function through the use of purposeful activities and development of compensatory strategies that enhance school performance. Occupational therapy provides and maintains adaptive equipment and assistive technology (e.g. splints, word processors, toileting equipment).

Occupational therapy may be recommended for a student whose physical needs and/or learning problems require such services and/or impede access to his/her educational program. These students may demonstrate skills that are below expectations commensurate with the student's total profile including cognitive development which adversely affects school performance. Normally, a physician's referral is required for a student to receive occupational therapy. The frequency and duration of services are determined by the IEP team in collaboration with the evaluating therapist (New York City Department of Education, 2011a).

What are orientation and mobility services?

Orientation and mobility services (O&M) became part of the federal law's list of related services with IDEA of 1997. O&M services are intended for children who are blind or have visual impairments, with the purpose of teaching them how to orient themselves in a range of environments (school, home, community) and to move safely within those environments (National Dissemination Center for Children with Disabilities, 2010).

O&M services are provided by qualified personnel to enable students to attain systematic orientation to and safe movement within their environments in school, home, and community. They include teaching children the following, as appropriate:

- spatial and environmental concepts and use of information received by the senses (such as sound, temperature, and vibrations) to establish, maintain, or regain orientation and line of travel (e.g. using sound at a traffic light to cross the street)

- to use the long cane or a service animal to supplement visual travel skills or as a tool for safely negotiating the environment for children with no available travel vision

- to understand and use remaining vision and distance low vision aids

- other concepts, techniques, and tools.

[34 C.F.R. 300.34(c)(7)]

O&M services are not intended for children with disabilities other than visual impairments. If such a child needs to learn how to safely navigate a variety of settings, that child would generally not receive O&M services but, rather, travel training. Travel training is included in the definition of special education and means providing instruction to children with significant cognitive disabilities, and any other children with disabilities who require this instruction, to enable them to develop an awareness of the environment in which they live and learn the skills necessary to move effectively and safely from place to place [34 C.F.R. 300.39(b)(4)].

What is parent counseling and training?

Parent counseling and training is an important related service that can help parents enhance the vital role they play in the lives of their children. Under IDEIA, parent counseling and training means:

- assisting parents in understanding the special needs of their child

- providing parents with information about child development, and

- helping parents to acquire the necessary skills that will allow them to support the implementation of their child's IEP or IFSP.

[34 C.F.R. 300.34(c)(8)]

The first two parts of this definition are longstanding in IDEIA. The last part—regarding helping parents acquire the necessary skills that will allow them to support the implementation of their child's IEP or IFSP—was added in IDEA 1997 to recognize the more active role of parents as participants in the education of their children and is retained in IDEIA. As with all related services, parent counseling and training would only be provided to parents if a child's IEP team determines that it is necessary for the child to receive FAPE.

What is physical therapy?

IDEIA defines physical therapy as "services provided by a qualified physical therapist" [34 C.F.R. 300.34(c)(9)]. These services generally address a child's posture, muscle strength, mobility, and organization of movement in educational environments. Physical therapy may be provided to prevent the onset or progression of impairment, functional limitation, disability, or changes in physical function or health resulting from injury, disease, or other causes.

An evaluation for physical therapy is conducted by a physical therapist using formal and informal assessment tools and techniques. Evaluations incorporate relevant data from family and school personnel to assess the student's current level of function and ability to participate in his/her educational program. Recommendations for service are based on whether physical therapy is required to enable the student to benefit from instruction (New York City Department of Education, 2011b).

Physical therapy emphasizes physical function and independence in various settings including the classroom, bathroom, gym, staircase, playground, and transitions between settings. Physical therapy uses manual/handling techniques, exercise, and sensory processing activities to maintain, improve, or restore function including gross motor development (e.g. mobility, ambulation, posture), neuromotor status (e.g. muscle tone, strength, balance, coordination), motor planning, and negotiating the environment.

School-based physical therapy addresses purposeful, goal-directed activities to improve student function within the educational environment, in the following areas (Los Angeles Unified School District, 2011a):

- motor planning

- sensorimotor coordination

- posture

- balance

- functional mobility

- activities of daily living

- accessibility

- environmental adaptations

- use of assistive devices.

Physical therapy also promotes function by adapting the environment, providing and maintaining seating, positioning, assistive technology, and mobility equipment, and by monitoring and managing orthoses and prostheses.

Physical therapy may be recommended for students whose physical needs require such services and/or impede access to their educational program. These students may demonstrate skills that are below expectations commensurate with their total profile including cognitive development which adversely affects school performance. Normally, a physician's referral is required for a student to receive physical therapy services. The frequency and duration of services are determined by the IEP team in collaboration with the evaluating therapist.

What are psychological services?

Under IDEIA, psychological services include:

- administering psychological and educational tests, and other assessment procedures

- interpreting assessment results

- obtaining, integrating, and interpreting information about child behavior and conditions relating to learning

- consulting with other staff members in planning school programs to meet the special educational needs of children as indicated by psychological tests, interviews, direct observation, and behavioral evaluations

- planning and managing a program of psychological services, including psychological counseling for children and parents

- assisting in developing positive behavioral intervention strategies.

[34 C.F.R. 300.34(c)(10)]

Psychological services are delivered as a related service when necessary to help eligible children with disabilities benefit from their special education. In some schools, these services are provided by a school psychologist, but some services are also appropriately provided by other trained personnel, including school social workers and counselors.

Further, the definition of psychological services uses the phrase "planning and managing a program of psychological services"—which includes "psychological counseling for children and parents." The more administrative nature of "planning and managing" is a telling difference in how counseling is included in the definitions of these two related services (National Dissemination Center for Children with Disabilities, 2010).

IDEIA's definition of psychological services also specifically mentions positive behavioral intervention strategies, often referred to as PBS or PBIS. Behavior is an area of great concern these days, and it is useful to know that many of IDEIA's provisions support taking a proactive approach to addressing behavior that interferes with a child's learning or the learning of others. For such a child, the IEP team must consider, if appropriate, strategies (including positive behavioral interventions, strategies, and supports) to address that behavior [34 C.F.R. 300.324(2)(i)].

The fact that psychological services can include "assisting in developing positive behavioral intervention strategies" does not mean that only the professionals who provide psychological services may provide such assistance or that they are even necessarily qualified to do so.

There are many professionals who might also play a role in developing and delivering positive behavioral intervention strategies. The standards for personnel who assist in developing and delivering positive behavioral intervention strategies will vary depending on the requirements of the state. Including the development and delivery of positive behavioral intervention strategies in the definition of psychological services is not intended to imply that school psychologists are automatically qualified to perform these duties or to prohibit other qualified personnel from providing these services, consistent with state requirements.

Who pays for counseling outside of school?

Payment by schools for counseling outside of school is an issue of much debate. IDEIA states: "Where the service is related to the special education program that it is necessary if the student is to benefit from special education, the service must be provided at the school's expense" [34 C.F.R. 300.24(b)(2)(13)].

Is a public agency responsible for paying for mental health services if the IEP team determines that a child with a disability requires these services to receive FAPE and includes these services in the child's IEP?

Yes. The IEP team for each child with a disability is responsible for identifying the related services that the child needs in order to benefit from special education and receive FAPE. These services must be included in the child's IEP in the statement of special education, related services, and supplementary aids and services, to be provided to, or on behalf of, the child to enable the child to advance appropriately toward attaining the annual goals, be involved and make progress in the general education curriculum, participate in extracurricular and other nonacademic activities, and be educated and participate with other children with and without disabilities in those activities [34 C.F.R. 300.320(a)(4)(i)–(iii)]. Mental health services provided as a related service must be provided at no cost to the parents [34 C.F.R. 300.101 and 300.17].

Note: The public agency would not be responsible for paying for mental health services that constitute medical treatment for a child by a licensed physician except to the extent that the services are for diagnostic and evaluation purposes only.

What is recreation?

Under IDEIA, recreation as a related service includes the following [34 C.F.R. 300.34(c)(11)]:

1. *Assessment of recreation and leisure functioning:* Assessment of recreation and leisure functioning is a procedure to determine the current functional strengths and needs of students with disabilities in terms of skills, abilities, and attitudes relative to recreation and leisure.

2. *Leisure education:* Leisure education provides students with recreational and educational instruction to promote positive attitudes toward leisure, recognition of the benefits of recreation involvement, the development of skills necessary for recreation participation (such as social, decision-making, and planning skills), knowledge of recreation resources, and attitudes and skills that facilitate independent, satisfying leisure experiences.

3. *Therapeutic recreation:* Therapeutic recreation is the use of recreation activities to habilitate or rehabilitate functional abilities, which contribute to behavioral change. Therapeutic recreation is a process involving assessment, development of goals and objectives, and the implementation, documentation, and evaluation of intervention strategies.

4. *Recreation in schools and community agencies:* Recreation in schools and community agencies involves the provision of recreation services that facilitate the full participation of children and youths with disabilities in school and community programs. Activities are used to promote health, growth, development, and independence through self-rewarding leisure pursuits.

Recreation services generally are intended to help children with disabilities learn how to use their leisure and recreation time constructively. Through these services, children can learn appropriate and functional recreation and leisure skills. Recreational activities may be provided during the school day or in after-school programs in a school or a community environment. Some school districts have made collaborative arrangements with the local parks and recreation programs or local youth development programs to provide recreational services (North Carolina Recreational Therapy, 2011).

What is rehabilitation counseling?

Rehabilitation counseling is a related service that is provided by qualified personnel in individual or group sessions that focus specifically on career development, employment preparation, achieving independence, and integration in the workplace and community of a student with a disability. The term also includes vocational rehabilitation services provided to a student with a disability by vocational rehabilitation programs funded under the Rehabilitation Act of 1973, as amended 29 U.S.C. 701 *et seq.* [34 C.F.R. 300.34(c)(12)].

What are school health and school nurse services?

School health services have long been a part of IDEIA's related services definition. In IDEIA, the term has been changed to "school health services" and "school nurse services."

School health services and school nurse services are health services that are designed to enable a child with a disability to receive FAPE as described in the child's IEP. School nurse services are services provided by a qualified school nurse. School health services are services that may be provided by either a qualified school nurse or other qualified person [34 C.F.R. 300.34(c)(13)].

Returning to an issue that was raised in the discussion about medical services (as a related service), many children with disabilities, especially those who are medically fragile, could not attend school without the supportive services of school nurses and other qualified people. Over the years, the extent of the health-related services that are provided in schools has grown, as might be expected when you consider medical advances in the last decade alone.

In *Cedar Rapids Community School District v. Garret F.*, the question of whether or not public agencies are responsible for providing health-related supports that are complex or continuous was settled. They are, only to the extent that the services allow a child to benefit from special education and enable a child with a disability to receive FAPE. What was previously called "school health services" in IDEA has been expanded to distinguish between services that are provided by a qualified nurse and those that may be provided by other qualified individuals.

States and local school districts often have guidelines that address school health services and school nurse services. These may include providing such health-related support as:

- special feedings

- clean intermittent catheterization

- suctioning

- the management of a tracheostomy

- administering and/or dispensing medications

- planning for the safety of a child in school

- ensuring that care is given while at school and at school functions to prevent injury (e.g. changing a child's position frequently to prevent pressure sores)

- chronic disease management

- conducting and/or promoting education and skills training for all (including the child) who serve as caregivers in the school setting.

Can school districts require parents to attend school with their child to perform health-related services?

No. School districts cannot require parents to attend school with their child to perform health-related services. Any such requirement would violate the IDEIA mandate of a free appropriate public education (FAPE) because it is not free to the parents if they must commit their time (Guersney and Klare, 2008).

What are social work services in schools?

Issues or problems at home or in the community can adversely affect a child's performance at school, as can a child's attitude or behavior in school. Social work services in schools may become necessary in order to help a child benefit from his/her educational program.

Social work services in schools include:

- preparing a social or developmental history on a child with a disability

- group and individual counseling with the child and family

- working in partnership with parents and others on those problems in a child's living situation (home, school, and community) that affect the child's adjustment in school

- mobilizing school and community resources to enable the child to learn as effectively as possible in his/her educational program

- assisting in developing positive behavioral intervention strategies.

[34 C.F.R. 300.34(c)(14)]

What are speech-language pathology services?

Speech-language pathology services include:

- identification of children with speech or language impairments

- diagnosis and appraisal of specific speech or language impairments

- referral for medical or other professional attention necessary for the habilitation of speech or language impairments

- provision of speech and language services for the habilitation or prevention of communicative impairments

- counseling and guidance of parents, children, and teachers regarding speech and language impairments.

[34 C.F.R. 300.34(c)(15)]

School-based speech-language therapy focuses on oral communication activities to support the student's ability to access his/her educational program in the following communication domains (Los Angeles Unified School District, 2011b):

- receptive/expressive/pragmatic language

- articulation/phonology

- voice

- fluency

- augmentative and alternative communication.

Speech and language therapy may be recommended for a student with a communication problem, including problems of language comprehension and expressive language which adversely affect school performance. In addition, it may be recommended for students with speech production skills whose speech is unintelligible or not commensurate with the student's total profile, including cognitive development which adversely affects his/her educational performance.

Speech and language therapy may be the most frequently requested related service, primarily because language is so closely related to education. Speech-language pathology services are provided by speech-language professionals and speech-language assistants, in accordance with state regulations, to address the needs of children and youth with disabilities affecting either speech or language.

Who is eligible for speech and language therapy?

Any student eligible for special education may receive speech and language therapy if he/she needs the service to benefit from special education. Special education students do not need to be identified for special education under the special education eligibility criteria for speech and/or language disorders in order to receive speech and language therapy as a related service (Pierangelo and Giuliani, 2012).

What are some of the issues facing parents and school districts regarding transportation, as a related service, of students with disabilities?

Transportation is specifically mentioned as a related service under IDEIA [34 C.F.R. 300.34; 20 U.S.C. 1401(26)]. Transportation includes travel to and from school and between schools; travel in and around school buildings; and specialized equipment such as special or adapted buses, lifts, and ramps, if required, to provide special transportation for a child with a disability. Unless the child is receiving homebound instruction, or in some type of residential educational program, it is logical that transportation from home to the educational setting is necessary for any child to receive educational benefit.

The issue of transportation is important because of the cost involved. In being responsible for transportation, schools must also provide specialized equipment if it is needed. The school may be required to purchase special lift equipment for a bus or other special equipment such as a van to ensure that the student can get to and from school and to benefit from school once the student is there.

It is assumed that most children with disabilities will receive the same transportation provided to children without disabilities in keeping with least restrictive environment requirements (see Chapter 9). Thus, transportation as a related service may also mean providing modifications and supports so that a child may ride the regular school bus transporting children without disabilities.

If a child needs transportation in order to benefit from special education, the service must be made available.

IDEIA requires that the school must reimburse parents if the school fails to provide appropriate transportation or where the parents and school agree to parent-provided transportation in lieu of school-provided transportation. However, where the parent is providing transportation as a matter of preference and the school has made available appropriate transportation services, the school need not reimburse the parents.

Public school districts must provide transportation to children with disabilities in two situations. These are:

1. If a district provides transportation to and from school for the general student population, then it must provide transportation for a child with a disability.

2. If a school district does not provide transportation for the general student population, then the issue of transportation for children with disabilities must be decided on a case-by-case basis if the IEP team has determined that transportation is needed by the child and has included it on his/her IEP.

Not all children with disabilities are eligible to receive transportation as a related service. A child's need for transportation as a related service and the type of transportation to be provided must be discussed and decided by the IEP team. If the team determines that the child needs this related service to benefit from his/her special education, a statement to that effect must be included in the IEP, along with relevant details and arrangements.

The IEP team is responsible for determining if transportation is required to assist a child with a disability to benefit from special education and related services, and how the transportation services should be implemented. The IEP should describe the transportation services to be provided, including transportation to enable a child with disabilities to participate in nonacademic and extracurricular activities in the manner necessary to afford the child an equal opportunity for participation in those services and activities to the maximum extent appropriate to the needs of that child [34 C.F.R. 300.107 and 300.117].

IDEIA does not require LEAs to transport children with disabilities in separate vehicles, isolated from their peers. In fact, many children with disabilities can receive the same transportation provided to nondisabled children, consistent with the least restrictive environment requirements [34 C.F.R. 300.114 through 300.120].

Each person, including a school bus driver, who collects or uses personally identifiable information concerning a child with a disability must receive training or instruction about the state's policies and procedures protecting the confidentiality of such information [34 C.F.R. 300.123]. To the extent appropriate, school personnel in LEAs should ensure that school bus drivers or other transportation providers are well informed about protecting the confidentiality of student information related to (1) the special needs of individual children with disabilities who ride on school buses with their general education peers, and (2) possible strategies and assistance that may be available to drivers (including the use of aides on buses).

Note: If the IEP team determines that transportation is required to assist a preschool child to benefit from special education, and includes transportation as a related service on the child's IEP, the LEA would be responsible for providing the transportation to and from the setting where the special education and related services are provided.

What is travel training?

Travel training means providing instruction to students with significant cognitive disabilities, as well as others, who need to develop an awareness of the environment in which they live and learn the skills necessary to move safely from school, home, work, and community [34 C.F.R. 300.39].

Travel training is most often designed to prepare a student with a disability for post-school activities. In general, students receive travel training as a related service between the ages of 15 and 21. However, it may be appropriate for some children to be introduced to travel training at an earlier age (Adoption Media, 2011).

Travel training is short-term, comprehensive, intensive instruction designed to teach students with disabilities how to travel safely and independently on public transportation. The goal of travel training is to train students to travel independently to a regularly visited destination and back. Specially trained personnel provide the travel training on a one-to-one basis. Students learn travel skills while following a particular route, generally to school or a worksite, and are taught the safest, most direct route. The travel trainer is responsible for making sure the student experiences and understands the realities of public transportation and learns the skills required for safe and independent travel.

The term "travel training" is often used generically to refer to a program that provides instruction in travel skills to individuals with any disability except visual impairment. Individuals who have a visual impairment receive travel training from orientation and mobility specialists. Travel trainers have the task of understanding how different disabilities affect a person's ability to travel independently, and devising customized strategies to teach travel skills that address the specific needs of people with those disabilities (National Information Center for Children and Youth with Disabilities, 1996).

The three goals of travel training are:

1. to improve student opportunities for community integration through independent travel and the use of public transportation

2. to increase students' independent functioning to enhance their post-school opportunities for supported employment, postsecondary education, vocational training, employment, and adult independent living options

3. to integrate acquired skills and behaviors into their everyday environment, as well as into instructional and vocational settings.

What is excluded as a related service?

IDEIA makes a specific *exception* to the list of related services: surgically implanted devices, including cochlear implants. This exception is new with IDEIA and shows the advance of time and technology. A relatively new technological development, the cochlear implant is a small, complex electronic device that can help to provide a sense of sound to a person who is profoundly deaf or severely hard of hearing. Although an implant does not restore normal hearing, it does give the recipient a useful representation of sounds in the environment and help him/her to understand speech (National Dissemination Center for Children with Disabilities, 2010).

Cochlear implants are not the only surgically implanted devices. Others include: insulin pump, baclofen pump, pacemaker, G-tube, and vagus nerve stimulator device.

There is an exception to note. If a child has a surgically implanted device, the scope of the public agency's responsibility to provide supportive related services in relation to that device is covered in IDEIA's provisions [34 C.F.R. 300.34(b)]. Public agencies are *not* responsible for optimizing these devices, maintaining them, or replacing them. Public agencies *are* responsible for routine checking to determine if the external component of a surgically implanted device is turned on and working and for providing other types of services the child needs, as determined by the IEP team, including:

- assistive technology (e.g. FM system)

- proper classroom acoustical modifications

- educational support services (e.g. educational interpreters)

- receiving the related services (e.g. speech and language services) that are necessary for the child to benefit from special education services.

Can artistic and cultural services, such as music therapy, be considered related services?

Yes. Related services can include artistic and cultural services that are therapeutic in nature, regardless of whether IDEIA identifies the particular therapeutic service as a related service. The list of related services in IDEIA is not exhaustive and may include other developmental, corrective, or supportive services (such as artistic and cultural programs, art, music, and dance therapy) if they are required to assist a child with a disability to benefit from special education in order for the child to receive FAPE. As is true regarding consideration of any related service for a child with a disability, the members of the child's IEP team must make individual determinations in light of each child's unique abilities and needs about whether an artistic or cultural service such as music therapy is required to assist the child to benefit from special education.

If a child's IEP team determines that an artistic or cultural service such as music therapy is an appropriate related service for the child with a disability, that related service must be included in the child's IEP under the statement of special education, related services, and supplementary aids and services to be provided to the child or on behalf of the child [34 C.F.R. 300.320(a)(4)]. These services are to enable the child to advance appropriately toward attaining the annual goals, to be involved and make progress in the general education curriculum, and to participate in extracurricular and other nonacademic activities, and to be educated and participate with other children with and without disabilities in those activities [34 C.F.R. 300.320(a)(4)(i)–(iii)]. If the child's IEP specifies that an artistic or cultural service such as music therapy is a related service for the child, then that related service must be provided at public expense and at no cost to the parents [34 C.F.R. 300.101 and 300.17].

What types of situations may require termination from related services?

Termination from related services may be appropriate when (New York City Department of Education, 2011d):

- a student can integrate his/her acquired skills into the everyday environment and successfully participate in his/her primary program without services or with declassification services for up to 12 months

- a student's skills have reached a plateau and little or no change is expected and the student can successfully participate in his/her primary program without services or with declassification services for up to 12 months

- a student has maximized his/her function in the educational setting in keeping with his/her abilities

- a student is able to function independently at a work site.

Individualized Education Programs (IEPs)

What is an individualized education program (IEP)?

The centerpiece of IDEIA is the requirement that each eligible student have an individualized education program (IEP). The contents of the IEP are designed to provide a road map for the child's educational programming during the course of the coming year. Under IDEIA, an "individualized education program" is a written statement for a child with a disability that is developed, reviewed, and revised in accordance with the law [34 C.F.R. 300.22]. The IEP is the primary mechanism for ensuring that students receive an appropriate education. An IEP summarizes all the information gathered concerning the student, sets the expectations of what the student will learn over the next year, and prescribes the types and amount of special services the student will receive.

The development of an IEP is a collaborative effort between the school district and parents to ensure that a student's special education program will meet his/ her individual needs and be appropriate (have meaningful educational benefit). All aspects of the student's special education program are directed by the IEP, including the goals of a student's program, the educational placement, and the special education and related services that the student will receive (Pierangelo and Giuliani, 2012; Pierangelo and Giuliani, 2007).

Does every student in special education have an IEP?

Yes. Every student who receives special education services *must* have an IEP [34 C.F.R. 300.23].

What must be included in an IEP?

IDEIA is very specific about the contents of an IEP. An IEP must include [34 C.F.R. 300.320; 20 U.S.C. 1414(d)(1)(A) and (d)(6)]:

1. A statement of the child's present levels of academic achievement and functional performance, including:

- how the child's disability affects the child's involvement and progress in the general education curriculum (i.e. the same curriculum as for nondisabled children), or

- for preschool children, as appropriate, how the disability affects the child's participation in appropriate activities.

2. A statement of measurable annual goals, including academic and functional goals designed to:

   - meet the child's needs that result from the child's disability to enable the child to be involved in and make progress in the general education curriculum, and

   - meet each of the child's other educational needs that result from the child's disability.

   Note: For children with disabilities who take alternate assessments aligned to alternate academic achievement standards, a description of benchmarks or short-term objectives should be included.

3. A description of:

   - how the child's progress toward meeting the annual goals will be measured

   - when periodic reports on the progress the child is making toward meeting the annual goals (such as through the use of quarterly or other periodic reports, concurrent with the issuance of report cards) will be provided.

4. A statement of the special education and related services and supplementary aids and services, based on peer-reviewed research to the extent practicable, to be provided to the child, or on behalf of the child, and a statement of the program modifications or supports for school personnel that will be provided to enable the child:

   - to advance appropriately toward attaining the annual goals

   - to be involved in and make progress in the general education curriculum and to participate in extracurricular and other nonacademic activities

   - to be educated and participate with other children with disabilities and nondisabled children in the activities described in this section.

5. An explanation of the extent, if any, to which the child will not participate with nondisabled children in the regular class and in the activities described above (see 4).

6. A statement of any individual appropriate accommodations that are necessary to measure the academic achievement and functional performance of the child on state- and district-wide assessments; and if the IEP team determines that

the child must take an alternate assessment instead of a particular regular state- or district-wide assessment of student achievement, a statement of why:

- the child cannot participate in the regular assessment

- the particular alternate assessment selected is appropriate for the child.

7. The projected date for the beginning of the services and modifications, and the anticipated frequency, location, and duration of those services and modifications.

8. *Transition services.* Beginning not later than the first IEP to be in effect when the child turns 16, or younger if determined appropriate by the IEP team, and updated annually, thereafter, the IEP must include:

- appropriate measurable postsecondary goals based upon age-appropriate transition assessments related to training, education, employment, and, where appropriate, independent living skills

- the transition services (including courses of study) needed to assist the child in reaching those goals.

9. *Transfer of rights at age of majority.* Beginning not later than one year before the child reaches the age of majority under state law, the IEP must include a statement that the child has been informed of his/her rights under Part B of the Act, if any, that will transfer to the child on reaching the age of majority.

What are present levels of educational performance (PLEP)?

All IEPs must contain a statement of the child's present level of educational performance (PLEP). The statement must include how the child's disability affects the child's involvement and progress in the general education curriculum [34 C.F.R. 300.320(a)(1)].

The present levels statement describes how a child is doing in school and identifies those areas where he/she is having difficulty. A clearly written and thorough PLEP is important, because it is the foundation for all of the IEP. Goals are written based upon a child's present levels. Special education and related services are provided based upon the child's present levels and the goals that result from those present levels.

A PLEP is used to serve as a bridge between the evaluation process and the annual goals written for the student. The statement of the present level of educational performance is important because it enables families, students, and educators to monitor student progress in the general curriculum. It summarizes and translates evaluation results into clear, understandable language. The present levels statement identifies and prioritizes the specific needs of the student (National Association of Special Education Teachers, 2011).

The present levels statement (Educational Service Unit 2, 2008; Florida Department of Education, 2001):

- is the cornerstone of the IEP document, the source that drives other IEP components, and the statement that links all components of the IEP together

- should identify how the student is currently functioning. The IEP team should develop statements that provide an accurate picture of the student and describe the skills, knowledge, or behaviors and any other areas that are important for the IEP team to address

- should describe the problems that interfere with the education of the student. The needs of the student must be set forth in the IEP so that all service providers know the level at which the student is functioning and so the team can set appropriate, meaningful annual goals for the student

- must contain current specific, measurable, objective baseline information for each area of need affected by the disability

- should link the evaluation results, the expectations of the general curriculum, and the goals for the student

- is an objective synthesis of all information relevant to the student's educational performance

- contains impartial, unbiased information based on a variety of factual sources

- identifies the sources of information, the strengths of the student, how the disability affects the student, and the priority educational needs of the student.

There is no requirement in the law that addresses how many present level statements are necessary. The IEP team will determine how many statements are necessary to provide enough information to develop annual goals and meet the student's needs appropriately.

If the child is new to special education, the information used to craft the "present levels" statement will come from the tests and observations done during the child's evaluation for eligibility. If the child's IEP is being revised, the information may come from evaluations done during the year. Teachers and others who work with the child may offer information gained during the child's day-to-day school routine. Parents also share information that help shape the child's "present levels" statement.

The statement of PLEP should be written in such a manner that a person could look at the statements from one year to the next and determine how much growth has occurred. It is important because it allows parents and professionals to monitor student progress in the general curriculum. Thus, the PLEP statement should be written in objective and measurable terms. It is very difficult, if not impossible, to write measurable IEP goals if the statement of PLEP is not written in a clear and measurable terms (National Association of Spcial Education Teachers, 2011).

What do present levels of educational performance describe for preschoolers?

For preschoolers, "present levels" is not addressing how the preschooler's disability affects his/her participation in the general education curriculum. For preschoolers, the statement needs to talk about how the disability affects the child's participation in appropriate activities—meaning preschool activities. Those are often different from what school-age children are involved in and include things like learning basic skills such as using scissors, coloring, grouping things, learning letters, playing children's games, and so on. So the "present levels" statement for a preschooler will describe how the child's disability affects his/her participation and success in the preschool environment (National Association of Special Education Teachers, 2011).

What are measureable annual goals?

Annual goals are statements of the major accomplishments expected for the student during the upcoming 12 months, and they must be able to be objectively measured (e.g. Alice will increase her reading decoding skills to fourth-grade level; Manuel will initiate appropriate conversation skills with classmates at least three times daily). Annual goals should be related to meeting the child's needs that result from the disability and to the extent possible enable the child to be involved in and make progress in the general curriculum [34 C.F.R. 300.320(a)(2)(i)].

In a manner of speaking, annual goals are like a road map. Where is the child heading this year? What will he/she work on, both academically and in terms of functional development? What does the IEP team feel the child can achieve by the end of the year—again, academically and functionally?

In the past, annual goals were paired with short-term objectives or benchmarks of progress. With the 2004 Amendments to IDEIA, this requirement has been removed. Now, benchmarks or short-term objectives are required only for children with disabilities who take alternate assessments aligned to alternate achievement standards [34 C.F.R. 300.320(a)(2)(ii)].

What are assistive technology devices and services?

IDEIA includes the definitions below.

Assistive technology device

The term "assistive technology device" means any item, piece of equipment, or product system, whether acquired commercially off the shelf, modified, or customized, that is used to increase, maintain, or improve functional capabilities of a child with a disability [34 C.F.R. 300.5; 20 U.S.C. 1401(1)].

Assistive technology service

The term "assistive technology service" means any service that directly assists a child with a disability in the selection, acquisition, or use of an assistive technology device. The term includes:

- the evaluation of the needs of such child, including a functional evaluation of the child in the child's customary environment

- purchasing, leasing, or otherwise providing for the acquisition of assistive technology devices by such child

- selecting, designing, fitting, customizing, adapting, applying, maintaining, repairing, or replacing of assistive technology devices

- coordinating and using other therapies, interventions, or services with assistive technology devices, such as those associated with existing education and rehabilitation plans and programs

- training or technical assistance for such child, or, when appropriate, the family of such child

- training or technical assistance for professionals (including individuals providing education and rehabilitation services) employers, or other individuals who provide services to, employ, or otherwise substantially involved in the major life functions of such child.

Assistive technology is important because, for some students, without assistive technology they would not have access to or be able to benefit from their educational program [34 C.F.R. 300.6; 20 U.S.C. 1401(2)].

Assistive technology devices or services are considered to be related services when the IEP team determines that the service(s) is required to assist a student with disabilities to benefit from his/her educational program (Pierangelo and Giuliani, 2009).

It is important that members of the IEP team recognize that technology is just one strategy in a multifaceted approach to addressing the needs and strengths of students with disabilities. IEP teams will therefore need to balance the degree of technology assistance with the student's learning potential, motivation, chronological age, and developmental level and goals/objectives, which include the following (California Department of Education, 2011):

- *Low-tech*: Equipment and other supports readily available in schools, including off-the-shelf items to accommodate the needs of students, which can be provided by general/special education through the student study team (SST)/ IEP processes (e.g. calculators, tape recorder, pencil grip, and larger pencils).

- *High-tech*: Supports students who may need more specialized equipment and support services beyond basic assistive technology, often students with low-incidence and/or significant/severe disabilities, who require more in-depth assessment (e.g. closed circuit television (CCTV), FM systems, augmentative communication devices, sound field systems, alternative computer access, and specialized software).

Technology devices purchased by the school district belong to the district. Distribution and use of devices are under the district's control as long as the needs designated in the IEP are being met. School district insurance policies usually cover devices purchased by the district for use by a child. Devices purchased with other funding sources may or may not be covered while on school premises. School staff and parents may want to investigate the district's property insurance to determine what is currently covered and whether or not the policy insures against loss or damage of assistive devices (PAVE, 2011).

In general, the school district is responsible for repair and maintenance of assistive devices used to support programs described in the IEP (Assistive Technology Partnership, 2008).

On a case-by-case basis, the use of school-purchased assistive technology devices in a child's home or in other settings is required if the child's IEP team determines that the child needs access to those devices in order to receive FAPE.

What does it mean that the IEP must contain an explanation for why the child will not participate with nondisabled children in the general education classroom and activities?

The IEP must also, if such is the case, contain an explanation for why a child with a disability will not participate with children without disabilities in the general education classroom and activities. This component of the IEP is the "extent of nonparticipation" [34 C.F.R. 300.320(a)(5)]. The presumption in IDEIA is that students with disabilities should, in most cases, be educated with their peers.

This provision highlights the value IDEIA places on educating children with disabilities, to the maximum extent appropriate, with children without disabilities. If a child's IEP places the child outside of the regular class, involvement in the general curriculum, and/or participation in extracurricular or nonacademic activities, the IEP must explain why.

What is required in the statement of any procedural modifications in the administration of state- or district-wide assessments of student achievement?

IDEIA requires that students with disabilities take part in state- or district-wide assessments. These are tests that are periodically given to all students to measure achievement. It is one way that schools determine how well and how much students are learning.

In the IEP, there must be a statement of any procedural modifications in the administration of state- or district-wide assessments of student achievement. For example:

- the student might need to take a state test in a small group instead of with an entire general education class

- the student might need extended time to take the test

- the student might need someone to read him/her the test.

If the IEP team determines the child will not participate in the assessment, the IEP needs to contain a statement as to why the assessment is not appropriate and the reason why a selected alternate assessment is appropriate for the child [34 C.F.R. 300.320(a)(2)(B)(ii)].

To support the participation of children with disabilities in such large-scale testing, accommodations or modifications may be necessary in how the test is administered or how a given child takes the test. It is the responsibility of the IEP team to decide how the student with a disability will participate, and then to document that decision in the child's IEP. Alternatively, the IEP team may decide that a particular test is not appropriate for a child. In this case, the IEP must include:

- an explanation of why that test is not suitable for the child, and

- how the child will be assessed instead (often called alternate assessment).

What does the IEP require in terms of dates, frequency, location, and duration of services?

The IEP must contain the date the services and modifications will begin as well as the expected frequency, location, and duration of the services [34 C.F.R. 300.320(a)(7)]. This component of the IEP is straightforward. The IEP must indicate the date on which it becomes effective and for how long it lasts. The IEP must specify how often services are to be provided and where they are to occur (e.g. in the general education setting or in a special education classroom or professional's office).

This is where the details are specified about the services that a child with a disability will receive—the when, where, how often, how long of service delivery. The service delivery statement in the IEP should include:

- how often the child will receive the service(s) (number of times per day or week)

- how long each "session" will last (number of minutes)

- where services will be provided (in the general education classroom or another setting such as a special education resource room), and

- when services will begin and end (starting and ending dates).

Does the IEP team need to consider extended school year (ESY) services?

Yes. The IEP team should also consider whether or not a child needs to receive services beyond the typical school year. This is called extended school year or ESY services. Some children receiving special education services may be eligible for ESY services. Clearly, this determination must be done on an individual basis. States and LEAs typically have guidelines for determining eligibility for ESY, but whether or not a child needs ESY in order to receive a free appropriate public education (FAPE) is a decision that is made by the IEP team. IDEIA states that:

1. Each public agency must ensure that extended school year services are available as necessary to provide FAPE.

2. Extended school year services must be provided only if the child's IEP team determines, on an individual basis that the services are necessary for the provision of FAPE to the child.

3. In implementing the requirements of this section, a public agency may NOT

    (i) Limit extended school year services to particular categories of disability, or

    (ii) Unilaterally limit the type, amount, or duration of those services.

[34 C.F.R. 303.106]

Some students need an extended school year (ESY) in order to prevent substantial regression during the summer. Students at risk of substantial regression may not be able to maintain developmental levels due to a loss of skill or knowledge during the months of July and August. This loss may be so severe as to require an inordinate period of review at the beginning of the school year to reestablish and maintain IEP goals and objectives mastered at the end of the previous school year. Candidates for consideration for ESY include:

- students with severe multiple disabilities whose programs consist primarily of habilitation and treatment

- students who are recommended for home and hospital instruction, whose special education needs are determined to be highly intensive, and who require a high degree of individualized attention and intervention

- students whose needs are so severe that they can be met only in a seven-day residential program

- students whose management needs are deemed highly intensive, who require a high degree of individualized attention/intervention

- students receiving other special education services who, because of their disabilities, exhibit the need for a 12-month special service and/or a program provided in a structured learning environment of up to 12 months' duration in order to prevent substantial regression.

(New York City Department of Education, 2004)

What are some factors to consider in deciding whether a child is eligible for ESY?

Extended school year services are among those services that must be considered in providing a FAPE for a student with a disability. In *Ruesch v. Fountain* (1994), the court ruled that:

> there is no requirement that extended school year services be part of every disabled child's Individualized Education Plan (IEP) even if there would be some benefit. Indeed, it appears that ESY services would appropriately be part of an [sic] FAPE for a relatively small number of disabled children. Nevertheless, although there is no requirement that all disabled children have ESY in their IEP, there is a legal obligation to consider and fairly evaluate the appropriateness of ESY in developing every IEP for every disabled child. (Maryland State Department of Education, 1999)

In *Ruesch v. Fountain*, the court listed six factors that the IEP team should consider in deciding if the child is eligible for ESY as a related service. ESY services must be provided if the student meets any one, or a combination, of these criteria. Summarized, these are (Concord Special Education Parent Advisory Committee, 2011; Maryland State Department of Education, 1999):

1. *Regression/recoupment:* The IEP team determines whether, without ESY services, there is a likelihood of substantial regression of critical life skills caused by the school break and a failure to recover those lost skills in a reasonable time following the school break.

2. *Degree of progress:* The IEP team reviews the student's progress towards IEP objectives on critical life skills and determines whether, without ESY services, the student's degree of progress toward those objectives will prevent the student from receiving some benefit from his/her educational program during the regular school year.

3. *Emerging skills/breakthrough opportunities:* The IEP team reviews all IEP objectives targeting critical life skills to determine whether any of these skills are at a breakthrough point. When critical life skills are at this point,

the IEP team determines whether the interruption of instruction on those objectives caused by the school break is likely to prevent the student from receiving some benefit from his/her educational program during the regular school year without ESY services.

4. *Interfering behavior(s):* The IEP team determines whether any interfering behavior(s), such as stereotypic, ritualistic, aggressive, or self-injurious behavior(s) targeted by IEP objectives, have prevented the student from receiving some benefit from his/her educational program during the previous school year without ESY services or whether the interruption of programming which addresses the interfering behavior(s) is likely to prevent the student from receiving some benefit from his/her educational program during the next school year without ESY services.

5. *Nature and/or severity of the disability:* The IEP team determines whether, without ESY services, the nature and/or severity of the student's disability is likely to prevent the student from receiving some benefit from his/her educational program during the regular school year.

6. *Special circumstances:* The IEP team determines whether, without ESY services, there are any special circumstances that will prevent the student from receiving some benefit from his/her educational program during the regular school year.

What are transition services?

"Transition services" means a coordinated set of activities for a child with a disability that:

1. is designed to be within a results-oriented process, that is focused on improving the academic and functional achievement of the child with a disability to facilitate the child's movement from school to post-school activities, including postsecondary education, vocational education, integrated employment (including supported employment), continuing and adult education, adult services, independent living, or community participation, and

2. is based on the individual child's needs, taking into account the child's strengths, preferences, and interests; and includes:

   • instruction

   • related services

   • community experiences

   • the development of employment and other post-school adult living objectives, and

- if appropriate, acquisition of daily living skills and provision of a functional vocational evaluation.

Transition services for children with disabilities may be special education, if provided as specially designed instruction, or a related service, if required to assist a child with a disability to benefit from special education [34 C.F.R. 300.43; 20 U.S.C. 1401(34)].

Broadly defined, transition is an all-inclusive process that focuses on improving a student's employment outcomes, housing options, and social networks after leaving school. The transition plan provides the framework for identifying, planning, and carrying out activities that will help a student make a successful transition to adult life. It identifies the type of skills to be learned, and which transition services will be provided, when they will be provided, and the party responsible for providing them. Involving a team of people drawn from different parts of the student's school and community life, the transition planning process focuses on the unique needs and goals of the student (National Transition Network, 1996).

Transition services cover a wide array of topics. When determining appropriate transition services for a student with a disability, certain areas should be addressed. These include (Island Tress Union Free School District, 2010):

- *Instructional activities:* Educational instruction that will be provided to the student to achieve the stated outcome(s) (e.g. special education course instruction, occupational education, and advanced placement courses).

- *Community integration:* Community-based experiences that will be offered or community resources utilized as part of the student's school program, whether utilized during school hours or after school hours, to achieve the stated outcome(s) (e.g. local employers, public library, local stores).

- *Post-high school:* Educational services that will be provided to the student to prepare for employment or other post-school activity.

- *Independent living:* Post-school activities that will determine what other skills or supports will be necessary for the student to succeed as independently as possible (e.g. include participation in a work experience program, information about colleges in which the student has an interest, and travel training).

- *Acquisition of daily living skills/functional vocational assessment:* Activities of daily living skills necessary to achieve the stated outcome(s) (e.g. dressing, hygiene, self-care skills, self-medication). If the vocational assessment has not provided enough information to make a vocational program decision, additional assessment activities can be performed to obtain more information about the student's needs, preferences, and interests.

Are students required to be involved in their transition planning?

Yes. Transition goals cannot be achieved in one year. Transition planning, services, and activities should be approached as a multi-year process. Young adults themselves, along with their parents, play an important role in the transition process. Granted, involving the student in his/her own transition planning is required by law, but perhaps the most important reason for student involvement in transition planning is to facilitate the development of his/her self-determination skills, for these are essential for the student to develop the ability to manage his/her own life (National Transition Network, 1996).

For the students themselves, the outcome or result sought via coordinated transition activities must be personally defined, taking into account a child's interests, preferences, needs, and strengths. This is why the public agency must invite the child with a disability to attend the IEP team meeting if a purpose of the meeting will be the consideration of the postsecondary goals for the child and the transition services needed to assist the child in reaching those goals [34 C.F.R. 300.321(b)(1)].

Note: If the student is not able to attend or doesn't attend, then the public agency "must take other steps to ensure that the child's preferences and interests are considered" [34 C.F.R. 300.321(b)(2)].

Are school districts required to ensure that the goal of employment or independent living is achieved?

No. School districts are not required to ensure that the goal of employment or independent living is achieved, but they must do more than provide opportunity and skills to simply apply to postsecondary programs. These are qualitative differences that are at the core of the district's duty to provide a program calculated to benefit each student.

When students are introduced to a variety of school and community experiences, and districts can demonstrate that school programs are designed to assist students to successfully meet social and vocational goals as well as graduation requirements, districts have prevailed in hearings. One administrative law judge commented that "the District was not required to provide every possible job experience," but was obligated to provide the student with experiences that were based on individual needs, preferences, and interests. However, the fact that a student meets graduation requirements does not relieve the district of the obligation to provide the transition services that fully implement and allow the student to complete the IEP program (Advocacy Institute, 2007).

Must an IEP include measurable postsecondary goals based on age-appropriate transition assessments for every 16-year-old student with a disability, regardless of the student's skill levels relating to education, employment, and training?

Yes. The IEP for each child with a disability, must, beginning not later than the first IEP to be in effect when the child turns 16, or younger if determined appropriate by the IEP team, and updated annually thereafter, include (1) appropriate measurable postsecondary goals based upon age-appropriate transition assessments related to training, education, employment, and, where appropriate, independent living skills; and (2) the transition services (including courses of study) needed to assist the child in reaching those goals. This requirement applies whether or not the child's skill levels related to training, education, and employment are age-appropriate. In all cases, the IEP team must develop the specific postsecondary goals for the child in light of the unique needs of the child as determined by age-appropriate transition assessments of the child's skills in these areas [34 C.F.R. 300.320(b)].

Must community access skills be included in the IEP as independent living skills?

Maybe. The IEP team must determine whether it is necessary to include appropriate measurable postsecondary goals related to independent living skills in the IEP for a particular child, and, if so, what transition services are needed to assist the child in reaching those goals. Under 34 C.F.R. 300.43, the term "transition services" is defined as "a coordinated set of activities for a child with a disability…to facilitate movement from school to post-school activities," and includes, among other activities, "independent living, or community participation." Based on the assessment of the student's independent living skills, the IEP team would need to determine whether transition services provided as community access skills are necessary for the child to receive FAPE. If so, those skills must be reflected in the transition services in the child's IEP.

If an IEP team chooses to address transition before age 16 (for example, at age 14), do the same requirements apply?

Yes. IDEIA requires that beginning not later than the first IEP to be in effect when the child turns 16, or younger if determined appropriate by the IEP team, and updated annually thereafter, the IEP must include (1) appropriate measurable postsecondary goals based upon age-appropriate transition assessments related to training, education, employment, and, where appropriate, independent living skills; and (2) the transition services (including courses of study) needed to assist the child in reaching those goals [34 C.F.R. 300.320(b)]. If the IEP team for a particular child with a disability determines that it is appropriate to address the requirements of 34 C.F.R. 300.320(b) for a child who is younger than age 16, then the IEP for that child must meet the requirements of 34 C.F.R. 300.320(b).

Must public agencies measure whether postsecondary goals have been met once a student has graduated or has aged out?

No. There is no requirement for public agencies to determine whether the postsecondary goals have been met once a child is no longer eligible for FAPE under IDEIA. A FAPE must be made available to all children residing in the state in mandatory age ranges [34 C.F.R. 300.101(a)]. However, the obligation to make FAPE available does not apply to children who have graduated from high school with a regular high school diploma [34 C.F.R. 300.102(a)(3)(i)] or to children who have exceeded the mandatory age range for provision of FAPE under state law [34 C.F.R. 300.102(a)(1)]. When a child's eligibility for FAPE terminates under these circumstances, the school district must provide a summary of the child's academic achievement and functional performance, including recommendations on how to assist the child in meeting the child's postsecondary goals. However, nothing in IDEIA requires the school district to measure the child's progress on these postsecondary transition goals, or provide any special education services to the child after the child has been graduated from a regular high school or exceeded the mandatory age range for FAPE.

What is the age of majority?

Age of majority is the legal age established under state law at which an individual is no longer a minor and, as a young adult, has the right and responsibility to make certain legal choices that adults make. Thus, when people use the term "age of majority," they are generally referring to the age at which a young person is considered to be an adult (National Center on Secondary Education and Transition, 2002).

What happens when a student reaches the age of majority?

The IEP must contain a statement one year before a student reaches the age of majority that the student has been informed of his/her rights which will transfer to the student at the age of majority [34 C.F.R. 300.320(c)]. State law determines whether and at what age rights transfer.

Some states have a legal process to determine if a student who receives special education and has reached the age of majority continues to need help in planning his/her IEP. Students may not necessarily have the ability to provide informed consent to their educational program even though they have not been determined to be incompetent. Such states have a mechanism to determine that a student with a disability, who has reached the age of majority under state law and has not been determined incompetent, still does not have the ability to provide informed consent with respect to his/her educational program. In such cases, the state shall establish procedures for appointing the parent, or, if the parent is not available, another appointed individual, to represent the educational interests of the student throughout the student's eligibility under IDEIA (National Center on Secondary Education and Transition, 2002).

What is progress monitoring?

IDEIA states that each child's IEP must contain a description of how the child's progress toward meeting the annual goals will be measured, and when periodic reports on the progress the child is making toward meeting the annual goals (such as through the use of quarterly or other periodic reports, concurrent with the issuance of report cards) will be provided [34 C.F.R. 300.320(a)(3)].

Progress monitoring is the method of formative assessment used to measure student's progress toward meeting a goal. Progress-monitoring procedures guide how data will be collected in order to make instructional decisions about the progress of the student and establish a decision-making plan for examining the data collected.

The progress-monitoring provision also requires that the IEP specify how the child's parents will be regularly informed of the child's progress toward the goals, and the extent to which progress is considered sufficient.

Progress monitoring helps IEP teams address any lack of expected progress toward the annual goals and make decisions concerning the effectiveness of curriculum delivery.

The information on how well a child must perform and how his/her progress will be measured is often called "evaluation criteria." Well-written evaluation criteria are stated in objective, measurable terms. For example, a child might be required to perform a task "with 90 percent accuracy" or get 18 out of 20 words correct in each of five trials. These are concrete numbers or scores, establishing what the IEP team considers an acceptable level of performance or progress for the child.

How often does the IEP team need to report progress to parents?

IDEIA's exact words refer to the periodic reporting of each child's progress, which gives parents, other members of the IEP team, and the public agency the opportunity to review the IEP and make adjustments if they are warranted. When a child does not make the progress expected, then it is essential to determine why and take corrective action.

IDEIA is less prescriptive about the timing of such reports than IDEA of 1997. IDEA 1997 required that parents of a child with a disability be informed of their child's progress "at least as often as parents of nondisabled children." This is no longer true.

It is also important to note that IDEIA does not require report cards or quarterly report cards. When IDEIA mentions them [34 C.F.R. 300.320(a)(ii)], they "are used as examples…of when periodic reports on the child's progress toward meeting the annual goals might be provided." According to the U.S. Department of Education, the specific times that progress reports are provided to parents and the specific manner and format in which a child's progress toward meeting the annual goals are reported is best left to state and local officials to determine.

Are school districts required to provide evidence of effectiveness for instructional programs recommended by the IEP team?

Yes. IDEIA adds an important new provision that the IEP team's choice of special education and related services be guided by peer-reviewed research whenever possible. In other words, instructional programs and other services should be supported by strong evidence of effectiveness. This is particularly important when determining instructional programs to address reading deficits, since there is a robust body of research showing the effectiveness of an array of reading programs.

With the passage of IDEIA, some new terms and concepts became part of the IEP process. One such is "peer-reviewed research." Although the term is not formally defined in IDEIA, peer-reviewed research generally refers to research that is reviewed by qualified and independent reviewers to ensure that the quality of the information meets the standards of the field before the research is published. However, there is no single definition of peer-reviewed research because the review process varies depending on the type of information to be reviewed.

States, school districts, and school personnel must select and use methods that research has shown to be effective, to the extent that methods based on peer-reviewed research are available. This does not mean that the service with the greatest body of research is the service necessarily required for a child to receive FAPE. Likewise, there is nothing in IDEIA to suggest that the failure of a public agency to provide services based on peer-reviewed research would automatically result in a denial of FAPE. The final decision about the special education, related services, and supplementary aids and services that are to be provided to a child must be made by the child's IEP team based on the child's individual needs (National Dissemination Center for Children with Disabilities, 2010).

When must an initial IEP be developed?

An initial IEP must be developed within 30 calendar days of a determination that a child requires special education and related services [34 C.F.R. 300.323(c)(1)].

Are educational placements based on the IEP?

Yes. Educational placement must be based on the IEP [34 C.F.R. 300.116]. Deciding the placement of a child before IEP development is a procedural violation of IDEIA.

Note: The IEP is not written for a specific location. The law requires that the IEP is developed first and then placement is determined. For information on this topic, see Chapter 9.

Who must be a part of the IEP team?

The IEP team consists of many different people. IDEIA mandates that certain individuals be a part of this team. The public agency must ensure that the IEP team for each child with a disability includes the following [34 C.F.R. 300.321; 20 U.S.C. 1414(d)(1)(B)–(d)(1)(D)]:

1. The parents of the child.

2. Not less than one regular education teacher of the child (if the child is, or may be, participating in the regular education environment).

3. Not less than one special education teacher of the child, or where appropriate, not less than one special education provider of the child.

4. A representative of the public agency who:

    • is qualified to provide, or supervise the provision of, specially designed instruction to meet the unique needs of children with disabilities

    • is knowledgeable about the general education curriculum, and

    • is knowledgeable about the availability of resources of the public agency.

5. An individual who can interpret the instructional implications of evaluation results.

6. The discretion of the parent or the agency, other individuals who have knowledge or special expertise regarding the child, including related services personnel as appropriate. (Note: The determination of the knowledge or special expertise of any individual must be made by the party—parents or public agency—who invited the individual to be a member of the IEP team.)

7. Whenever appropriate, the child with a disability.

8. *Transition services participants (when appropriate).* The public agency must invite a child with a disability to attend the child's IEP Team meeting if a purpose of the meeting will be the consideration of the postsecondary goals for the child and the transition services needed to assist the child in reaching those goals. If the child does not attend the IEP Team meeting, the public agency must take other steps to ensure that the child's preferences and interests are considered.

Note: To the extent appropriate, with the consent of the parents or a child who has reached the age of majority, the public agency must invite a representative of any participating agency that is likely to be responsible for providing or paying for transition services.

Why are parents on the IEP team?

Since the passage of Public Law 94-142 in 1975, parents have been recognized as vital members of the IEP team. Everyone agrees that parents have an enduring and passionate interest in the well-being and education of their children. So it makes perfect sense that Congress would ensure that parents are represented on the IEP team, front and center. The school must invite the parents to the IEP meeting early enough to ensure that one or both parents have the opportunity to attend and participate. The notice must include the purpose of the meeting, its time and location, and who will attend.

Typically, parents know their child very well—not just the child's strengths and weaknesses, but all the little qualities that make their child unique. Parents' knowledge can keep the team focused on the "big picture" of the child; they can help the team to create an IEP that will work appropriately for the child. Parents can describe what goals are most important to them and to their child, share their concerns and suggestions for enhancing their child's education, and give insights into their son or daughter's interests, likes and dislikes, and learning styles. By being an active IEP team member, parents can also infuse the IEP planning process with thought about long-term needs for the child's successful adult life (National Dissemination Center for Children with Disabilities, 2010).

Can parents bring a lawyer to an IEP meeting?

Yes. The importance of parental participation in the development of the IEP cannot be overestimated. IDEIA requires parental participation at every meaningful stage of the educational process, and the development of the IEP is perhaps the most critical part of the process. Therefore, the parents have the right to have legal counsel at the IEP meeting if they believe the lawyer's knowledge and expertise would be helpful (Pierangelo and Giuliani, 2007).

Are all members of the IEP team mandated to be in attendance at an IEP meeting?

No, provided certain conditions are met. A member of the IEP team is not required to attend an IEP team meeting, in whole or in part, if the parent of a child with a disability and the public agency agree, in writing, that the attendance of the member is not necessary because the member's area of the curriculum or related services is not being modified or discussed in the meeting.

A member of the IEP team may be excused from attending an IEP team meeting, in whole or in part, when the meeting involves a modification to or discussion of the member's area of the curriculum or related services, if:

- the parent, in writing, and the public agency consent to the excusal, and

- the member submits, in writing to the parent and the IEP team, input into the development of the IEP prior to the meeting.

[34 C.F.R. 300.321(e)]

Is parental participation required at IEP team meetings?

Yes, unless the public agency is unable to convince the parents that they should attend.

Each public agency must take steps to ensure that one or both of the parents of a child with a disability are present at each IEP team meeting or are afforded the opportunity to participate, including [34 C.F.R. 300.322; 20 U.S.C. 1414(d)(1)(B)(i)]:

- notifying parents of the meeting early enough to ensure that they will have an opportunity to attend, and

- scheduling the meeting at a mutually agreed time and place.

The notice required must:

- indicate the purpose, time, and location of the meeting and who will be in attendance, and

- inform the parents of the provisions regarding required IEP team members [see 34 C.F.R. 300.321].

For a child with a disability, beginning not later than the first IEP to be in effect when the child turns 16, or younger if determined appropriate by the IEP team, the notice also must indicate that a purpose of the meeting will be the consideration of the postsecondary goals and transition services for the child [34 C.F.R. 300.320] and that the agency will invite the student and identify any other agency that will be invited to send a representative.

If neither parent can attend an IEP team meeting, the public agency must use other methods to ensure parent participation, including individual or conference telephone calls, consistent with the guidelines under IDEIA related to alternative means of meeting participation [34 C.F.R. 300.328].

A meeting may be conducted without a parent in attendance if the public agency is unable to convince the parents that they should attend. In this case, the public agency must keep a record of its attempts to arrange a mutually agreed time and place, such as:

- detailed records of telephone calls made or attempted and the results of those calls

- copies of correspondence sent to the parents and any responses received

- detailed records of visits made to the parent's home or place of employment and the results of those visits.

The public agency must take whatever action is necessary to ensure that the parent understands the proceedings of the IEP team meeting, including arranging for an interpreter for parents with deafness or whose native language is other than English.

The public agency must give the parent a copy of the child's IEP at no cost to the parent.

When must an IEP be in effect?

IDEIA sets forth very specific guidelines as to when IEPs must be in effect [34 C.F.R. 300.323; 20 U.S.C. 1414(d)(2)(A)–(C)].

At the beginning of each school year, each public agency must have in effect, for each child with a disability within its jurisdiction, an IEP, as defined under IDEIA [34 C.F.R. 300.320].

In the case of a child with a disability aged three through five (or, at the discretion of the SEA, a two-year-old child with a disability who will turn age three during the school year), the IEP team must consider an individualized family service plan (IFSP) that contains the IFSP content (including the natural environments statement) described in the law (see Chapter 13 for a detailed description of the IFSP).

Each public agency must ensure that:

- a meeting to develop an IEP for a child is conducted within 30 days of a determination that the child needs special education and related services

- as soon as possible following development of the IEP, special education and related services are made available to the child in accordance with the child's IEP

- the child's IEP is accessible to each regular education teacher, special education teacher, related services provider, and any other service provider who is responsible for its implementation

- each teacher and provider is informed of his/her specific responsibilities related to implementing the child's IEP; and the specific accommodations, modifications, and supports that must be provided for the child in accordance with the IEP.

What happens to a student's IEP if he/she transfers out of district or to a new state?

If a child with a disability (who had an IEP that was in effect in a previous public agency in the same state) transfers to a new public agency in the same state, and enrolls in a new school within the same school year, the new public agency (in consultation with the parents) must provide FAPE to the child (including services comparable to those described in the child's IEP from the previous public agency), until the new public agency either:

- adopts the child's IEP from the previous public agency, or

- develops, adopts, and implements a new IEP.

If a child with a disability (who had an IEP that was in effect in a previous public agency in another state) transfers to a public agency in a new state, and enrolls in a new school within the same school year, the new public agency (in consultation with the parents) must provide the child with FAPE (including services comparable to those described in the child's IEP from the previous public agency), until the new public agency:

- conducts an evaluation as detailed under IDEIA [34 C.F.R. 300.304–306] (if determined to be necessary by the new public agency), and

- develops, adopts, and implements a new IEP, if appropriate.

To facilitate the transition for a child described above:

- the new public agency in which the child enrolls must take reasonable steps to promptly obtain the child's records, including the IEP and supporting documents and any other records relating to the provision of special education or related services to the child, from the previous public agency in which the child was enrolled [34 C.F.R. 99.31(a)(2)], and

- the previous public agency in which the child was enrolled must take reasonable steps to promptly respond to the request from the new public agency.

What does IDEIA mandate regarding the development of an IEP?

In developing each child's IEP, the IEP team must consider the following:

- the strengths of the child

- the concerns of the parents for enhancing the education of their child

- the results of the initial or most recent evaluation of the child, and

- the academic, developmental, and functional needs of the child.

[34 C.F.R. 300.324(a)(1)]

The IEP team is legally required to take into consideration special factors of children when they arise. The IEP team must:

- in the case of a child whose behavior impedes the child's learning or that of others, consider the use of positive behavioral interventions and supports, and other strategies, to address that behavior

- in the case of a child with limited English proficiency, consider the language needs of the child as those needs relate to the child's IEP

- in the case of a child who is blind or visually impaired, provide for instruction in Braille and the use of Braille unless the IEP team determines, after an evaluation of the child's reading and writing skills, needs, and appropriate reading and writing media (including an evaluation of the child's future needs for instruction in Braille or the use of Braille), that instruction in Braille or the use of Braille is not appropriate for the child

- consider the communication needs of the child, and, in the case of a child who is deaf or hard of hearing, consider the child's language and communication needs, opportunities for direct communications with peers and professional personnel in the child's language and communication mode, academic level, and full range of needs, including opportunities for direct instruction in the child's language and communication mode; and

- consider whether the child needs assistive technology devices and services.

[34 C.F.R. 300.324(a)(2)]

A regular education teacher of a child with a disability, as a member of the IEP team, must, to the extent appropriate, participate in the development of the IEP of the child, including the determination of:

- appropriate positive behavioral interventions and supports and other strategies for the child

- supplementary aids and services, program modifications, and support for school personnel.

[34 C.F.R. 300.324(a)(3)]

In making changes to a child's IEP after the annual IEP team meeting for a school year, the parent of a child with a disability and the public agency may agree not to convene an IEP team meeting for the purposes of making those changes, and instead may develop a written document to amend or modify the child's current IEP. If changes are made to the child's IEP, the public agency must ensure that the child's IEP team is informed of those changes [34 C.F.R. 300.324(a)(4)].

To the extent possible, the public agency must encourage the consolidation of reevaluation meetings for the child and other IEP team meetings for the child [34 C.F.R. 300.324(a)(5)].

Changes to the IEP may be made either by the entire IEP team at an IEP team meeting, or by amending the IEP rather than by redrafting the entire IEP. Upon request, a parent must be provided with a revised copy of the IEP with the amendments incorporated [34 C.F.R. 300.324(a)(6)].

What does IDEIA mandate regarding the review and revisions of an IEP?

Under IDEIA, each public agency must ensure that the IEP team:

1. reviews the child's IEP periodically, but not less than annually, to determine whether the annual goals for the child are being achieved, and

2. revises the IEP, as appropriate, to address:

   • any lack of expected progress toward the annual goals described in §300.320(a)(2), and in the general education curriculum, if appropriate

   • the results of any reevaluation

   • information about the child provided to, or by, the parents

   • the child's anticipated needs, or

   • other matters.

[34 C.F.R. 300.324(b)(1)]

In conducting a review of the child's IEP, the IEP team must consider special factors (as described in the section on the development of IEPs above) [34 C.F.R. 300.324(b)(2)].

A regular education teacher of the child, as a member of the IEP team, must participate in the review and revision of the IEP of the child [34 C.F.R. 300.324(b)(3)].

The IEP team of a child with a disability who is convicted as an adult under state law and incarcerated in an adult prison may modify the child's IEP or placement if the state has demonstrated a bona fide security or compelling interest that cannot otherwise be accommodated.

Is an IEP meeting required before a public agency places a child with a disability in, or refers a child to, a private school or facility?

Yes. Before a public agency places a child with a disability in, or refers a child to, a private school or facility, the agency must initiate and conduct a meeting to develop an IEP for the child [34 C.F.R. 300.325; 20 U.S.C. 1412(a)(10)(B)].

The agency must ensure that a representative of the private school or facility attends the meeting. If the representative cannot attend, the agency must use other methods to ensure participation by the private school or facility, including individual or conference telephone calls.

After a child with a disability enters a private school or facility, any meetings to review and revise the child's IEP may be initiated and conducted by the private school or facility at the discretion of the public agency.

If the private school or facility initiates and conducts these meetings, the public agency must ensure that the parents and an agency representative:

- are involved in any decision about the child's IEP, and

- agree to any proposed changes in the IEP before those changes are implemented.

Even if a private school or facility implements a child's IEP, responsibility for compliance with this part remains with the public agency and the SEA.

Can students be declassified from special education?

Yes. During annual, requested, and triennial reviews of a student's IEP, the IEP team should determine if that student no longer requires special education services because his/her needs can be met in the general education setting without special education supports.

Upon review, the IEP team may recommend the decertification of a student from special education with the provision of appropriate support services for up to one year following the student's declassification. Students who continue to require ongoing special education services for more than a year are not eligible for declassification support services.

Declassification support services are direct or indirect services intended to support the decertified student while he/she makes the transition from a special program to a general education program with no other special education services. Declassification services include, but are not limited to, the following:

- services that provide instructional support or remediation

- instructional modifications

- individual and/or group speech-language services

- individual and/or group counseling.

The declassification support services to be provided must be indicated on the student's exiting IEP which recommends decertification. Their frequency and duration must be specified and appropriate school staff to implement the services must be assigned (New York City Department of Education, Office of Special Education Initiatives, 2011).

The **Least Restrictive Environment** (LRE)

Chapter

9

What is the least restrictive environment (LRE)?

The IEP team makes two separate determinations: what the child should be learning and where a child should learn. The intersection of those two determinations is that particular child's least restrictive environment (Pawlisch, 2000).

Under IDEIA, the "least restrictive environment," or LRE, requires that each public agency ensure that:

- to the maximum extent appropriate, children with disabilities, including children in public or private institutions or other care facilities, are educated with children who are nondisabled, and

- special classes, separate schooling, or other removal of children with disabilities from the regular educational environment occurs only if the nature or severity of the disability is such that education in regular classes with the use of supplementary aids and services cannot be achieved satisfactorily.

[34 C.F.R. 300.114(a)(2)(i); 20 U.S.C. 1412(a)(5)]

This requirement applies to nonacademic activities and extracurricular activities—for example, lunch and recess—as well as academic activities [34 C.F.R. 300.117; 20 U.S.C. 1412(a)(5)(B)].

IDEIA guarantees students with disabilities the right to be educated with their peers in the general education classroom to the maximum extent appropriate. The IEP team determines the supports and accommodations necessary for successful participation in the general education classroom and other special education services as needed. According to the No Child Left Behind (NCLB) legislation, schools are responsible for ensuring that students with disabilities make "adequate yearly progress." One component of implementing IDEA and NCLB legislation is determining effective practices to educate students with disabilities in general education classes alongside their peers without disabilities (Georgia Department of Education, 2011).

With respect to the IDEIA, how is the term "placement" defined?

Neither federal nor state regulations provide a regulatory definition for this term, but the federal Office of Special Education Programs (OSEP) has provided some clarity regarding what constitutes placement. It has stated that placement involves the substance of the student's IEP, the services, the supports, or any other aspect of a free appropriate public education (FAPE)—that is, the program itself; not just the physical location or setting. In determining the educational placement for a student, the first line of inquiry is whether his/her IEP can be implemented satisfactorily in the regular educational environment with the provision of supplementary aids and services (State of New Mexico Department of Education, 2003).

Who has the decision-making responsibility for placement?

The overriding rule is that placement must be made on an individual basis. The educational placement decision must be made by the IEP team. The term "placement" means the setting in which special education services are provided, not the specific classroom teacher or school.

If there is disagreement between the parents and the district over the placement decision and a hearing is initiated by the parents, the child must "stay put" unless a temporary placement is agreed upon by the district and the parents (Pierangelo and Giuliani, 2012).

The IEP team makes the least restrictive environment (LRE) decisions, including the specific determinations of appropriate educational services, location, and building or facility (Pawlisch, 2000). In determining the educational placement of a child with a disability, including a preschool child with a disability, each public agency must ensure that the placement decision is made by a group of persons, including the parents, and other persons knowledgeable about the child, the meaning of the evaluation data, and the placement options, and is made in conformity with the LRE provisions of IDEIA.

What does "maximum extent appropriate" mean?

The IEP team is responsible for identifying the student's needs and the appropriate placement in which these needs can be met. Placement decisions should begin with the least restrictive environment. All possible placement alternatives should be considered to ensure that services are delivered in the LRE (Texas Education Agency, 2009).

What are supplementary aids and services?

Before an IEP team determines that special education and related services should be provided outside of the regular education classroom, the full range of supplementary aids and services that could be provided to facilitate the student's success in the regular education classroom must be considered.

"Supplementary aids and services" means aids, services, and other supports that are provided in regular education classes, other education-related settings, and in extracurricular and nonacademic settings, to enable children with disabilities to be educated with nondisabled children to the maximum extent appropriate [34 C.F.R. 300.42; 20 U.S.C. 1401(33)].

Although determinations of what supplementary aids and services are appropriate for a particular student must be made on an individual basis, some supplementary aids and services that educators have used successfully include providing a special seating arrangement for a child, raising the level of a child's desk, allowing the child more time to complete a given assignment, working with the parents to help the child at home, and providing extra help to the child before, during, or after the school day. Other accommodations could involve providing a particular assistive technology device for the child or modifying the child's desk in some manner that facilitates the child's ability to write or hold books (Pawlisch, 2000).

What is the course of instruction for students with disabilities?

The course of instruction for the vast majority of students with disabilities should be the general education curriculum, unless otherwise stated on the student's IEP. General education curriculum for school-aged students refers to the content of the curriculum and not the language of instruction or the setting in which it is provided. The general education curriculum can be delivered in a language other than English, at different instructional levels to meet the needs of individual students, and in different settings to meet the student's individual needs, including the general education environment, a special class environment, at home, or in a hospital (New York City Department of Education, Office of Special Education Initiatives, 2011).

Is there an absolute right to have the child placed in the school closest to home?

No. IDEIA contains several requirements governing the location of the educational placement. Unless the IEP requires otherwise, the child should be placed in the school where he/she would attend were there no disability [34 C.F.R. 300.116(c); 20 U.S.C. 1412(a)(5)]. There is, however, no absolute right to have the child placed in the school closest to home.

To the greatest extent possible, the goal is for students with disabilities to attend the schools they would normally attend if they did not require special education services to address their learning needs. It is at the neighborhood school or the "home-zoned school," surrounded by siblings and friends, that services to meet the full range of the student's needs are to be provided whenever possible.

Benefits of home-zoned school placement include (New York City Department of Education, Office of Special Education Initiatives, 2011):

- membership in one's community

- development of long-term relationships with peers

- reinforcement of building-level "ownership" of the student

- promotion of "natural proportions" of students with disabilities in each school

- enhanced opportunities for parent involvement.

Are school districts permitted to use funding from IDEIA to pay for special education and related services and supplementary aids and services provided in a regular class or other education-related locations, even if one or more of children without disabilities benefit from the services?

Yes, in certain cases. If special education and related services are being provided in a regular education classroom to meet the requirements of the IEP for a child with a disability, federal regulations permit other children to benefit. However, the regulations do not permit Part B funds to be expended in a regular class except for special education and related services and supplementary aids and services for a child with a disability in accordance with the child's IEP. In such circumstances, no time and effort records are required under federal law, thus reducing unnecessary paperwork (Pawlisch, 2000).

What does "inclusion" mean?

IDEIA does not include the term "inclusion" and consequently a legal definition has not been established. Inclusion, in its broadest meaning, implies that students with disabilities are a part of the overall school community and should be included in all activities associated with the school.

Inclusion is understood in the field of special education to mean a policy or philosophy that supports the creation of a system in which all children with disabilities attend their home school with their age and grade peers, while also holding that for some students a regular education setting may not be the appropriate education option. Inclusive education programs are typically thought of to "include" students rather than merely "mainstreaming" them—a term used in the years before the regulations emphasized the creation of a system that strives to produce better outcomes for all students (State of New Mexico Department of Education, 2003).

Some of the confusion over the use of "inclusion" rises from its inconsistent use. As educators have worked to include students with disabilities in the general curriculum, the term "inclusion" has been used to describe this effort. In general, "inclusion" means that students with disabilities participate in the same activities as their peers without disabilities, including general education classes, extracurricular organizations, and social activities. The term "inclusion" also implies that students are provided services and supports in the general education setting before being removed to a special education classroom or excluded from an activity (Georgia Department of Education, 2011).

Is "LRE" the same thing as "inclusion"?

No. The U.S. Department of Education's Office of Special Educations Programs (OSEP) has stated that inclusion is not the same thing as the IDEA's mandate for educating students in the LRE. All placement decisions (that is, the spot on the continuum of alternative placements that describes the level of services and supports a student's needs) must be determined on a case-by-case basis according to the individual needs of the student. LRE determinations require an individualized inquiry into the unique educational needs of each eligible student in determining the possible range of aids and supports that are needed to facilitate the student's placement in the regular educational environment before a more restrictive placement is considered (State of New Mexico Department of Education, 2003).

What procedures must be followed when determining the educational placement decision of a child with a disability?

Under IDEIA, the IEP team must adhere to the following procedures when determining the educational placement decision of a child with a disability, including a preschool student with a disability (Alaska State Department of Education, 2007):

- *Placement based on IEP:* The placement decision must be based on the child's IEP.

- *Placement decision after IEP:* The placement decision must be made after the IEP is completed. Placement decisions for students with disabilities are to be based on an existing IEP, and therefore must be made after the development of the IEP [34 C.F.R. 300.116(b)(2)]. A decision to place a child with a disability prior to developing an IEP upon which to base that decision constitutes a violation of IDEIA and can lead to a finding that the decision would not provide the child with FAPE.

- *Placement decision made by the IEP team:* The placement decision must be made by the IEP team and must consider the continuum of placement options. All options must be available for consideration, even if a school site or district has a policy of being fully inclusive. The IEP team must include persons knowledgeable about the child, the meaning of the evaluation data, and the placement options.

- *Draw on a variety of sources:* In making the placement decision, the IEP team must use information drawn from a variety of sources including teacher recommendations and parent input. Information may include achievement data, performance on social and behavior rating scales, and language spoken in the home.

- *Continuum of alternative placements:* Each district must have a continuum of alternative placements available at all times to meet the individual needs of children with disabilities.

- *Consideration of harmful effects:* In selecting the placement, consideration must be given to any potential harmful effect on the child or on the quality of services.

- *Removal only when unsatisfactory achievement documented:* Special classes, separate schooling, or other removal of children with disabilities from the regular classroom environment may occur only when the nature or severity of the disability is such that education in regular classes with the use of supplementary aids and services cannot be achieved satisfactorily.

- *Involvement with peers who do not have disabilities:* Children with disabilities, including preschool children with disabilities, have the right to be educated in the regular setting to the greatest extent possible with their peers who do not have disabilities. This provision includes children with disabilities placed in a public or private institution or other care facility. The placement decision is not where the child is educated, but rather with whom.

- *Modifications in the general education curriculum are not a basis for removal:* A child cannot be removed from education in age-appropriate regular classrooms solely because of needed modifications in the general education curriculum.

- *Placement in home school or closest to home:* A child with disabilities should be enrolled in the school he/she would attend if not disabled, unless the IEP requires another arrangement. If the child cannot be educated in the neighborhood school, the child must be provided an educational program as close to home as possible.

- *Variety of educational programs and services equally available:* Each district shall ensure that children with disabilities have the variety of educational programs and services available to children without disabilities.

- *Participation in nonacademic and extracurricular activities:* Children with disabilities must be allowed to participate with other children who do not have disabilities in nonacademic and extracurricular services and activities to the maximum extent appropriate.

- *Age-appropriate placements:* In recommending a placement outside the regular classroom environment, the IEP team shall recommend placement in classrooms and schools with similar-age peers.

- *Placement is determined annually:* The placement, including the justification, must be considered at least annually.

- *Parent refusal to initial consent for services:* If the parent refuses to initial consent to services, the LEA shall not be required to provide special education services to the child.

What are questions to ask to determine compliance with LRE requirements?

Questions to ask to determine compliance with LRE requirements include, but are not limited to (Alaska State Department of Education, 2007):

- Can education in the regular classroom be achieved satisfactorily with the use of supplemental aids and services?

- Have steps been taken to accommodate the child in a regular education environment?

- Have more than mere token gestures been made to accommodate the child?

- Will the child benefit from regular education?

- What has been the child's overall educational experience in regular education environments?

- What effect does the presence of the child with a disability have on a regular classroom environment?

- If education cannot be satisfactorily achieved in a regular classroom, has the child been included with children without disabilities to the maximum extent appropriate? For example, has the school taken intermediate steps, such as placing the child in regular education for some academic classes and in special education for others; including the child in nonacademic classes only; or providing interaction with students without disabilities during lunch and recess?

What is the continuum of placement options available to children with special needs?

IDEIA requires that each public agency ensure that a continuum of alternative placements is available to meet the needs of children with disabilities for special education and related services. The continuum required must:

- include the alternative placements listed in the definition of special education under IDEIA [34 C.F.R. 300.38] (instruction in regular classes, special classes, special schools, home instruction, and instruction in hospitals and institutions), and

- make provision for supplementary services (such as resource room or itinerant instruction) to be provided in conjunction with regular class placement.

[34 C.F.R. 300.115]

The continuum of alternative placements includes the following options (Alaska State Department of Education, 2007):

- *The regular classroom with additional support services:* The child remains in the regular classroom. The teacher and/or child are provided with special equipment and supplies, special transportation, paraprofessional services, or other supportive services. The regular education classroom teacher or paraprofessional conducts classroom activities, while the special education teacher or therapist works with the regular education classroom teacher or paraprofessional to implement the IEP.

- *The regular classroom with direct services from special education personnel:* The child remains in the regular classroom. A special education teacher or therapist works with the regular education teacher and provides instruction in the regular class to an eligible child whose identified needs can be met with part-time support. The instruction may be on an individual or small-group basis and is always coordinated with the regular class activities.

  The term "co-teaching" refers to when a special education teacher and a general education teacher share the teaching responsibilities for a class which includes students with and without disabilities. Both teachers are equally responsible for planning, the delivery of instruction, grading, IEP implementation, and classroom management for all students. Instruction is enhanced for students when there are two teachers in a room with different areas of expertise. The general education teacher provides expertise in the content area while the special education teacher provides expertise in differentiating instruction.

  Teachers need professional learning opportunities on collaboration, differentiated instruction, the models of co-teaching, and how to ensure that both teachers are used effectively. In addition, teachers need time to plan collaboratively on a regular basis for instruction, assessment, and classroom management. In addition, school personnel should collaborate with parents of students with disabilities to determine if co-taught classes are appropriate for their child with a disability (Georgia Department of Education, 2011).

- *The regular educational environment with special education itinerant or resource support:* The child receives as much of the regular classroom instruction as appropriate. Additional educational experiences are provided by a special education teacher or therapist in a pull-out program designed to meet identified needs. The duration of time spent with the teacher or therapist is determined by the degree of intervention necessary to meet the child's needs. The instruction may be provided on an individual or small-group basis and is always coordinated with the regular class activities.

- *The regular education environment with self-contained classroom support:* The child receives any regular education classroom instruction from which he/she can benefit. The majority of instruction is provided in a self-contained classroom. Interaction with nondisabled peers may occur in the regular classroom, and in nonacademic and extracurricular activities as determined by the IEP team.

- *Full-time instruction in a separate day school:* The child receives all instruction in a separate day school. These experiences are supplemented by involvement in those parts of the regular school program that are appropriate.

- *Home or hospital instruction:* The home or hospital program consists of instructional and/or supportive services provided by the school to a child in his/her home, in a convalescent home, or in a hospital. A physician must certify in writing and the IEP provide that the child's bodily, mental, or emotional condition does not permit attendance at a school.

- *Institutional services:* The child resides in an institutional setting and receives all instruction in this setting. Involvement with nondisabled peers is provided as indicated in the IEP.

What factors may not be considered when determining the placement of a student?

Schools may not make placement decisions based solely on factors such as the following:

- category of disability

- severity of disability

- availability of educational or related services

- availability of space

- administrative convenience.

Funding concerns cannot be used as a reason for not providing appropriate programs or services. If funding is a problem, the school district must explore other ways of serving the student (Illinois State Board of Education, 2011).

When determining the location of services, should the IEP team consider the educational and nonacademic benefits to the child with a disability?

Yes. When determining the location of services, the IEP team should consider both the educational and the nonacademic benefits to the child with a disability. The IEP team should also consider, if applicable, the degree of disruption to the education of other students. In determining the location in which a child with behavioral problems will be educated, the IEP team must consider strategies, including positive behavioral interventions, strategies, and supports to address the child's behavior. However, if a student with a disability has behavioral problems that are so disruptive in a regular classroom that, even with the use of supplementary aids and services, the education of other students is significantly impaired, the regular education classroom is not appropriate to meet the student's needs (Pawlisch, 2000).

Must an IEP meeting occur in order to change a student's placement?

Yes, if the change involves a material change in the substance of the program itself—nature, frequency, or duration of special education and related services. Therefore, any proposal that would move the student in either direction along the continuum constitutes a proposed change in placement that triggers the district's obligation to:

- convene a properly composed IEP team meeting to make this decision, and

- provide prior written notification to the parents regarding this change before it is implemented (prior notice by the public agency).

On the other hand, as long as a schedule change (e.g. services on Tuesday as opposed to Thursday) or a location change (e.g. services in Room 18 as opposed to Room 11 with no change in the service delivery configuration) does not involve a substantial or material alteration in the student's IEP supports and services or conflict with any other provision of FAPE as detailed in the student's IEP, a schedule or location change would not require an IEP meeting or prior written notification, or necessitate parental consent. Again, these kinds of decisions must be determined on a case-by-case basis by the IEP team and not by any blanket or system-wide effort to move the district forward to meet the LRE mandate (State of New Mexico Department of Education, 2003).

What are the LRE considerations for students moving from one grade level to the next?

Under IDEIA, each public agency shall ensure that a continuum of alternative placements is available for students as they move from one grade level to another and/or one campus to another. A child with a disability must not be removed from education in age-appropriate general education classrooms solely because of needed modifications in the general education curriculum. Placement decisions should *not* be based on (Texas Education Agency, 2009):

- administrative convenience
- the previous year's placement decision
- existing instructional settings and/or programs
- lack of support staff and/or resources or space, or
- lack of staff development and/or training.

Are school districts required to provide full continuums of services and locations in every school within its jurisdiction?

No. The school district is not required to provide full continuums of services and locations in every school within its jurisdiction. Neither is a school district required to provide full continuums of services, locations, and buildings or facilities within its borders (Pawlisch, 2000).

Does a child have to fail in the regular education classroom before the IEP team considers another location in which to provide services?

No. A student need not fail in the regular classroom before another location can be considered. Conversely, a student does not need to demonstrate that he or she will be able to achieve satisfactorily in the regular classroom as a prerequisite for providing services in that location (Pawlisch, 2000).

Who is responsible for payment when a child with a disability is educated in a residential placement?

It is the responsibility of the school district (LEA). If placement in a public or private residential program is necessary to provide special education and related services to a child with a disability, the program, including non-medical care and room and board, must be at no cost to the parents of the child [34 C.F.R. 300.104].

Does the IEP team always need to justify the educational placement of a child with a disability?

Yes. The IEP team must provide a written statement on the IEP justifying the need for special education services that are more restrictive than full-time services in the regular classroom [34 C.F.R. 300.116; 34 C.F.R. 300.117].

Placement is considered after the child's educational services are determined. Removal of children from the regular education environment shall occur only when the nature or severity of the disability is such that education in regular classes with the use of supplementary aids and services cannot be achieved satisfactorily. Justification for placement statements must document that other placement options were considered, as well as the reasons they were rejected.

The IEP team must provide a written statement on the IEP justifying the need for special education services that are more restrictive than full-time services in the regular classroom. Such a statement justifying a more restrictive placement should answer the following questions, as applicable:

1. What supplemental aids and services (i.e. curriculum adaptation, paraprofessional assistance, assistive technology, resource or itinerant instruction) have been considered to address the child's needs?

2. Based on factors identified in the present level of academic achievement and functional performance, and/or in the child's educational goals and objectives, did the team consider the need to:

   a. develop a behavior intervention plan?

   b. furnish additional training to the service provider?

   c. address the developmental level of the child's language skills and social skills?

3. What factors identified in the present level of academic achievement and functional performance and/or in the child's educational goals and objectives require placement in a self-contained classroom in a local school building rather than in a regular classroom with itinerant or resource support?

4. What factors identified in the present level of academic achievement and functional performance and/or in the educational goals and objectives require placement in a self-contained classroom in a special school building, rather than in a self-contained classroom in the child's home school or in a regular classroom with itinerant or resource support?

5. What factors identified in the present level of academic achievement and functional performance and/or in educational goals and objectives require placement in an institutional setting or a private day school under contractual

agreement, rather than in a self-contained classroom in the local district or in a regular classroom with itinerant or resource support?

Must there be parental consent before the initial placement of a child in special education?

Before the initial placement of a child in special education, the child's parents must provide the school district with written consent. Only a parent, a guardian, a person acting as a parent, or a surrogate parent can provide consent for initial placement in special education (Pierangelo and Giuliani, 2012).

How often does the child's educational placement need to be determined?

The child's educational placement must be determined at least annually by the IEP team [C.F.R. 300.116(b)(1); 20 U.S.C. 1412(a)(5)]. A justification should again be stated for continuing a child in a present placement or for changing the child's placement.

Must the LEA ensure that extended school year (ESY) services are available if necessary to provide a FAPE?

Yes. The LEA must ensure that extended school year services are available if necessary to provide a FAPE [34 C.F.R. 300.106(b)(2)(i)].

The term "extended school year services" means special education and related services that are provided to a child with a disability:

- beyond the normal school year of the public agency

- in accordance with the child's IEP

- at no cost to the parents of the child, and

- meet the standards of the SEA.

Although ESY services are subject to debate, in general, ESY services are necessary to a FAPE when the benefits a child with a disability gains during a regular school year will be significantly jeopardized if he/she is not provided with an educational program during the summer months.

Is the LEA allowed to pursue an out-of-district placement for a child with a disability?

Yes. If the district determines that a student's IEP cannot reasonably be implemented within the district, the district may pursue an out-of-district placement. If a student who requires special education and related services is placed outside the student's resident district by the district, it is the sending district's responsibility to ensure that an IEP is developed and implemented. The sending district is also responsible for all costs associated with the transfer. The district must obtain the consent of the student's parent before the student may be transferred to an out-of-district placement. The withholding of consent by a parent does not relieve a school district of the obligation to provide special education and related services to the student. Only in the event that no in-state placement is available in which a free appropriate education can be provided may the student be placed outside the state (Alaska State Department of Education, 2007).

If the LEA recommends a private placement, what is its responsibility?

As part of the continuum of educational placements required to be made available, the LEA must include private educational programs when it is unable to provide a FAPE within the public school system. If a child is placed in a private special education program, the LEA is responsible for ensuring, in fact, that the IEP meets all the criteria that would be required were the child placed in public school [34 C.F.R. 300.146(a)].

The LEA placing the child in a program outside of the public school must ensure that the private education be provided at no cost to the parents, and that the child placed has all the rights of a child who is directly served by the LEA.

Does a parentally placed private school child with a disability have the same right to receive some or all of the special education and related services that he/she would receive if enrolled in a public school?

No. Even if the LEA is able to provide a FAPE in the public schools to a child, the parents may choose to place the child in a private program. A parentally placed private school child with a disability, however, does not have the same right to receive some or all of the special education and related services that he/she would receive if enrolled in a public school [34 C.F.R. 300.137(a); 20 U.S.C. 1412(a)(10)(a)]. The LEA need not pay for the general education of the child at the private placement if the placement was made unilaterally by the parent.

When the LEA is prepared to provide a FAPE in the public school, but the parents unilaterally decide to place the child in a parochial school, is the LEA required to provide special education and related services for the child at the parochial school?

No. The LEA is not obligated to provide services at a parochial school because the LEA has little obligation to provide educational services at any private school. May the school provide services? Yes, and many schools do, but are they obligated to do so when placement is done unilaterally by the parent? No, they are not (Guersney and Klare, 2008).

When a parent disagrees with the LEA regarding the placement decision, what is an LEA required to do?

The IEP meeting serves as a communication vehicle between parents and school personnel and enables them, as equal participants, to make joint, informed decisions regarding the child's placement. Parents are considered equal partners with school personnel in making these decisions (Pawlisch, 2000).

The IEP team should work toward consensus, but the public agency has ultimate responsibility to ensure that the child receives FAPE. Both state and federal law contain provisions under procedural safeguards on how to proceed whenever a parent does not agree with an IEP team's determination of a child's initial or continued placement.

If parents disagree with the initial placement proposed by the LEA and refuse to grant consent for placement, the LEA may not place the child in special education. The LEA may use various forms of dispute resolution options to resolve the refusal to consent (see Chapter 10).

Dispute Resolution Options in Special Education

This chapter will focus on various ways to address situations in which parents and school districts do not agree on a matter or issues pertaining to a child with a disability. There are both "informal" approaches" and "formal" approaches. The law (IDEIA) provides several approaches that parents and schools can use to help resolve disputes.

In this chapter certain abbreviations will be used:

- *LEA: Local education agency* or *LEA* means a public board of education (e.g. school district) or other public authority legally constituted within a state for either administrative control or direction of, or to perform a service function for, public elementary or secondary schools in a city, county, township, school district, or other political subdivision of a state, or for a combination of school districts or counties as are recognized in a state as an administrative agency for its public elementary schools or secondary schools [34 C.F.R. 300.28; 20 U.S.C. 1401(19)].

- *SEA: State educational agency* or *SEA* means the state board of education or other agency or officer primarily responsible for the state supervision of public elementary schools and secondary schools, or, if there is no such officer or agency, an officer or agency designated by the governor or by state law [34 C.F.R. 300.41; 20 U.S.C. 1401(32)].

What approaches are there to dispute resolution in special education?

In all cases where a family and school disagree, it is important for both sides to first discuss their concerns and try to compromise. There are several, relatively informal ways in which parents and school staff might attempt to work out disagreements regarding a child's special education program (National Dissemination Center for Children with Disabilities, 2010a). The two most frequently used "informal" methods are:

- IEP review meeting
- facilitated IEP meeting.

IDEIA provides more formal approaches for resolving disputes between parents and school districts. These include:

- mediation
- filing a state complaint
- resolution meetings
- due process hearings.

Each of these six approaches for resolving disputes will be discussed in this chapter.

» I. IEP REVIEW MEETING

What is an IEP review meeting?

Under IDEIA, the school system is responsible for determining when it is necessary to conduct an IEP meeting. The child's IEP team is responsible for reviewing the child's IEP periodically, but not less than annually, and revising the child's IEP, if appropriate. In addition, the parents of a child with a disability have the right to request an IEP meeting at any time [34 C.F.R. 300.324(a)(6)(B)].

What types of disputes might be resolved through an IEP review meeting?

After the annual IEP review has taken place, if a parent has concerns about his/her child's rate of progress, the appropriateness of the services provided to the child, or the child's educational placement, it would be appropriate for the parent to request that the IEP team reconvene. At that meeting, the parent and public agency can discuss the parent's concerns and, it would be hoped, as collaborative members of the IEP team, work toward a solution that is agreeable to all.

The solution doesn't have to be permanent. It is not uncommon for IEP teams to agree on a temporary compromise—for example, to try out a particular plan of instruction or classroom placement for a certain period of time that the child's IEP is in effect. During (or at the end of) that period, the school can check the child's progress. Team members can then meet again and discuss how the child is doing, how well the temporary compromise addressed the original concern, and what to do next. The trial period may help parents and the school come to a comfortable agreement on how to help the child [34 C.F.R. 300.324(a)(6)(B)].

Does the entire team have to be at an IEP review meeting?

Not necessarily. A new provision in IDEIA allows changes to be made to the child's IEP, following the annual IEP team review, without convening the full IEP team [34

C.F.R. 300.324(a)(4)]. In making changes to a child's IEP after the annual IEP team meeting for a school year, the parent of a child with a disability and the public agency may agree not to convene an IEP team meeting for the purposes of making those changes, and instead may develop a written document to amend or modify the child's current IEP. If changes are made to the child's IEP, the public agency must ensure that the child's IEP team is informed of those changes.

Simply stated, the parent and the public agency may agree not to convene an IEP team meeting for the purpose of making changes to the child's IEP. In some cases, the parties may be able to resolve a disagreement by conducting a review of the child's IEP and amending it as appropriate, without convening the entire IEP team.

What are the benefits of resolving a dispute through an IEP review?

Because parents and the public agency are partners in ensuring the child is provided an appropriate education, and sometimes will be working together for many years—in some cases, the child's entire school career—it is in everyone's best interest, especially the child's, that the IEP team members communicate with one another, respectfully and honestly (National Dissemination Center for Children with Disabilities, 2010a).

» II. FACILITATED IEP MEETING

What is a facilitated IEP team meeting?

A facilitated IEP meeting is an IEP meeting that includes an impartial facilitator who promotes effective communication and assists an IEP team in developing an acceptable IEP. The facilitator keeps the team focused on the proper development of the IEP while addressing conflicts that arise (Minnesota Special Education Mediation Service, 2011).

Conducting a facilitated IEP team meeting is quickly becoming the most recognized strategy for improving the effectiveness and efficiency of IEP meetings. The use of externally facilitated IEP meetings is growing nationally. The purpose of the facilitation process is to develop and sustain collaborative relationships between team members and to preserve and maintain a productive relationship between families and schools (Conflict Resolution Program, 2011).

In 2005, President Bush's Commission on Excellence in Special Education recommended using skilled facilitators to guide IEP meetings in a situation where parties are having difficulty reaching agreement so that the process can result in win-win solutions for the child (New Mexico Public Education Department, Special Education Bureau, 2006).

When relationships between parents and schools are strained, facilitated meetings may be beneficial (The Consortium for Appropriate Dispute Resolution in Special

Education, 2011). Using a trained facilitator has been found to be an effective means to keep IEP teams focused on the development of the educational program for the student while addressing some of the conflicts and disagreements that may arise from inadequate communication. The facilitator will utilize skills that create an environment in which the IEP team members, school personnel, and parents can listen to each other and work together in developing high-quality education programs for students suspected of or identified as having disabilities (Maryland State Department of Education, Division of Special Education/Early Intervention Services, 2007).

Is IEP facilitation mentioned in IDEIA?

No. IEP facilitation is not mentioned in IDEIA and is not one of the dispute resolution options described in the law's procedural safeguards. Since IDEIA does not address IEP facilitation, there is no requirement for school systems to provide an impartial facilitator for IEP team meetings (The Consortium for Appropriate Dispute Resolution in Special Education, 2011).

Who can request an IEP meeting be facilitated?

A facilitator may be requested by the parent or the school. However, both parties must agree to use this voluntary process (Maryland State Department of Education, Division of Special Education/Early Intervention Services, 2007).

Who does the IEP facilitator serve?

The role of an IEP facilitator is to ensure that the IEP team members do their best thinking and interact respectfully, that the perspectives of all participants are heard, and that the IEP team focuses on future action. Thus, an IEP facilitator serves the whole group rather than an individual, and assists the group with the process of the IEP meeting rather than the content of the IEP. The agenda for a facilitated IEP meeting is the IEP process, and the focus of the meeting is the student and his/her needs (New Mexico Public Education Department, Special Education Bureau, 2006).

Is the facilitator a decision maker at the IEP meeting?

No. The role of the facilitator is to facilitate communication among the IEP team members and assist them to develop an effective IEP for the student. The facilitator models effective communication skills and offers ways to address and resolve conflicts in the development of the IEP. Facilitators are trained in effective communication and ways to address and resolve conflicts. The members of the IEP team are the decision makers (Consortium for Appropriate Dispute Resolution in Special Education, 2011).

What is the difference between an internal facilitator and an external facilitator?

When a member of the IEP team facilitates the meeting (or, in some instances, students may lead their own IEP meetings), this is an example of an internal facilitator. When IEP teams reach an impasse or meetings are expected to be contentious, an independent (external) facilitator, who is not affiliated with the team or school district, may help guide the process. The external facilitator keeps members of the IEP team focused on the development of the IEP and will foster effective communication in order to complete the development of a high-quality IEP (National Dissemination Center for Children with Disabilities, 2010b).

How does facilitation differ from mediation under IDEIA?

IEP facilitation should not be confused with mediation. Mediation may be used to deal with a broader range of issues in special education than in an IEP meeting. Mediation is typically used when there is a significant disagreement that the parties are otherwise unable to resolve. A trained impartial mediator brings the parties together to work with each other to resolve a variety of disagreements, often including those unrelated to the student's IEP (Maryland State Department of Education, Division of Special Education/Early Intervention Services, 2007).

Although facilitated IEP team meetings are emerging as a means to avoid conflicts and/or to resolve conflicts prior to requesting mediation or filing a due process complaint, it is not required under IDEIA. States or local school systems are not required to offer the service. Some other differences between IEP facilitation and mediation include:

- The facilitation occurs at a regular IEP team meeting.

- The IEP meeting is generally run by the school system in the same manner as an IEP meeting that is not being facilitated.

- There is no written agreement other than a written IEP for the student and the prior notice requirement of IDEIA.

The purpose of a facilitated IEP meeting is to develop an acceptable IEP and involves the required IEP team members, in addition to the facilitator. Mediation also differs from IEP facilitation in that it involves a smaller, balanced number of participants and may deal with a broader range of issues unrelated to the IEP (Minnesota Special Education Mediation Service, 2011).

What are the benefits of an IEP facilitator?

Facilitators are individuals with a background in special education who have experience and training in IEP development, special education law, and facilitation methods. They are not decision makers but instead model effective communication skills and offer ways to address and resolve issues related to the IEP development. Facilitators are impartial and do not represent the parent, the school district. or the state.

A facilitator can be expected to (Maryland State Department of Education, Division of Special Education/Early Intervention Services, 2007):

- assist the team in establishing an agenda

- guide the discussion and keep the focus on the student

- make sure everyone has a chance to speak and be heard

- help resolve disagreements

- use communication skills to help parents and school personnel to work together to make decisions about the program

- help team members develop and ask clarifying questions about issues that may have occurred in the past

- help to keep the team on task and within the time allotted for the meeting

- remain impartial, not take sides, place blame, impose a decision on the group, nor offer an opinion on the appropriateness of a decision.

The IEP facilitator can help support the full participation of all parties. The facilitator does not impose a decision on the group; the facilitator clarifies points of agreement and disagreement and can model effective communication and listening for the IEP team members. When disagreements arise, the facilitator can help encourage the members to identify new options. Most importantly, the impartial facilitator ensures that the meeting remains focused on the child.

Key strengths of using a facilitator include:

- A facilitated IEP meeting can resolve concerns at the lowest level possible— no state involvement or need to go to a formal complaint.

- Unlike mediation, a facilitated IEP meeting does not require a separate IEP meeting to formalize the agreements that are reached.

- The challenges of communication during an IEP meeting where parties are encountering continued difficulty may best be handled by an impartial facilitator not affiliated with the school or family—that is, someone who has no past experience with the group members and will not have any continued relationship with those members.

- The facilitator enables the IEP team to build and improve strong relationships among its individual members, problem-solve as a group, reach true consensus, focus on the student's needs, and experience an efficient and productive meeting where effective communication skills are practiced.

- The presence of an IEP facilitator eliminates the need to have someone at the table having to play the dual role of participant and facilitator.

A facilitator provides expert guidance through the implementation of a compliant IEP meeting while focusing attention on the process of the meeting. An IEP meeting facilitator can help a team resolve differences not only more immediately but where they originate. The role of the facilitator is to assist team members in communicating effectively in order to reach decisions that are in the best interest of the student. The facilitator is not a member of the IEP team or an advocate for any person on the team. His/her responsibility is to the whole team rather than an individual. He/she will not offer advice, suggestions, solutions, or legal interpretation (Conflict Resolution Program, 2011).

Other benefits of IEP facilitation include:

- planning and designing the meeting process, in partnership with the parties

- setting a positive and welcoming tone for the meeting

- clarifying the purpose of the meeting, the ground rules, the desired outcomes, the process to be used, and the roles of each person

- keeping the discussion focused on the child

- drawing out opinions and encouraging full participation from all IEP team members

- monitoring the pace of the meeting

- maintaining neutrality, reflecting content and process back to the group.

When should parents *not* use IEP facilitation as a method of dispute resolution?

If parents find themselves doing any of the following, then it is time to consider whether IEP facilitation is really a worthwhile option:

- spending more time putting out fires than working on activities that promote student achievement and success

- sensing that the discussions and/or interactions at IEP meetings are creating an acrimonious climate that might lead to a formal complaint

- attending multiple IEP meetings for the same student to address persistent issues with little or no resolution or a completed quality plan.

The facilitated IEP process is designed to work best when the dispute is child- or situation-specific. If parents find that they are facing a dispute that raises systemic concerns or a situation in which the parties do not appear to be solution-oriented, then this process is most likely not a viable option (New Mexico Public Education Department, Special Education Bureau, 2006).

Is procedural notice to parents required for a facilitated IEP meeting?

Yes, as in any IEP meeting, the notification procedures found in IDEIA apply. Districts must give parents proper notice, including the place and time where the meeting will occur, who will attend, and the purpose of the meeting. Parents and the school district may bring an advocate or other people who have knowledge or special expertise regarding the child to the meeting (Consortium for Appropriate Dispute Resolution in Special Education, 2011).

How do parents request a facilitated IEP meeting?

Although access to IEP facilitators is increasing, not all states or districts make IEP facilitation available to parents and educators. Parents interested in having an externally facilitated IEP meeting should begin by contacting their school district to explore their options and inquire about availability. Parents can also contact their state education agency or parent center for information about the availability and use of IEP meeting facilitators (Consortium for Appropriate Dispute Resolution in Special Education, 2011).

How long does the facilitated IEP meeting take?

A facilitated IEP meeting may take longer than a standard IEP meeting, but typically does not exceed four hours. A facilitated IEP meeting can always be reconvened if consensus on the IEP is not reached at the first meeting.

Where and when is a facilitated IEP meeting held?

Similar to any IEP meeting, a facilitated IEP meeting is scheduled by the district and is held at a time and place mutually agreed to by the parent and school. The district must give proper notice to the parent, including the purpose, the time and place where the meeting will occur, and who will attend. Just as in any IEP meeting, parents can bring an advocate or other people at their discretion (Minnesota Special Education Mediation Service, 2011).

Who is required to attend a facilitated IEP meeting?

The required members of the IEP team (see Chapter 8) must attend the meeting unless the LEA and parent have agreed in writing to excuse one or more members. The LEA must follow the federal regulation regarding excusals. It is recommended that all the required members attend a facilitated IEP team meeting in order to resolve the concerns and/or issues.

Both parties have the right to invite to the meeting others who have special expertise and/or knowledge about the child. The child should attend whenever it is appropriate. The child must be invited when transition is discussed. Signatures on the IEP and other forms indicate the member was in attendance and participated in the development of the IEP. If a member is not in attendance, then he/she must not sign any form(s).

IEP meetings, including facilitated meetings, should not be adversarial and it is strongly recommended by many states that both parties refrain from inviting attorneys. If one party plans to invite an attorney to the meeting, then he/she must inform the other party and the facilitator (North Carolina Department of Public Instruction, 2011).

How is the confidentiality of the student and family maintained with the facilitator?

The parent must provide their consent to allow the school to share confidential information about the student with the facilitator. This is required under the Family Education Rights Privacy Act (Maryland State Department of Education, Division of Special Education/Early Intervention Services, 2007).

Who pays for the facilitator?

IEP facilitation is provided at no cost to parents. One of the objectives in using the facilitated IEP meeting is to reduce costs and avoid more adversarial procedures such as due process hearings (Consortium for Appropriate Dispute Resolution in Special Education, 2011; Maryland State Department of Education, Division of Special Education/Early Intervention Services, 2007).

Do all school districts have to offer facilitated IEP team meetings?

No. Since IDEIA does not address IEP facilitation, there is no requirement in IDEIA for school systems to provide an impartial facilitator for IEP team meetings. Although the use of IEP facilitation has become more popular, facilitators may not be available in all school districts and are not required (Consortium for Appropriate Dispute Resolution in Special Education, 2011).

What if the facilitated IEP meeting does not result in an acceptable IEP?

Parents have not forfeited their rights to other forms of dispute resolution if the facilitated IEP meeting does not result in an acceptable IEP (Consortium for Appropriate Dispute Resolution in Special Education, 2011).

» III. MEDIATION

What is mediation?

Mediation is a voluntary process that may be used to resolve disputes between school systems and the parents of a child with a disability. Mediation is a dispute-resolution and collaborative problem-solving process in which a trained impartial party facilitates a negotiation process between parties who have reached an impasse. The role of the mediator is to facilitate discussion, encourage open exchange of information, assist the involved parties in understanding each other's viewpoints, and help the parties reach mutually agreeable solutions (National Dissemination Center for Children with Disabilities, 2010c).

Mediation is entirely voluntary. Although each mediation situation is unique, generally both parties to the mediation will come to the mediation session prepared to explain their own position and listen and respond to the other party's position. The mediator will facilitate a discussion but does not "take sides" or give an opinion on the issues being disputed. The mediator works with the parties to help them express their views and positions and to understand each other's perspectives. The mediator helps the parties generate potential solutions and helps them communicate and negotiate. If an agreement is reached to resolve the dispute, the mediator helps the parties record their agreement in a written, signed document (State Education Department of New York, Office of Vocational and Educational Services for Individuals with Disabilities, 2001).

In mediation, an impartial third-party mediator helps parents and school staff clarify the issues and underlying concerns, explore interests, discuss options, and reach mutually satisfying agreements that address the needs of the student. The mediator does not decide how to resolve the dispute—that is left in the hands of the parent(s) and the school personnel. When the parties resolve all or some of the issues, they work together with the mediator to put their agreement in writing (CADRE, 2007).

Mediation is less stressful than formal hearings, less time-consuming, and can improve relationships between educators and parents. Mediation can help the parties envision other alternatives to their original positions (National Dissemination Center for Children with Disabilities, 2010c). The collaborative problem-solving meeting encourages mutual respect, promotes communication, and often provides the basis for positive working relationships between the parent(s) and school staff (U.S. House of Representatives, Committee on Education and the Workforce, 2005).

Why would parents and school districts want to use mediation as a dispute-resolution option?

When parents and schools disagree on special education programs for students with disabilities (and negotiations in IEP team meetings have stalled), reaching a resolution can be difficult. However, parents may want to avoid a more adversarial due process hearing and/or want to attempt to resolve the matter without attorney involvement. In this type of situation, mediation is often considered.

Parents and school districts will use mediation as an attempt to bring about a peaceful settlement or compromise between parties to a dispute through the objective intervention of a neutral party. Mediation is an opportunity for parents and school officials to sit down with an independent mediator and discuss a problem, issue, concern, or complaint in order to resolve the problem amicably without going to due process (U.S. House of Representatives, Committee on Education and the Workforce, 2005).

Mediation provides a positive, less adversarial approach to resolving disputes between parents and school systems. With the assistance of a skilled and impartial facilitator (the mediator), the parties involved in the dispute are encouraged to communicate openly and respectfully about their differences and to come to an agreement. The decision-making power always resides with the participants in mediation.

Does IDEIA afford mediation as an option for dispute resolution?

Yes. Each public agency must ensure that procedures are established and implemented to allow parties, to resolve disputes through a mediation process [34 C.F.R. 300.506(a); 20 U.S.C. 1415(e)(1)].

What sets mediation apart from other special education meetings?

Mediation differs from other special education or IEP meetings in that:

- Mediation is conducted by a neutral third party.

- Mediation can uncover new approaches that the parties haven't previously explored.

- Participants are encouraged to examine the reasons behind their conclusions and reevaluate their thinking.

- Mediation provides a structured, problem-solving approach that ensures that all participants are able to express their perspectives while being treated fairly and impartially.

- A mediator's questions may encourage new thought, elicit new options, and provide a format in which people can communicate with each other differently. The parties often reach a different outcome than they reached in previous special education meetings.

What are the benefits of using mediation to resolve a dispute?

Although mediation cannot guarantee specific results, it can be an efficient and effective method of dispute resolution between the parents and the school district or, as appropriate, the SEA or other public agency.

As part of its technical assistance and dissemination (TA&D) network, the United States Office of Special Education Programs has funded a center that specializes in dispute resolution, including mediation. It is called CADRE, the Center for Appropriate Dispute Resolution in Special Education, also known as the National Center on Dispute Resolution.

Through its work in dispute resolution, CADRE (2007) has identified a range of benefits of mediation for parents, educators, and services providers, including:

- Special education issues are complex and can best be solved by working together.

- Mediation often results in lowered financial and emotional costs, especially when compared to a due process hearing. It also tends to be faster and less adversarial.

- Given its voluntary nature and the ability of the parties to devise their own remedies, mediation often results in written agreements because parties have an increased commitment to, and ownership of, the agreement.

- Remedies are often individually tailored and contain workable solutions that are easier for the parties to implement since they have both been involved in developing the specific details of the implementation plan. Because the parties reach their own agreement, as opposed to having a third party decide the solution, they are generally more likely to follow through and comply with the terms of that agreement.

- Families can maintain an ongoing and positive relationship with the school and benefit from partnering with educators or service providers in developing their child's program.

- Research shows that people tend to follow the terms of their mediated agreements.

How is mediation different from a due process hearing?

At mediation, the mediator facilitates communication between the school district and the child's parent or guardian to help them reach agreement regarding the issue(s) on which they disagree. At a due process hearing, the hearing officer renders a decision on the issue(s) based on evidence and testimony. Other differences include those listed below.

Mediation

- Informal process that takes about 2–5 hours.

- Voluntary participation for parents and school districts.

- Attorneys need not be present and parties speak for themselves.

- Discussion allows participants to focus on the student's future educational program together.

- Parties shape their own agreements through collaborative problem solving.

- When resolution is reached, the parties usually leave the mediation with a written agreement.

Due process hearing

- Formal legal proceeding that takes about 1–3 days.

- Mandatory participation upon hearing request by either parents or school districts.

- Attorneys are generally present and usually speak on behalf of the participants.

- Evidence and sworn testimony are presented as the legal basis for a decision about the student's educational program.

- Hearing officer makes a decision based on a determination of the facts and law.

What are the procedural requirements of mediation?

Mediation may be requested by the child's parent, guardian, or surrogate parent, by organizations, groups, or school personnel. The procedures must ensure that the mediation process:

- is voluntary on the part of the parties

- is not used to deny or delay a parent's right to a hearing on the parent's due process complaint, or to deny any other rights afforded under Part B of IDEIA, and

- is conducted by a qualified and impartial mediator who is trained in effective mediation techniques.

[34 C.F.R. 300.506(b)(1)(i–iii)]

How would school districts know what mediators are available?

The state must maintain a list of individuals who are qualified mediators and knowledgeable in laws and regulations relating to the provision of special education and related services [34 C.F.R. 300.506(3)(i); 20 U.S.C. 1415(e)(2)(C) and (D)].

How are mediators selected?

The SEA must select mediators on a random, rotational, or other impartial basis [34 C.F.R. 300.506(b)(3)(ii); 20 U.S.C. 1415(e)(2)(C) and (D)].

Does IDEIA address the impartiality of mediators?

Yes. An individual who serves as a mediator:

- may not be an employee of the SEA or the LEA that is involved in the education or care of the child, and

- must not have a personal or professional interest that conflicts with the person's objectivity.

[34 C.F.R. 300.506(c); 20 U.S.C. 1415(e)]

The role of the mediator is to help the parties to discuss the issues respectfully and to consider alternatives to the dispute. The mediator does not make decisions, but may ask questions and make suggestions for both parties to consider. If the parties do not agree with the suggestions, the mediator does not push for their acceptance. The mediator guides the discussion so that the parties can effectively problem-solve the disputed issues.

Who bears the cost of mediation?

Neither parents nor school districts are responsible for the costs of special education mediation. Such costs are the responsibility of the State Education Department [34 C.F.R. 300.506(b)(4); 20 U.S.C. 1415(e)(2)(D)].

When and where are mediation sessions held?

Each session in the mediation process must be scheduled in a timely manner and must be held in a location that is convenient to the parties to the dispute [34 C.F.R. 300.506(b)(5); 20 U.S.C. 1415(e)(2)(E)].

Who can attend a mediation session?

Generally, the parent(s) or guardian(s) and a representative of the school district attend mediation. Since mediation is intended to improve communication, the parties represent themselves in discussions regardless of who accompanies them. The school district representative who attends the mediation should be adequately informed and authorized by the school district to enter into an appropriate agreement. Either party may be accompanied by others, including an attorney (State Education Department of New York, Office of Vocational and Educational Services for Individuals with Disabilities, 2001).

Are attorneys' fees reimbursed for mediation?

No, attorneys' fees cannot be reimbursed for mediation (State Education Department of New York, Office of Vocational and Educational Services for Individuals with Disabilities, 2001).

What happens if the parties resolve the dispute through mediation?

If the parties resolve a dispute through the mediation process, the parties must execute a legally binding agreement that sets forth that resolution and:

- states that all discussions that occurred during the mediation process will remain confidential and may not be used as evidence in any subsequent due process hearing or civil proceeding [34 C.F.R. 300.506(b)(6)(i)]

- is signed by both the parent and a representative of the agency who has the authority to bind such agency [34 C.F.R. 300.506(b)(6)(ii); 20 U.S.C. 1415(e)(2)(F)].

A written, signed mediation agreement is enforceable in any state court of competent jurisdiction or in a district court of the United States.

Are discussions during mediation confidential?

Yes. Discussions that occur during the mediation process must be confidential and may not be used as evidence in any subsequent due process hearing or civil proceeding of any federal court or state court. Only the written mediation agreement may be presented as evidence at an impartial hearing subsequent to a mediation session. No summary of actual discussions or offers of settlement will be permitted [34 C.F.R. 300.506(b)(8); 20 U.S.C. 1415(e)(2)(G)]. If the parties resolve a dispute through the mediation process, the parties must execute a legally binding agreement that includes a statement that all discussions that occurred during the mediation process will remain confidential.

Must a written mediation agreement be kept confidential?

IDEIA does not specifically address whether the mediation agreement itself must remain confidential. However, the confidentiality provisions in the Part B regulations of IDEIA and the Family Educational Rights and Privacy Act (FERPA) and its regulations apply. Further, there is nothing in IDEIA that would prohibit the parties from agreeing voluntarily to include in their mediation agreement a provision that limits disclosure of the mediation agreement, in whole or in part, to third parties.

How is a mediation agreement enforced?

If the parties resolve the dispute through the mediation process, they must execute a legally binding agreement that states the resolution and is signed by both the parent and a representative of the agency who has authority to bind the agency. This is clearly stated at 34 C.F.R. 300.506(b)(6). A written, signed mediation agreement is enforceable in any state court of competent jurisdiction (a court that has the authority under state law to hear this type of case) or in a district court of the United States (CADRE, 2007).

If, at the conclusion of the 30-day resolution period, the LEA and parents wish to continue the mediation process, must the hearing officer agree to the extension?

No. The regulations contemplate that the parties may agree in writing to continue the mediation at the end of the 30-day resolution period. Therefore, such agreements would not require hearing officer involvement or approval.

Each hearing and review involving oral arguments must be conducted at a time and place that is reasonably convenient to the parents and child involved, and a hearing officer may grant specific extensions of time at the request of either party [34 C.F.R. 300.515]. Therefore, to the extent that the hearing officer already has established a hearing schedule that is inconsistent with the extension agreed upon by the parties, it would be appropriate to notify the hearing officer of the agreement and any scheduling conflicts in order to revise the hearing schedule.

How does the use of mediation affect parents' other due process rights?

Use of mediation to resolve a parent's concern does not in any way affect (deny or delay) the parent's other rights to due process, such as the right to a due process hearing. A parent can request a due process hearing at any time before, during, or after the mediation. Requesting a hearing prior to or in the absence of mediation does not constitute that a person has failed to exhaust administrative remedies, which has to do with awarding attorneys' fees in subsequent hearings. Mediation does not diminish or limit the due process rights of a parent (State Education Department of New York, Office of Vocational and Educational Services for Individuals with Disabilities, 2001).

» IV. STATE COMPLAINTS

What is a state complaint?

A state complaint is a written, signed letter directed to the State Department of Education, which alleges that a public agency responsible for the education of a student with disabilities violated a requirement of the Individuals with Disabilities Education Act (IDEA) and accompanying state and federal regulations. The complaint may be filed on behalf of an individual student or a group of students that were affected by the alleged violation (Maryland State Department of Education, Division of Special Education/Early Intervention Services, 2011).

Who may file a state complaint?

Any individual or organization who believes that an LEA has violated IDEIA or the State Department's Rules and Regulations on Special Education can file. This includes a parent/parents or any other concerned individual or organization (Utah Department of Education, 2011). This is an important difference between state complaints and mediation and due process complaints. Those two dispute resolution options—due process complaints and mediation—require either the child's parent or the public agency to initiate the process. The person who files a state complaint is referred to as the "complainant."

Where does IDEIA talk about state complaints?

IDEIA does not include state complaint procedures. Rather, it requires each state to adopt its own written state complaint procedures. These regulations are found at 34 C.F.R. 300.151 through 300.153.

The written procedures that a state adopts must [34 C.F.R. 300.151(a)]:

- provide a way for individuals and organizations to file a state complaint with the state education agency (SEA), and

- if the state so chooses, also provide a way for a complaint to be filed with the school system itself and have the school system's decision on the complaint be reviewed by the SEA.

These procedures must be widely disseminated to parents and other interested individuals, including parent training and information centers, protection and advocacy agencies, independent living centers, and other appropriate entities.

Because the SEA has a general supervisory obligation and authority for special education systems in the state, its procedures for resolving state complaints must include remedies when a failure to provide appropriate services is found. This includes:

- corrective action appropriate to address the needs of the child (such as compensatory services or monetary reimbursement)

- how appropriate services for all children with disabilities will be provided in the future.

Thus, as the Department of Education has observed, state complaint procedures are directly under the control of the SEA, and provide parents and the school district "with mechanisms that allow them to resolve differences without having to resort to a more costly and cumbersome due process complaint, which, by its nature, is litigious" (71 Fed. Reg. 46606).

What information must a state complaint include?

First, a state complaint must be *signed* and *written*. It must also include [34 C.F.R 300.153(b)]:

- a statement that the school system has violated a requirement of Part B of IDEIA

- the facts on which this statement is based

- the signature and contact information for the complainant.

If the alleged violation is with respect to a specific child, the complaint must also include [34 C.F.R 300.153(b)]:

- the name and address of the child

- the name of the school the child is attending

- a description of the "nature of the problem of the child," including facts related to the problem, and

- a proposed resolution of the problem to the extent known and available to the party at the time the complaint is filed.

Each SEA must develop a model form to assist parents and other parties in filing a state complaint. However, the SEA or local education agency (LEA) may *not* require the use of its model forms. Another form or document may be used so long as the form or document includes the content required for filing a state complaint [34 C.F.R. 300.509(b)].

When filing a state complaint, who needs to receive a copy of the complaint?

A copy of any complaint sent to the state must also be sent to the public agency against which the complaint is made. It is recommended that the copy of the complaint be sent for the attention of the Director of Special Education for the public agency. This permits the public agency to review the complaint and consider resolving it as quickly as possible (Maryland State Department of Education, Division of Special Education/ Early Intervention Services, 2011).

What types of complaints will not be investigated by the state under its special education general supervisory responsibilities?

The state does not investigate complaints regarding personnel matters, complaints that do not allege a violation of state or federal special education requirements, and other matters that do not fall within the state's authority to monitor and enforce, such as alleged violations of the Rehabilitation Act of 1973. The state does not investigate allegations that the school did not implement any agreements between a public agency and parents of a student with a disability that were developed as a result of mediation, a resolution meeting, or other settlement agreement (Maryland State Department of Education, Division of Special Education/Early Intervention Services, 2011).

Is the complaint filed with the SEA?

Yes. But it is also important to note that the complainant must also send a copy to the LEA or school system serving the child at the same time the state complaint is filed with the SEA. This is a new provision, found at 34 C.F.R. 300.153(d).

Why was this new provision added? As the U.S. Department of Education explains:

> The purpose…is to ensure that the public agency involved has knowledge of the issues and an opportunity to resolve them directly with the complaining party at the earliest possible time. The sooner the LEA knows that a complaint is filed and the nature of the issue(s), the quicker the LEA can work directly with the complainant to resolve the complaint. (71 Fed. Reg. 46606)

What happens if the complainant doesn't include all required information?

This question arises because IDEA's due process procedures specify what must occur if the SEA receives a due process complaint that is insufficient [34 C.F.R. 300.508(d)]—"Sufficiency of complaint." Unlike due process, however, the Part B regulations governing the state complaint process do not even *mention* "sufficiency of complaint."

When an SEA receives a complaint that is not signed or does not include contact information, the SEA may choose to dismiss the complaint. In general, an SEA should adopt proper notice procedures for such situations. For example, an SEA could provide notice indicating that the complaint will be dismissed for not meeting the content requirements or that the complaint will not be investigated and timelines not commence until the missing content is provided.

What will the state do when it receives a complaint that meets the requirements?

The state will respond to the written complaint in writing. The written response will notify the complainant and the public agency against which the complaint is filed that the complaint was received and specify the allegations subject to the investigation. It will also identify the staff person assigned to investigate the complaint and the steps that the public agency may take to resolve the complaint, and describe the procedures that will be used in the investigation (Maryland State Department of Education, Division of Special Education/Early Intervention Services, 2011).

What is the SEA's obligation when it receives a state complaint?

The SEA must ensure that state complaints are resolved within 60 days from the date the complaint is filed (unless an extension of the timeline is permitted). Here is a rundown of the basic steps involved in resolving a state complaint. The SEA must [34 C.F.R. 300.152(a) and (b)(2)]:

- carry out an independent on-site investigation, if the SEA determines that an investigation is necessary

- give the complainant the opportunity to submit additional information about the complaint, either orally or in writing

- provide the public agency with the opportunity to respond to the state complaint

- review all relevant information, make an independent determination on the complaint, and issue a written decision to the complainant

- have procedures to ensure effective implementation of the SEA's final decision.

What are the timelines for filing a state complaint?

The complaint must allege a violation that occurred no more than one year prior to the date the state receives the complaint [34 C.F.R. 300.153(c)].

Previously, complaints could be filed for alleged violations that occurred up to *three* years prior to the date the complaint was received. The "one-year timeline is reasonable," the Department explains, and "will assist in smooth implementation of the State complaint procedures…[and will] help ensure that problems are raised and addressed promptly" (71 Fed. Reg. 46606).

The Department also points out that states may choose to accept and resolve complaints outside the one-year timeline, just as they are free to add additional protections in other areas that are not inconsistent with IDEIA's requirements.

How soon must the SEA resolve a state complaint?

The timeline for the resolution of a state complaint is 60 days (Utah Department of Education, 2011). The specific activities associated with resolving the complaint must take place within that time limit. These include:

- conducting an independent on-site investigation, if the SEA determines that an investigation is necessary

- giving the complainant the opportunity to submit additional information, either orally or in writing

- providing the public agency with the opportunity to respond to the complaint

- having the SEA or the public agency responsible for resolving the complaint review all relevant information and make an independent determination

- issuing a final decision on the allegations in the state complaint.

The SEA's complaint procedures must permit that 60-day timeline to be extended only if exceptional circumstances exist or if the parent and the public agency agree to extend the time to engage in mediation (or other alternative means of dispute resolution, if available).

If the complaint is filed by an individual or organization other than the parent, the timeline may also be extended through agreement between the public agency and the other individual or organization filing a complaint if mediation (or other alternative means of dispute resolution) is available to the individual or organization under state procedures [34 C.F.R. 300.152(b)(1)(ii)].

This means that the fact that the parties agree to use mediation is not sufficient by itself to warrant an extension of the 60-day timeline. The complainant and the public agency must also agree to extend the timeline as a result of the decision to use mediation.

Can the public agency attempt to resolve the complaint before an investigation occurs?

Yes. It is suggested that the public agency contact the complainant as soon as it is aware of the complaint to discuss the alleged violation(s) and any remedy requested. The public agency may wish to resolve the complaint with the complainant by providing the remedy requested, or some other agreed-upon remedy reached through mediation or a less formal process. Should the public agency offer to resolve the complaint by providing the requested remedy, or the parties agree that the matter has been resolved, the state will consider the matter closed and no further investigation of the specific complaint will occur. If the public agency conducts an internal investigation into the allegation and determines that a violation occurred, it may acknowledge the violation and propose a corrective action that addresses the loss of services to the named student(s) and make corrections to address the future provision of services for all students with disabilities, as appropriate (Maryland State Department of Education, Division of Special Education/Early Intervention Services, 2011).

Must a state complaint be investigated if it is resolved through mediation?

If the parties resolve the issues involved in a state complaint, the SEA need take no further action. An agreement reached through mediation is legally binding. Such an agreement is enforceable in an appropriate state or federal court and is not subject to the SEA's approval. This is one reason why the Department of Education encourages parties to resolve complaints "at the local level without the need for the SEA to intervene" (71 Fed. Reg. 46605).

What happens if a state complaint and a due process complaint are filed to resolve the same issue?

According to IDEA's regulations, the SEA must set aside any part of the state complaint that is being addressed in the due process hearing until the conclusion of the hearing. But any issue in the state complaint that is *not* a part of the due process hearing action must be resolved using the time limit and state complaint procedures described above [34 C.F.R. 300.152(c)(1)].

If an issue included in a state complaint has *previously* been decided in a due process hearing that involved the same parties, the due process decision is binding on that issue, and the SEA must inform the complainant to that effect [34 C.F.R. 300.152(c)(2)].

Can the SEA's decision be appealed?

IDEA neither prohibits nor requires that a state's complaint procedures include a way to appeal the SEA's decision on a state complaint. The Department observes that "States are in the best position to determine what, if any, appeals process is necessary to meet each State's needs, consistent with State law" (71 Fed. Reg. 46607).

Regardless of the state's policies regarding appeal of the SEA's final decision, the Department makes sure to point out, after that decision is issued, that a party who disagrees with it (and has the right to request a due process hearing) may initiate a due process hearing, given the following two conditions:

- that the subject of the state complaint involves an issue about which a due process hearing can be filed, and

- the two-year statute of limitations for due process hearings (or other time limit imposed by sate law) has not expired.

» V. RESOLUTION MEETING

What is a resolution meeting?

The resolution meeting was a step added to the due process complaint procedure in IDEIA when parents file a due process complaint. With the Individuals with Disabilities Education Improvement Act, Congress recognized the need to provide additional opportunities for early dispute resolution. The resolution process was added as another way schools and parents can work out their differences whenever a parent has filed a due process complaint ([34 C.F.R. 300.510(a)(2)]; Partners Resources Network, Inc., 2011).

Before a due process hearing can occur, the parents and the school district must participate in a resolution meeting. The purpose of this meeting is for parents to be able to discuss the issues and the facts that are the basis of the due process complaint and to provide the school the opportunity to resolve the issues (North Dakota Department of Instruction, 2011). IDEIA makes the purpose of the resolution meeting very clear. The meeting provides an opportunity "for the parent of the child to discuss their due process complaint, and the facts that form the basis of the due process complaint, so that the LEA has the opportunity to resolve the dispute that is the basis for the due process complaint" [34 C.F.R. 300.510(a)(2)].

When a parent (not a school district) files a due process complaint, a resolution meeting is intended to create an early opportunity for parents and school district officials to come to an agreement about the issues that have led up to or resulted in a due process complaint (Disability Rights Education and Defense Fund, 2008). At the meeting, the parent explains the reason for the complaint and proposes a solution, and school personnel have the opportunity to respond and resolve the conflict.

Does the resolution process apply when a public agency (e.g. school district) files a due process complaint?

No. IDEIA does not require a public agency to convene a resolution meeting when the public agency files a due process complaint. However, the public agency and parent may choose to engage voluntarily in mediation to resolve the issue.

Note: Since the resolution process is not required under the regulations when a public agency files a complaint, the 45-day timeline for issuing a written decision begins the day after the public agency's due process complaint is received by the other party and the SEA.

What are the benefits of participating in a resolution meeting?

There are many benefits of resolution meetings (see North Dakota Department of Instruction, 2011; Partners Resources Network, Inc., 2011; Consortium for Appropriate Dispute Resolution in Special Education and Technical Assistance: ALLIANCE for Parent Centers, 2008; Disability Rights Education and Defense Fund, 2008). They include:

- It is an important additional opportunity to talk things over.

- It is potentially less adversarial than a due process hearing.

- It offers an opportunity to develop a mutually agreeable solution.

- It offers the possibility of repaired communication and relationship.

- The meeting may result in an agreement that is legally binding and enforceable in court.

- The informality of the resolution meeting provides an opportunity for the parents to meet with the special education director and other educators, perhaps for the first time since the development of issues, regarding the education of their child. This meeting may improve communication and future collaboration.

- The resolution meeting is an opportunity for educators to establish, or reestablish, trust with the parents. As the parents and educators work on building trust, they may choose to contact each other in the future, before differences escalate.

What are the concerns about the resolution meeting?

Although there are many benefits of resolution meetings, there are also various concerns which need to be understood and taken into consideration on the part of the parent and the school district (see North Dakota Department of Instruction, 2011; Partners Resources Network, Inc., 2011; Consortium for Appropriate Dispute

Resolution in Special Education and Technical Assistance: ALLIANCE for Parent Centers, 2008; Disability Rights Education and Defense Fund, 2008). These include:

- Going in unprepared reduces the chance of a good agreement.

- Some situations could benefit from a third-party facilitator.

- The meeting and preparations can be emotionally demanding.

- There is no guarantee that an agreement will be reached.

- The confidentiality of discussions is not protected in the same way that it is in the mediation process.

- The resolution meeting is required. When parties are forced to meet, rather than just have the option to meet "voluntarily" (as in mediation), they may just go through the process and have no real interest to settle.

- An unfortunate consequence of the resolution meeting is that it may cause additional delay and expense for the parties.

- Either the parents or school may not be willing to discuss the issues contained in the due process hearing request—and may just remain "positioned" during the resolution meeting rather than take the opportunity to talk about possible options to resolve the situation.

- The resolution meeting may not include all of the appropriate members from the IEP team to discuss and help resolve the disagreement.

- IDEIA requires the school district to respond to a parent's request for a due process hearing within ten days. The parent might decide to wait to schedule the resolution meeting until after receiving the school's response, which may slow the process.

Is there a required agenda for a resolution meeting?

No. However, parents most likely will be offered a chance to further discuss the concerns they raised in their due process complaint and how they might be addressed. The meeting is more likely to result in an agreement if the parents and the school staff listen carefully to each other (Partners Resources Network, Inc., 2011).

Who pays for the resolution meeting?

There is no cost to parents. It is the school district's responsibility to convene the resolution meeting. Unless the parents' attorney is involved, the only cost for parents is the time to prepare and participate (Consortium for Appropriate Dispute Resolution in Special Education and Technical Assistance: ALLIANCE for Parent Centers, 2008).

Can parents and/or the school district withdraw from an agreement reached at a resolution meeting?

Either the parents or the school district can withdraw from any agreement that is reached at the resolution meeting within three business days of the agreement's execution. If the district does not withdraw from the agreement during that period, it is legally required to follow through. The agreement can be enforced in court (Consortium for Appropriate Dispute Resolution in Special Education and Technical Assistance: ALLIANCE for Parent Centers, 2008).

What happens if parents do not reach an agreement in the resolution meeting?

If parents and the district do not come to resolution, parents may proceed to a due process hearing. The 45-day timeline for the due process hearing starts the next day. An impartial hearing officer must issue a decision within 45 days after the beginning of the due process hearing. Parents and the district also may consider going to mediation instead of having a resolution meeting (North Dakota Department of Instruction, 2011; Partners Resources Network, Inc., 2011; Consortium for Appropriate Dispute Resolution in Special Education and Technical Assistance: ALLIANCE for Parent Centers, 2008).

Who can attend the resolution meeting?

The parents and any IEP team members who have specific knowledge of the facts in the due process complaint and the LEA representative who has decision-making authority attend the resolution meeting. The parents and the school district decide who they would like to have participate. Attorneys from the school district may attend only if the parents bring their attorney to the meeting. It may be appropriate to have the child attend the meeting [34 C.F.R. 300.510(a)(1)].

Are resolution meetings confidential?

No. There is no legal requirement to keep discussions in the resolution meeting confidential. IDEIA is silent on the issue of keeping matters discussed during resolution meetings confidential. A confidentiality agreement, however, could be considered for the parents and school district to sign at the beginning of the meeting (Partners Resources Network, Inc., 2011).

Are facilitators available for the resolution meeting?

Maybe. Since IDEIA does not require the use of facilitators, some states or school districts provide facilitators for resolution meetings whereas others do not. The answer to this question varies depending on where parents live (Partners Resources Network, Inc., 2011).

Can the resolution meeting be waived?

Yes, if certain conditions are met. The resolution meeting may be mutually waived by a written statement signed by all parties. If parents and the school representative agree, they may waive their right to participate in the resolution meeting. Then, they have two options:

- proceed to a due process hearing

- request mediation instead.

Mediation is the better option when requested as early in the dispute as possible and when the participants need assistance to resolve a specific issue. Under federal and state law, mediation may be used for disputes that deal with evaluation, disability, identification, placement, IEP issues, or provision of free appropriate public education (FAPE). These categories are very broad and can fit most any issue that comes up related to special education (Disability Rights Education and Defense Fund, 2008).

What is the timeline for a resolution meeting?

IDEIA requires the resolution meeting to be held within 15 days of the school district receiving notice of the parents' due process hearing request (Wisconsin Special Education Mediation System, 2011):

- If the school district fails to hold the resolution meeting within 15 days of receiving notice of a parent's due process complaint or fails to participate in the resolution meeting, the parent may ask the hearing officer to begin the due process hearing timeline.

- The failure of the parent to participate in the resolution meeting will delay the timelines for the resolution process and due process hearing until the meeting is held (except where the parties have jointly agreed to waive the resolution meeting or to use mediation).

- The resolution meeting may be held in one or more sessions within 30 days of receiving notice of the parents' due process hearing request.

- If the school district does not resolve the due process hearing complaint to the satisfaction of the parents *within 30 days*, the due process hearing may proceed. The timelines for the due process start at this point (on day 31).

Is there an expedited resolution meeting timeline?

IDEIA specifies requirements for expedited resolution meetings, such as when there is an appeal of discipline action. Unless the parents and school district agree in writing to waive the resolution meeting, or agree to use mediation (Wisconsin Special Education Mediation System, 2011):

- a resolution meeting must occur within seven days of receiving notice of the due process complaint, and

- unless the matter has been resolved to the satisfaction of both parties within 15 days of the receipt of the due process complaint, the due process hearing may proceed.

Can attorney fees be awarded at a resolution meeting?

No attorney fees are awarded in the resolution meeting, since this meeting shall not be considered to be (Wisconsin Special Education Mediation System, 2011):

- a meeting convened as a result of an administrative hearing or judicial action, or

- an administrative hearing or judicial action for purposes of 34 C.F.R. 300.517 (attorney fees).

What happens when a resolution of a dispute is reached?

If a resolution of the dispute is reached during the resolution meeting (National Dissemination Center for Children with Disabilities, 2010a):

- It must be put in a written agreement.

- Both the parent and the school representative must sign the agreement.

- Either the parents or school district may void the agreement within three business days.

- This document is enforceable in state or federal court.

- Parties may want to consult their attorneys to review a draft of the agreement before signing.

- If the agreement deals with IEP-related issues, this information needs to be incorporated into the IEP as soon as possible.

Is information discussed at a resolution meeting allowed to be introduced at a due process hearing?

In general, yes. Unlike mediation, IDEIA does not require that discussions in resolution meetings remain confidential. Therefore, absent an agreement by the parties to the contrary, either party may, at a due process hearing, introduce information discussed during the resolution meeting when presenting evidence and confronting or cross-examining witnesses. Nothing in the IDEIA would prevent the parties from voluntarily agreeing that the resolution meeting discussions will remain confidential, including prohibiting the introduction of those discussions at any subsequent due process hearing. However, neither an SEA nor an LEA can require the parties to enter into such an agreement as a condition of participation in the resolution meeting (National Dissemination Center for Children with Disabilities, 2010a).

In the event that an agreement is not reached during the resolution meeting, must mediation continue to be available?

Yes. IDEIA requires that the public agency ensure mediation is available "to allow parties to disputes involving any matter under this part, including matters arising prior to the filing of a due process complaint, to resolve disputes through a mediation process." It is important to note that mediation is voluntary and must be agreed to by both parties [34 C.F.R. 300.506].

Does the 30-day resolution period apply if the parties elect to use mediation rather than convene a resolution meeting?

Yes. If the parties choose to use mediation rather than participate in a resolution meeting, the 30-day resolution period is still applicable. The resolution period applies to the use of mediation after the filing of a complaint requesting a due process hearing [34 C.F.R. 300.510(c)].

Must the LEA continue its attempts to convince a parent to participate in a resolution meeting throughout the 30-day resolution period?

Yes. If a parent fails to participate in a resolution meeting, an LEA must continue to make reasonable efforts throughout the remainder of the 30-day resolution period to convince the parent to participate in a resolution meeting. The regulations permit an LEA, at the conclusion of the 30-day resolution period, to request that a hearing officer dismiss the complaint when an LEA is unable to obtain the participation of a parent in a resolution meeting despite making reasonable efforts to do so and has documented its efforts.

If a party fails to participate in the resolution meeting, must the other party seek the hearing officer's intervention?

Yes. IDEIA provides that an LEA may request a hearing officer to dismiss a complaint when the LEA has been unable to obtain the participation of the parent in a resolution meeting despite making reasonable efforts to do so [34 C.F.R. 300.510(b)(4)]. If an LEA fails to hold a resolution meeting within the required timelines or fails to participate in a resolution meeting, the parent may seek the intervention of a hearing officer to begin the due process hearing timeline. The hearing officer's intervention will be necessary to either dismiss the complaint or to commence the hearing, depending on the circumstances [34 C.F.R. 300.510(b)(5)].

» VI. DUE PROCESS COMPLAINT

What is a due process complaint?

A due process complaint is an administrative hearing on a special education issue that is not agreed upon between a student's parent (or an adult student) and the school district. An impartial hearing officer is assigned to hear testimony, receive evidence, and render a decision [34 C.F.R. 300.507; 34 C.F.R. 300.520(a)(1)(ii)].

Who may file a due process complaint?

A due process complaint may be filed by the local education agency (LEA) or the parent [34 C.F.R. 300.307; 34 C.F.R. 300.30]. A student 18 years or older may file the request on his/her own [34 C.F.R. 300.507; 34 C.F.R. 300.520(a)(1)(ii)].

What is the subject matter of a due process complaint?

A due process complaint involves the proposal or refusal to initiate or change the identification, evaluation, or educational placement of a child with a disability or the provision of a free and appropriate public education (FAPE) to the child [34 C.F.R. 300.507(a)].

Is there a timeframe as to when the due process complaint must be filed?

Yes. The due process complaint must allege a violation that occurred not more than two years before the date the parent or public agency knew or should have known about the alleged action that forms the basis of the due process complaint, or, if the state has an explicit time limitation for filing a due process complaint, in the time allowed by that state law [34 C.F.R. 300.507(a)(2)].

The timeline does not apply to a parent if the parent was prevented from filing a due process complaint due to specific misrepresentations by the LEA that it had resolved the problem forming the basis of the due process complaint or the LEA's withholding of information from the parent that was required under this part to be provided to the parent [34 C.F.R. 300.511(f)].

Does the school district need to provide the parents with information about legal services if they file a due process complaint?

Yes. The public agency must inform the parent of any free or low-cost legal and other relevant services available in the area if the parent requests the information or the parent or the agency files a due process complaint [34 C.F.R. 300.507(b); 20 U.S.C. 1415(b)(6)].

Do all states have to have due process procedures?

Yes. IDEIA requires that all public agencies must have procedures that require either party, or the attorney representing a party, to provide to the other party a due process complaint (which must remain confidential). The party filing a due process complaint must forward a copy of the due process complaint to the state education agency [34 C.F.R. 300.508(a)(1–2)].

Can a party have a hearing on a due process complaint until the party, or the attorney representing the party, files a due process complaint?

No. A party may not have a hearing on a due process complaint until the party, or the attorney representing the party, files a due process complaint [34 C.F.R. 300.508(c)].

What is a "sufficient" due process complaint?

The due process complaint must contain specific information in order to be considered "sufficient." Under IDEIA [34 C.F.R. 300.508(b)], the due process complaint must include:

- the name of the child
- the address of the residence of the child
- the name of the school the child is attending
- in the case of a homeless child or youth (within the meaning of section 725(2) of the McKinney-Vento Homeless Assistance Act [42 U.S.C. 11434a(2)]),

available contact information for the child, and the name of the school the child is attending

- a description of the nature of the problem of the child relating to the proposed or refused initiation or change, including facts relating to the problem, and

- a proposed resolution of the problem to the extent known and available to the party at the time.

Does the complaint have to be sufficient?

Yes. The due process complaint must be deemed sufficient unless the party receiving the due process complaint notifies the hearing officer and the other party in writing, within 15 days of receipt of the due process complaint, that the receiving party believes the due process complaint does not meet the requirements.

Within five days of receipt of notification, the hearing officer must make a determination on the face of the due process complaint of whether the due process complaint meets the requirements and must immediately notify the parties in writing of that determination [34 C.F.R. 300.508(d)(1–2)].

What steps are available to the complaining party if a hearing officer rules that the due process complaint is "insufficient"?

If the hearing officer determines the due process complaint is "insufficient," the hearing officer's decision will identify how the notice is insufficient, so that the filing party can amend the notice, if appropriate.

A party may amend its due process complaint only if the other party consents in writing to the amendment and is given the opportunity to resolve the due process complaint through a meeting [34 C.F.R. 300.510] (i.e. resolution meeting or if the parties choose to use mediation); or the hearing officer grants permission to amend the complaint at any time not later than five days before the due process hearing begins [34 C.F.R. 300.508(d)(3)].

If a party files an amended due process complaint, the timelines for the resolution meeting and resolution period begin again with the filing of the amended due process complaint [34 C.F.R. 300.508(d)(4)]. If the hearing officer determines that the complaint is insufficient and the complaint is not amended, the complaint may be dismissed.

A party may refile a due process complaint if the complaint remains within the applicable timelines for filing [34 C.F.R. 300.507(a)(2) and 300.511(f)]—generally, within two years or an explicit timeline established under state law, unless an exception applies.

When can a party amend a due process complaint?

A party may amend its due process complaint only if:

- the other party consents in writing to the amendment and is given the opportunity to resolve the due process complaint through a meeting, or

- the hearing officer grants permission, except that the hearing officer may only grant permission to amend at any time not later than five days before the due process hearing begins.

[34 C.F.R. 300.508(d)(3)]

Is the local education agency required to respond to a parent's due process complaint?

Yes. If the LEA has not sent a prior written notice to the parent regarding the subject matter contained in the parent's due process complaint, the LEA must, within ten days of receiving the due process complaint, send to the parent a response that includes [34 C.F.R. 300.503(b)]:

- an explanation of why the agency proposed or refused to take the action raised in the due process complaint

- a description of other options that the IEP team considered and the reasons why those options were rejected

- a description of each evaluation procedure, assessment, record, or report the agency used as the basis for the proposed or refused action, and

- a description of the other factors that are relevant to the agency's proposed or refused action.

Note: A response by an LEA shall not be construed to preclude the LEA from asserting that the parent's due process complaint was insufficient, where appropriate [34 C.F.R. 300.508(e)].

How would parents know how to draft a due process complaint?

Under IDEIA, the SEA must develop model forms to assist parents in filing a due process complaint and to assist parents and other parties in filing a state complaint. However, the SEA or LEA may not require the use of the model forms. Parents, public agencies, and other parties may use the appropriate model form or another form or other document, as long as the form or document that is used meets, as appropriate, the content requirements for filing a due process complaint [34 C.F.R. 300.509; 20 U.S.C. 1415(b)(8)].

When the local education agency is notified of a parent's due process complaint, what must it do?

Within 15 days of receiving notice of the parent's due process complaint, and prior to the initiation of a due process hearing, the LEA must convene a resolution meeting with the parent and the relevant member or members of the IEP team who have specific knowledge of the facts identified in the due process complaint that:

- includes a representative of the public agency who has decision-making authority on behalf of that agency, and

- may not include an attorney of the LEA unless the parent is accompanied by an attorney.

The purpose of the meeting is for the parent of the child to discuss the due process complaint and the facts that form the basis of the due process complaint, so that the LEA has the opportunity to resolve the dispute that is the basis for the due process complaint.

The meeting need not be held if:

- the parent and the LEA agree in writing to waive the meeting, or

- the parent and the LEA agree to use the mediation process.

Note: The parent and the LEA determine the relevant members of the IEP team to attend the meeting [34 C.F.R. 300.510(a)(1–4)].

If a resolution to the dispute is reached at the meeting, the parties must execute a legally binding agreement that is:

- signed by both the parent and a representative of the agency who has the authority to bind the agency, and

- enforceable in any state court of competent jurisdiction or in a district court of the United States, or, by the SEA, if the State has other mechanisms or procedures that permit parties to seek enforcement of resolution agreements.

If the parties execute an agreement, a party may void the agreement within three business days of the agreement's execution [34 C.F.R. 300.510(e)].

What are the timelines for the due process hearing to occur?

Due process hearings must be held and a final decision issued within 45 calendar days following the end of a resolution period.

If the LEA has not resolved the due process complaint to the satisfaction of the parent within 30 days of the receipt of the due process complaint, the due process hearing may occur.

The 45-day timeline for issuing a final decision begins at the expiration of this 30-day period.

Except where the parties have jointly agreed to waive the resolution process or to use mediation, the failure of the parent filing a due process complaint to participate in the resolution meeting will delay the timelines for the resolution process and due process hearing until the meeting is held.

If the LEA is unable to obtain the participation of the parent in the resolution meeting after reasonable efforts have been made (and documented), the LEA may, at the conclusion of the 30-day period, request that a hearing officer dismiss the parent's due process complaint.

If the LEA fails to hold the resolution meeting within 15 days of receiving notice of a parent's due process complaint or fails to participate in the resolution meeting, the parent may seek the intervention of a hearing officer to begin the due process hearing timeline [34 C.F.R. 300.510(b)(1–5)].

Must each party disclose to the other parties all of the evaluations completed by the date of the due process hearing?

Yes. At least five business days prior to a due process hearing, each party must disclose to all other parties all evaluations completed by that date and recommendations based on the offering party's evaluations that the party intends to use at the hearing. A hearing officer may bar any party that fails to comply with this requirement from introducing the relevant evaluation or recommendation at the hearing without the consent of the other party [34 C.F.R. 300.512(b)].

What are the requirements to be a hearing officer presiding over a due process hearing?

The hearing officer has an important role as the individual who presides over a due process hearing. At a minimum, a hearing officer [34 C.F.R. 300.511(c)]:

- must not be an employee of the SEA or the LEA that is involved in the education or care of the child

- must not be a person having a personal or professional interest that conflicts with the person's objectivity in the hearing

- must possess knowledge of, and the ability to understand, the provisions of the Act, federal and state regulations pertaining to the Act, and legal interpretations of the Act by federal and state courts

- must possess the knowledge and ability to conduct hearings in accordance with appropriate, standard legal practice

- must possess the knowledge and ability to render and write decisions in accordance with appropriate, standard legal practice

- must not be an employee of the agency solely because he/she is paid by the agency to serve as a hearing officer.

What are the rights of parties at a due process hearing?

Any party to a due process hearing has the right to:

- be accompanied and advised by counsel and by individuals with special knowledge or training with respect to the problems of children with disabilities, except that whether parties have the right to be represented by non-attorneys at due process hearings is determined under state law

- present evidence and confront, cross-examine, and compel the attendance of witnesses

- prohibit the introduction of any evidence at the hearing that has not been disclosed to that party at least five business days before the hearing

- obtain a written, or, at the option of the parents, electronic, verbatim record of the hearing, and

- obtain written, or, at the option of the parents, electronic findings of fact and decisions.

[34 C.F.R 300.512(a)]

Also, parents involved in hearings must be given the right to:

- have the child who is the subject of the hearing present

- open the hearing to the public, and

- have the record of the hearing and the findings of fact and decisions provided at no cost.

[34 C.F.R. 300.512(c)]

Can the party requesting the due process hearing raise issues at the due process hearing that were not raised in the due process complaint?

No. The party requesting the due process hearing may not raise issues at the due process hearing that were not raised in the due process complaint. Only issues raised in the due process complaint can be addressed in the hearing unless the other party agrees otherwise [34 C.F.R. 300.511(d)].

If there are issues in dispute that are not mentioned in the due process complaint notice, then a party requesting the due process has three options [34 C.F.R. 300.508(d)(3)]:

1. The party may ask the other party to agree in writing that the issues can be raised during the hearing.

2. The party may seek to amend its request.

3. The party may file another due process complaint to address the other issues.

Who has the burden of proof in an IDEIA due process hearing?

Burden of proof, as a legal term, refers to "the duty to prove disputed fact." In criminal cases, the burden of proof always rests on the prosecutors. In civil cases, the burden is usually carried by the party filing the complaint or bringing the action. In due process hearings, which party has the burden of proof (the parent or the public agency) varies from state to state and even, sometimes, within a state. Thus, individuals involved in a due process hearing will need to find out how their state or locale addresses the question of burden of proof.

The question of which party has the burden of proof in an IDEIA due process hearing—the parent or public agency—was addressed in the Supreme Court case *Shaffer v. Weast* (546 U.S. 2005). On November 14, 2005, the U.S. Supreme Court ruled that in an administrative hearing under the Individuals with Disabilities Education Act (IDEA), the party initiating the appeal and seeking relief bears the burden of proof.

Although the IDEIA is silent on the issue of burden of proof, the Supreme Court has held that, unless state law assigns the burden of proof differently, in general, the party who requests the hearing will have the burden of proving their case. Check your specific state law to find out who has the burden of proof in an IDEIA due process hearing.

How is a decision about whether a child received a FAPE determined by a hearing officer?

A hearing officer's determination of whether a child received FAPE must be based on substantive grounds. In matters alleging a procedural violation, a hearing officer may find that a child did not receive a FAPE only if the procedural inadequacies:

- impeded the child's right to a FAPE

- significantly impeded the parent's opportunity to participate in the decision-making process regarding the provision of a FAPE to the parent's child, or

- caused a deprivation of educational benefit.

[34 C.F.R. 300.513]

Are decisions at due process hearings final?

Yes. A decision made in a hearing is final, except that any party involved in the hearing may appeal the decision [34 C.F.R. 300.514(a)].

How does the appeal process work?

If there is an appeal, the SEA must conduct an impartial review of the findings and decision appealed. The official conducting the review must:

- examine the entire hearing record

- ensure that the procedures at the hearing were consistent with the requirements of due process

- seek additional evidence if necessary

- afford the parties an opportunity for oral or written argument, or both, at the discretion of the reviewing official

- make an independent decision on completion of the review, and

- give a copy of the written, or, at the option of the parents, electronic findings of fact and decisions to the parties.

The decision made by the reviewing official is final unless a party brings a civil action [34 C.F.R. 300.514(b)(2); 20 U.S.C. 1415(g) and (h)(4), 1415(i)(1)(A), 1415(i)(2)].

What are the timelines and convenience of hearings and reviews?

The public agency must ensure that not later than 45 days after the expiration of the 30-day period:

- a final decision is reached in the hearing, and

- a copy of the decision is mailed to each of the parties.

The SEA must ensure that not later than 30 days after the receipt of a request for a review:

- a final decision is reached in the review, and

- a copy of the decision is mailed to each of the parties.

A hearing or reviewing officer may grant specific extensions of time beyond the periods set out at the request of either party.

Each hearing and each review involving oral arguments must be conducted at a time and place that is reasonably convenient to the parents and child involved [34 C.F.R. 300.515; 20 U.S.C. 1415(f)(1)(B)(ii), 1415(g), 1415(i)(1)].

Can parties bring a civil action with respect to the due process complaint notice requesting a due process hearing?

Yes. Any party aggrieved by the findings and decision made who does not have the right to an appeal has the right to bring a civil action with respect to the due process complaint notice requesting a due process hearing. The action may be brought in any state court of competent jurisdiction or in a district court of the United States without regard to the amount in controversy. (Amount on controversy denotes the amount at stake in a lawsuit.)

The party bringing the action shall have 90 days from the date of the decision of the hearing officer or, if applicable, the decision of the state review official, to file a civil action, or, if the state has an explicit time limitation for bringing civil actions under Part B of the Act, in the time allowed by that state law.

In any action brought under this section, the court:

- receives the records of the administrative proceedings

- hears additional evidence at the request of a party, and

- basing its decision on the preponderance of the evidence, grants the relief that the court determines to be appropriate.

The district courts of the United States have jurisdiction of actions brought under section 615 of the Act without regard to the amount in controversy [34 C.F.R. 300.516(a–c)].

What is the child's status during the pendency of any administrative or judicial proceeding regarding a due process complaint notice requesting a due process hearing?

During the pendency of any administrative or judicial proceeding regarding a due process complaint notice requesting a due process hearing, unless the state or local agency and the parents of the child agree otherwise, the child involved in the complaint must remain in his/her current educational placement.

If the complaint involves an application for initial admission to public school, the child, with the consent of the parents, must be placed in the public school until the completion of all the proceedings.

If the complaint involves an application for initial services under this part from a child who is transitioning from Part C of the Act to Part B and is no longer eligible for Part C services because the child has turned three years of age, the public agency is not required to provide the Part C services that the child had been receiving. If the child is found eligible for special education and related services under Part B, and the parent consents to the initial provision of special education and related services, then the public agency must provide those special education and related services that are not in dispute between the parent and the public agency.

If the hearing officer in a due process hearing conducted by the SEA, or a state review official in an administrative appeal agrees with the child's parents that a change of placement is appropriate, that placement must be treated as an agreement between the state and the parents [34 C.F.R. 300.518(a–d); 20 U.S.C. 1415(j)].

Can the hearing officer award attorney fees?

No. If the parents prevail in the due process hearing or upon appeal, a court may award some or all of the attorney fees they have paid in conjunction with the due process hearing. Only a court can award attorney fees to the parents. The special education due process hearing officer has no authority to do so. However, there may be limitations on the amount paid. For example, if it is found that the parents prolonged the process or if the fees charged are more than the hourly rate usually charged, the judge has the authority to reduce the award paid to the parents.

The school may be awarded attorney fees if a parent files a complaint or subsequent cause of action that is frivolous, unreasonable, or without foundation, or against the attorney of a parent who continued to litigate after the litigation clearly became frivolous, unreasonable, or without foundation. The school may be awarded attorney fees if the parent's request for a due process hearing or subsequent cause of action was presented for any improper purpose, such as to harass, to cause unnecessary delay, or to needlessly increase the cost of litigation.

In determining the amount of the reimbursement of attorney fees, the judge must follow federal regulations [34 C.F.R. 300.517] and state law.

Discipline of **Students** with **Disabilities**

When did the federal law add explicit new provisions regarding the discipline of students with disabilities?

In 1997, the federal law (IDEA) added explicit new provisions regarding the discipline of students with disabilities. IDEIA of 2004 has kept these provisions and added new requirements for the discipline of children with disabilities (Pierangelo and Giuliani, 2008).

Why did the federal law add explicit new provisions regarding the discipline of students with disabilities?

The federal law added explicit new provisions regarding the discipline of students with disabilities to protect the rights of children with disabilities and their parents, while at the same time address the concerns of school administrators and teachers regarding school safety and order. They were also intended to help schools respond appropriately to a child's behavior and promote the use of appropriate behavioral interventions to prevent troubling behavior from recurring.

The protections in IDEA of 1997 regarding discipline were designed to prevent the type of often speculative and subjective decision making by school officials that led to widespread abuses of the rights of children with disabilities to an appropriate education in the past. For example, in *Mills v. Board of Education of the District of Columbia* (1972) the court recognized that many children were being excluded entirely from education merely because they had been identified as having a behavior disorder (see Chapter 1).

IDEA of 1997 recognized that it was extremely important that the provisions of the law concerning the amount of time a child with a disability can be removed from his/her regular placement for disciplinary reasons should only be called into play if the removal constitutes a change of placement and the parent objects to proposed action by school officials (or objects to a refusal by school officials to take an action) and requests a due process hearing. The discipline rules established under the law concerning the amount of time a child can be removed from his/her current placement essentially were set up as exceptions to the generally applicable requirement that a child remains in his/her current placement during the pendency of due process, and subsequent judicial, proceedings.

Finally, IDEA of 1997 established that if school officials believe that a child's placement is inappropriate, they can work with the child's parent through the IEP and placement processes to come up with an appropriate placement for the child that will meet the needs of the child and result in his/her improved learning and the learning of others and ensure a safe environment (Office of Special Education and Rehabilitative Services, 1999).

How are discipline cases handled for children with disabilities?

IDEIA permits school personnel to consider any unique circumstances on a case-by-case basis when determining whether a change of placement is appropriate for a child with a disability. The same discipline may not be appropriate for all students, even students involved in the same incident. IDEIA specifically states that school personnel may consider any unique circumstances on a case-by-case basis when determining whether a change in placement is appropriate for a child with a disability who violates a code of student conduct [34 C.F.R. 300.530].

At first glance, this provision may appear to give school personnel the authority to unilaterally determine a change of placement for a child, but this is not so. School personnel must exercise this new authority on a case-by-case basis and may only exercise their discretion on a case-by-case basis to allow removals for unique circumstances if the other disciplinary procedures have been satisfied.

Are the disciplinary measures available to the school the same for students with disabilities as for students without disabilities?

Sometimes. In general, as long as the child's educational placement does not change, the disciplinary measures available to the school are the same for students with disabilities as for other students [34 C.F.R. 300.530(b)(1); 20 U.S.C. 1415(k)]. For example, a child with a disability can get detention or have to stay after school for misconduct in the same manner and for the same reason as a child without a disability.

What are short-term disciplinary actions?

IDEIA provides that a student with a disability can be removed from his/her current placement for up to ten cumulative school days for any violation of school rules to the extent that removal would be applied to a student without disabilities. In such a case, an LEA need not provide services for ten school days or less if services are not provided to a student without disabilities who is similarly removed.

Under the federal law, school personnel may remove a child with a disability who violates a code of student conduct from his/her current placement to an appropriate interim alternative educational setting, another setting, or suspension, for not more than ten consecutive school days (to the extent that those alternatives are applied to children without disabilities), and for additional removals of not more than ten consecutive school days in that same school year for separate incidents of misconduct [34 C.F.R. 300.530(b)(1)].

IDEIA draws a distinction between short-term disciplinary actions and long-term disciplinary actions. The line of demarcation is ten school days.

What is a change of placement?

School personnel have the authority to make additional removals of a child with a disability for not more than ten consecutive school days in the same school year for separate incidents of misconduct—as long as those removals do not constitute a change of placement. A change of placement occurs if:

1. the removal is for more than ten consecutive school days, or

2. the child has been subjected to a series of removals that constitute a pattern:

    a. because the series of removals total more than ten school days in a school year

    b. because the child's behavior is substantially similar to the child's behavior in previous incidents that resulted in the series of removals, and

    c. because of such additional factors as the length of each removal, the total amount of time the child has been removed, and the proximity of the removals to one another.

The public agency determines on a case-by-case basis whether a pattern of removals constitutes a change of placement [34 C.F.R. 300.536].

Is parent notification required during disciplinary procedures involving a change of placement?

Yes. Parent notification is a very important aspect of implementing IDEA's discipline procedures [34 C.F.R 300.504]. On the date when the decision is made to make a removal that constitutes a change of placement of a child with a disability because of a violation of a code of student conduct, the local education agency (school district) must notify the parents of that decision and provide the parents the procedural safeguards notice [34 C.F.R. 300.530(h)].

If specific concerns arise that a child may need special education and related services due to his/her pattern of behavior, must such concerns be submitted in writing to school officials in order for the public agency to be deemed to have knowledge that the child is a child with a disability?

No. Teachers or other local education agency (LEA) personnel are not required to submit a written statement expressing specific concerns about a pattern of behavior demonstrated by the child in order for the public agency to be deemed to have knowledge that the child is a child with a disability [34 C.F.R. 300.534(b)(3)]. Although a written statement is not necessary, the teacher of the child or other LEA personnel must express their specific concerns directly to the special education director or other supervisory personnel within the agency. In addition, state Child Find policies and procedures may provide guidelines regarding how teachers and other LEA personnel should communicate their specific concerns regarding a child's pattern of behavior. If the state's or LEA's Child Find or referral procedures do not specify how such communication should occur, the state or LEA is encouraged to change its guidelines to provide a method for communicating direct expressions of specific concerns regarding a child's pattern of behavior.

What is a manifestation determination hearing?

Under IDEIA, a manifestation determination is defined as:

- Within 10 school days of any decision to change the placement of a child with a disability because of a violation of a code of student conduct, the LEA, the parent, and relevant members of the child's IEP Team (as determined by the parent and the LEA) must review all relevant information in the student's file, including the child's IEP, any teacher observations, and any relevant information provided by the parents to determine:

    (e)(1)(i) If the conduct in question was caused by, or had a direct and substantial relationship to, the child's disability; or

    (e)(1)(ii) If the conduct in question was the direct result of the LEA's failure to implement the IEP.

- The conduct must be determined to be a manifestation of the child's disability if the LEA, the parent, and relevant members of the child's IEP Team determine that a condition in either paragraph (e)(1)(i) or (e)(1)(ii) of this section was met.

- If the LEA, the parent, and relevant members of the child's IEP Team determine the condition described in paragraph (e)(1)(ii) of this section was met, the LEA must take immediate steps to remedy those deficiencies.

[34 C.F.R. 300.530(e)]

Manifestation determination hearings follow disciplinary actions by the school that result in suspension, expulsion, or a change in placement. If a disciplinary action involves a request for a suspension or other actions involving removal from a program for more than ten days, the IEP team must meet to determine whether the misconduct resulted from the disability. This is referred to as a manifestation determination hearing (Pierangelo and Giuliani, 2008).

Before a long-term suspension or expulsion can be initiated within a school system for a student with a disability, the IEP team must conduct a "manifestation determination."

In this meeting the IEP team must determine whether the behavior exhibited by the student that resulted in expulsion was a result of the disability. For example, did a student who lifted a pair of blunt-end paper scissors to scare another child do so because he was impulsive due to ADHD or did he do so simply as an act of aggression?

What questions must be answered at a manifestation determination hearing?

The two questions that must be answered at a manifestation determination meeting are:

1. Was the conduct in question caused by, or had a direct and substantial relationship to, the child's disability?

2. Was the conduct a direct result of the LEA's failure to implement the IEP?

To complete a manifestation determination, school personnel should carefully consider the student's disability and the nature of the behavior to determine the possible relationship [34 C.F.R. 300.530(e)].

What is the timeframe for a manifestation determination hearing to occur?

A manifestation determination hearing must occur within ten days after the date on which the decision was made to recommend a suspension or expulsion [34 C.F.R. 300.530(e)].

What is the scope of review at a manifestation determination hearing?

To complete a manifestation determination, school personnel should carefully consider the student's disability and the nature of the behavior to determine the possible relationship.

IDEIA states that the LEA, the parent, and relevant members of the child's IEP team must review "all relevant information in the student's file, including the child's IEP, any teacher observations, and any relevant information provided by the parents" as part of conducting a manifestation determination [34 C.F.R. 300.530(e)(1)]. This list is not exhaustive, according to the U.S. Department of Education. It may include other relevant information in the child's file, including placement appropriateness, supplementary aids and services, and if the behavior intervention strategies were appropriate and consistent with the IEP.

Representative questions that can be reviewed in this process include the following:

- Does the disability lead to impulsivity?

- Does the disability lead to violence or defiance?

- Is the specific problem an example of the behavioral concerns caused by the disability?

- Does the disability limit the student's ability to handle stressful situations?

- Does the disability interfere with a student's ability to build or maintain appropriate peer and/or teacher relationships?

- Does the disability interfere with the ability of the student to express appropriate feelings?

If, by using questions such as these, professionals determine that the behavior does not reflect a manifestation of the student's disability, the disciplinary procedures that would be relevant and appropriate are similar to those that are applicable to students without disabilities.

At the manifestation determination hearing, is it recommended for parents to engage the services of an educational legal advocate or a special education lawyer?

Yes. At the manifestation determination hearing, it is highly recommended for parents to engage the services of an educational legal advocate or a special education lawyer, who can help them make certain needed procedures are followed in the hearing (Gindis, 2006).

What happens if a student's behavior is *not* a manifestation of the disability?

If a student's behavior is not a manifestation of the disability, the school is authorized to impose the same penalty as would be applicable to a student without a disability who has committed the same infraction. The law specifically says that the penalty can be applied "in the same manner and for the same duration" as it would be for the student without a disability.

However, IDEIA clearly requires a FAPE to be provided to all children with disabilities between ages 3 and 21, including those who have been suspended or expelled [20 U.S.C. 1412(a)(1)(A); 34 C.F.R. 300.101].

The right to a FAPE for children with disabilities who have been suspended or expelled begins on the 11th day in the school year that they are removed from their current educational placement [34 C.F.R. 300.530(c)].

Because of the FAPE provision, alternate educational programming must be provided.

The provision states that, irrespective of the manifestation determination, a student with a disability removed for disciplinary reasons must continue to receive educational services so as to enable the student to continue to participate in the general curriculum, although in another setting, and to progress toward meeting the goals set out in the student's IEP.

A manifestation determination of "no" means either that:

- the child's behavior was not caused by or did not have a direct and substantial relationship to the child's disability, or

- the child's behavior was not the direct result of the LEA's failure to implement the IEP.

In either case of "no," school personnel have the authority to apply the relevant disciplinary procedures to the child with disabilities in the same manner and for the same duration as the procedures would be applied to a child without disabilities, except—*and this is very important*—for whatever special education and related services the school system is required to provide the child with disabilities [34 C.F.R. 300.530(d)].

What happens if a student's behavior is a manifestation of the disability?

Under IDEIA [34 C.F.R. 300.530(f)], if the LEA, the parent, and relevant members of the IEP team make the determination that the conduct was a manifestation of the child's disability, the IEP team must:

- Either—

  ○ Conduct a functional behavioral assessment, unless the LEA had conducted a functional behavioral assessment before the behavior that resulted in the change of placement occurred, and implement a behavioral intervention plan for the child, or

- If a behavioral intervention plan already has been developed, review the behavioral intervention plan, and modify it, as necessary, to address the behavior, and

- Except as provided in paragraph (g) of this section (Special Circumstances of weapons, drugs, and serious bodily injury), return the child to the placement from which the child was removed, unless the parent and the LEA agree to a change of placement as part of the modification of the behavioral intervention plan.

There are two scenarios under which the manifestation determination would be "yes." These are when [34 C.F.R. 300.530(f)]:

1. *The conduct is directly related to the child's disability:* If the group finds that the child's misconduct had a direct and substantial relationship to his/her disability, then the group must also reach a manifestation determination of "yes." Such a determination carries with it two immediate considerations:

   a. Functional behavioral assessment (FBA): Has the child had one? Does one need to be conducted?

   b. Behavioral intervention plan (BIP): Does the child have one? If so, does it need to be reviewed and revised? Or if the child does not have one, does one need to be written?

   Thus, if a child's misconduct has been found to have a direct and substantial relationship to his/her disability, the IEP team will need to immediately conduct a FBA of the child, unless one has already been conducted.

2. *The LEA fails to implement the IEP:* If the IEP team determines that the child's misconduct was the direct result of the LEA's failure to implement the child's IEP, the "LEA must take immediate steps to remedy those deficiencies." Unless the behavior involved one of the special circumstances—weapons, drugs, or serious bodily injury—the child would be returned to the placement from which he/she was removed as part of the disciplinary action. However, the parent and LEA can agree to a change of placement as part of the modification of the behavioral intervention plan.

Under what circumstances must an IEP team use a functional behavioral assessment (FBA) and behavior intervention plan (BIP)?

FBAs and BIPs are required when the LEA, the parent, and the relevant members of the child's IEP team determine that a student's conduct was a manifestation of his/her disability under the law [34 C.F.R. 300.530(f); 34 C.F.R. 300.530(e)]. If a child's misconduct has been found to have a direct and substantial relationship to his/her disability, the IEP team will need to conduct an FBA of the child, unless one has already been conducted. Similarly, the IEP team must write a BIP for this child, unless one already exists. If a BIP already exists, then the IEP team will need to review the plan and modify it, as necessary, to address the behavior.

An FBA focuses on identifying the function or purpose behind a child's behavior. Typically, the process involves looking closely at a wide range of child-specific factors (e.g. social, affective, environmental). Knowing why a child misbehaves is directly helpful to the IEP team in developing a BIP that will reduce or eliminate the misbehavior.

For a child with a disability whose behavior impedes his/her learning or that of others, and for whom the IEP team has decided that a BIP is appropriate, or for a child with a disability whose violation of the code of student conduct is a manifestation of the child's disability, the IEP team must include a BIP in the child's IEP to address the behavioral needs of the child. A BIP takes the observations made in an FBA and turns them into a concrete plan of action for managing a student's behavior.

Is consent required to do an FBA for a child?

Yes. As with other individualized evaluation procedures, parental consent is required for an FBA to be conducted as part of the initial evaluation or a reevaluation [34 C.F.R. 300.300(a) and (c)].

If a parent disagrees with the results of an FBA, can the parent obtain an independent educational evaluation (IEE) at public expense?

Yes. The parent of a child with a disability has the right to request an IEE of the child [34 C.F.R. 300.502], if the parent disagrees with an evaluation obtained by the public agency. However, the parent's right to an IEE at public expense is subject to certain conditions, including the LEA's option to request a due process hearing to show that its evaluation is appropriate [34 C.F.R. 300.502(b)(2) through (b)(5)]. The U.S. Department of Education has clarified previously that an FBA that was not identified as an initial evaluation, was not included as part of the required triennial reevaluation, or was not done in response to a disciplinary removal, would nonetheless be considered a reevaluation or part of a reevaluation under IDEIA because it was an individualized evaluation conducted in order to develop an appropriate IEP for the child. Therefore, a parent who disagrees with an FBA that is conducted in order to develop an appropriate IEP also is entitled to request an IEE. Subject to the conditions in IDEIA [34 C.F.R. 300.502(b)(2) through (b)(5)], the IEE of the child will be at public expense.

What recourse does a parent have if he/she disagrees with the determination that his/her child's behavior was not a manifestation of the child's disability?

If the parents of a child with a disability, the LEA, and the relevant members of the child's IEP team cannot reach consensus or agreement on whether the child's behavior was or was not a manifestation of the disability, the public agency must make the determination and provide the parent with written notice [34 C.F.R. 300.503]. The parent of the child with a disability has the right to exercise his/her procedural safeguards by requesting mediation and/or a due process hearing to resolve a disagreement about the manifestation determination [34 C.F.R. 300.506 and 300.532(a)]. A parent also has the right to file a state complaint alleging a violation related to the manifestation determination [34 C.F.R. 300.153] (see Chapter 10).

Are there any "special circumstances" in which the school is authorized to take disciplinary action whether the student's behavior is a manifestation of the disability or not?

Yes. Congress has identified special circumstances in which the school is authorized to take disciplinary action whether the student's behavior is a manifestation of the disability or not [34 C.F.R. 300.530(g)].

Under IDEIA, school personnel may remove a student to an interim alternative educational setting for not more than 45 school days without regard to whether the behavior is determined to be a manifestation of the child's disability, if the child:

1. carries a weapon to or possesses a weapon at school, on school premises, or at a school function under the jurisdiction of an SEA or an LEA

2. knowingly possesses or uses illegal drugs, or sells or solicits the sale of a controlled substance, while at school, on school premises, or at a school function under the jurisdiction of an SEA or an LEA, or

3. has inflicted serious bodily injury upon another person while at school, on school premises, or at a school function under the jurisdiction of an SEA or an LEA.

[34 C.F.R. 300.530(g)]

On the date the decision is made to make a removal that constitutes a change of placement of a child with a disability because of a violation of a code of student conduct, the LEA must notify the parents of that decision and provide the parents the procedural safeguards notice [34 C.F.R. 300.504].

In order to understand the special circumstances described above, the following definitions apply:

- *Controlled substance* means a drug or other substance identified under schedules I, II, III, IV, or V in section 202(c) of the Controlled Substances Act [21 U.S.C. 812(c)].

- *Illegal drug* means a controlled substance, but does not include a controlled substance that is legally possessed or used under the supervision of a licensed health care professional or that is legally possessed or used under any other authority under that Act or under any other provision of federal law (71 Fed. Reg. 46723).

- *Serious bodily injury* is defined strictly, as that which involves substantial risk of death, extreme physical pain, protracted and obvious disfigurement, or protracted loss or impairment of the function of a bodily member, organ, or mental faculty (71 Fed. Reg. 46723).

- *Weapon* means a device, instrument, material, or substance, animate or inanimate, that is used for, or is readily capable of, causing death or serious bodily injury, except that such term does not include a pocket knife with a blade of less than 2½ inches in length [18 U.S.C. 930(g)(2)].

Note that the child doesn't have to use the weapon; he/she may merely possess it. It is also enough for a child with a disability to knowingly possess an illegal drug; he/she doesn't have to be caught using the drug. In contrast, for drug violations involving controlled substances, IDEIA means that the child must sell or solicit the sale of a controlled substance.

In all three instances, the law specifically states that the student can be removed "without regard to whether the behavior is determined to be a manifestation of the student's disability."

What are the consequences involving special circumstances?

When a student with a disability has committed a weapons or drug violation, or inflicted serious bodily injury on another person, school personnel may remove that child to an interim alternative educational setting for not more than 45 school days without regard to whether the behavior is determined to be a manifestation of the child's disability [34 C.F.R. 300.530(g)].

Other provisions of IDEA's discipline procedures apply under special circumstances—for example:

- conducting the manifestation determination [34 C.F.R. 300.530(e)]

- notifying parents [34 C.F.R. 300.530(h)]

- determining the extent of services that must be provided to the child [34 C.F.R. 300.530(d)(1)].

Can parents challenge manifestation determination or any decision regarding placement with a right to have an expedited due process hearing?

Yes. The parents of a child with a disability who disagree with any decision regarding placement [34 C.F.R. 300.530 and 300.531], or the manifestation determination [34 C.F.R. 300.530(e)], or with the LEA's belief that maintaining the current placement of the child is substantially likely to result in injury to the child or others, may appeal the decision by requesting a hearing [34 C.F.R. 300.532].

Parents may challenge a manifestation determination decision or any decision regarding placement with a right to have an expedited due process hearing. The right to an expedited hearing means that it takes place within 20 school days and results in a decision within ten school days thereafter.

If a parent appeals the decision of the manifestation determination hearing, what options does the hearing officer of the appeal have?

In making a determination, the hearing officer may either [34 C.F.R. 300.511]:

- return the child with a disability to the placement from which the child was removed if the hearing officer determines that the removal was a violation of the law [34 C.F.R. 300.530] or that the child's behavior was a manifestation of the child's disability, or

- order a change of placement of the child with a disability to an appropriate interim alternative educational setting for not more than 45 school days if the hearing officer determines that maintaining the current placement of the child is substantially likely to result in injury to the child or to others.

What is the appropriate placement of a student with a disability during an appeal of a manifestation determination decision?

When an appeal has been made by either the parent or the LEA [34 C.F.R. 300.532], the child must remain in the interim alternative educational setting pending the decision of the hearing officer or until the expiration of the time period specified in the law, whichever occurs first, unless the parent and the SEA or LEA agree otherwise [20 U.S.C. 1415(k)(4)(A)].

What are the protections for a child who has not been determined to be eligible for special education and related services who has engaged in behavior that violated a code of student conduct?

A child who has not been determined to be eligible for special education and related services who has engaged in behavior that violated a code of student conduct may assert any of the protections provided under IDEIA if the public agency had knowledge that the child was a child with a disability before the behavior that precipitated the disciplinary action occurred.

A public agency must be deemed to have knowledge that a child is a child with a disability if before the behavior that precipitated the disciplinary action occurred:

1. the parent of the child expressed concern in writing to supervisory or administrative personnel of the appropriate educational agency, or a teacher of the child, that the child is in need of special education and related services

2. the parent of the child requested an evaluation of the child pursuant to IDEIA [34 C.F.R. 300.300 through 300.311], or

3. the teacher of the child, or other personnel of the LEA, expressed specific concerns about a pattern of behavior demonstrated by the child directly to the director of special education of the agency or to other supervisory personnel of the agency.

A public agency would not be deemed to have knowledge if the parent of the child had not allowed an evaluation of the child pursuant to IDEIA [34 C.F.R. 300.300 through 300.311] or had refused services under IDEIA.

If a public agency does not have knowledge that a child is a child with a disability prior to taking disciplinary measures against the child, the child may be subjected to the disciplinary measures applied to children without disabilities who engage in comparable behaviors.

If a request is made for an evaluation of a child during the time period in which the child is subjected to disciplinary measures, the evaluation must be conducted in an expedited manner.

Until the evaluation is completed, the child remains in the educational placement determined by school authorities, which can include suspension or expulsion without educational services.

If the child is determined to be a child with a disability, taking into consideration information from the evaluation conducted by the agency and information provided by the parents, the agency must provide special education and related services [34 C.F.R. 300.534; 20 U.S.C. 1415(k)(5)].

Do IDEIA's discipline procedures allow school systems to report crimes that are committed by children with disabilities?

Yes. IDEIA makes clear that schools are not prohibited from reporting a crime committed by a child with a disability to appropriate authorities [34 C.F.R. 300.535]. Similarly, the law does not prevent state law enforcement and judicial authorities from exercising their responsibilities. The agency reporting the crime must ensure that copies of the special education and disciplinary records are transmitted for consideration by the appropriate authorities—however, only to the extent that the transmission is permitted by the Family Educational Rights and Privacy Act (FERPA), a federal law that protects the privacy of children's education records.

Under FERPA, personally identifiable information (such as the child's status as a special education child) can only be released with parental consent, except in certain very limited circumstances. Therefore, the transmission of a child's special education and disciplinary records without parental consent is permissible only to the extent that such transmission is permitted by the Family Educational Rights and Privacy Act [20 U.S.C. 1415(k)(6)] (see Chapter 12).

Chapter

12

Confidentiality of Information and Education Records

What laws address confidentiality of student records in special education?

Through the process of determining eligibility and placement, designing an individualized education program (IEP), and providing that program, very personal and sensitive information about students and families is created, collected, and shared. This often includes information about the social, emotional, and educational status of the student. Such information must be held confidentially and must only be shared with individuals who need the information to provide services to the student or who have a legitimate educational need for the information.

Confidentiality is the legally required process of keeping secret. In special education, it is the legally and ethically required principle and practice that compels professionals not to disclose identifying or other significant information about the parties without legal authority and the written consent of the involved parties to do so.

The Individuals with Disabilities Education Improvement Act (IDEIA) and the Family Education Rights and Privacy Act (FERPA) contain provisions that protect the confidentiality of student records. These laws also provide parents the right to review and inspect records. A school district will assume that each parent has the right to inspect and review his/her child's education records unless the district has received legal documents limiting parent access to those records (U.S. Department of Education, 2011).

What is the Family Education Rights and Privacy Act (FERPA)?

The Family Educational Rights and Privacy Act (FERPA) [20 U.S.C. 1232g; 34 C.F.R. Part 99] is a federal law that protects the privacy of student education records. The law applies to all schools that receive funds under an applicable program of the U.S. Department of Education.

FERPA gives parents certain rights with respect to their children's education records. These rights transfer to the student when he/she reaches the age of 18 or attends a school beyond the high school level.

Under FERPA:

- Parents or eligible students have the right to inspect and review the student's education records maintained by the school. Schools are not required to provide copies of records unless, for reasons such as great distance, it is impossible for parents or eligible students to review the records. Schools may charge a fee for copies.

- Parents or eligible students have the right to request that a school correct records which they believe to be inaccurate or misleading. If the school decides not to amend the record, the parent or eligible student then has the right to a formal hearing. After the hearing, if the school still decides not to amend the record, the parent or eligible student has the right to place a statement with the record setting forth his/her view about the contested information.

Generally, schools must have written permission from the parent or eligible student in order to release any information from a student's education record. However, FERPA allows schools to disclose those records, without consent, to the following parties or under the following conditions [34 C.F.R. 99.31]:

- school officials with legitimate educational interest

- other schools to which a student is transferring

- specified officials for audit or evaluation purposes

- appropriate parties in connection with financial aid to a student

- organizations conducting certain studies for or on behalf of the school

- accrediting organizations

- to comply with a judicial order or lawfully issued subpoena

- appropriate officials in cases of health and safety emergencies

- state and local authorities, within a juvenile justice system, pursuant to specific state law.

Schools may disclose, without consent, "directory" information such as a student's name, address, telephone number, date and place of birth, honors and awards, and dates of attendance. However, schools must tell parents and eligible students about directory information and allow parents and eligible students a reasonable amount of time to request that the school not disclose directory information about them. Schools must notify parents and eligible students annually of their rights under FERPA. The actual means of notification (special letter, inclusion in a PTA bulletin, student handbook, or newspaper article) is left to the discretion of each school (U.S. Department of Education, 2011).

What does "personally identifiable" mean?

Personally identifiable [34 C.F.R. 300.32; 20 U.S.C. 1415(a)] means information that has:

- the child's name, the name as the parent, or the name of another family member

- the child's address

- a personal identifier, such as the child's social security number or student number, or

- a list of personal characteristics or other information that would make it possible to identify the child with reasonable certainty.

What notice must be given to parents regarding confidentiality?

The state educational agency must give notice that is adequate to fully inform parents about confidentiality of personally identifiable information, including:

- a description of the extent to which the notice is given in the native languages of the various population groups in the state

- a description of the children on whom personally identifiable information is maintained, the types of information sought, the methods the state intends to use in gathering the information (including the sources from whom information is gathered), and the uses to be made of the information

- a summary of the policies and procedures that participating agencies must follow regarding storage, disclosure to third parties, retention, and destruction of personally identifiable information, and

- a description of all of the rights of parents and children regarding this information, including the rights under the Family Educational Rights and Privacy Act (FERPA) and its implementing regulations in 34 C.F.R. Part 99.

Before any major identification, location, or evaluation activity (also known as Child Find), the notice must be published or announced in newspapers or other media, or both, with circulation adequate to notify parents throughout the state of the activity to locate, identify, and evaluate children in need of special education and related services [34 C.F.R. 300.612; 20 U.S.C. 1412(a)(8); 1417(c)].

What are considered "education records"?

Under FERPA [20 U.S.C. 1232(g); 34 C.F.R. 300.611] "education records" are defined as records that are:

- directly related to a student, and

- maintained by an educational agency or institution or by a party acting for the agency or institution.

Such records may include:

- written documents (including student advising folders)

- computer media

- microfilm and microfiche

- video or audio tapes or CDs

- film

- photographs.

Any record that contains personally identifiable information that is directly related to the student is an education record under FERPA. This information can also include records kept by the school in the form of student files, student system databases kept in storage devices such as servers, or recordings or broadcasts which may include student projects (Van Dusen, 2004).

What are *not* considered education records?

The term "education records" does not include:

1. records of instructional, supervisory, and administrative personnel and educational personnel ancillary thereto which are in the sole possession of the maker thereof and which are not accessible or revealed to any other person except a substitute

2. records maintained by a law enforcement unit of the educational agency or institution that were created by that law enforcement unit for the purpose of law enforcement

3. in the case of persons who are employed by an educational agency or institution but who are not in attendance at such agency or institution, records made and maintained in the normal course of business which relate exclusively to such person in that person's capacity as an employee and are not available for use for any other purpose, or

4. records on a student who is 18 years of age or older, or is attending an institution of postsecondary education, which are made or maintained by a physician, psychiatrist, psychologist, or other recognized professional or paraprofessional acting in his/her professional or paraprofessional capacity, or assisting in that capacity, and which are made, maintained, or used only in connection with the provision of treatment to the student, and are not available to anyone other than persons providing such treatment, except that

such records can be personally reviewed by a physician or other appropriate professional of the student's choice.

What are the two types of education records?

There are two types of education records as defined under FERPA. Each type of education record is afforded different disclosure protections. Therefore, it is important for faculty and staff to know the type of education record that is being considered for disclosure.

1. Directory information

Some information in a student's education record is defined as "directory information" under FERPA. Under a strict reading of FERPA, the school may disclose this type of information without the written consent of the student. However, the student can exercise the option to restrict the release of directory information by submitting a formal request to the school to limit disclosure. Directory information may include:

- name
- address
- phone number and email address
- dates of attendance
- degree(s) awarded
- enrollment status
- major field of study.

Although it is not specifically required by FERPA, institutions should always disclose to the student that such information is considered by the school to be directory information and, as such, may be disclosed to a third party upon request. Institutions should err on the side of caution and request, in writing, that the student allow the school to disclose directory information to third parties (Van Dusen, 2004).

2. Non-directory information

"Non-directory information" is any education record not considered directory information. Non-directory information must not be released to anyone without prior written consent. Further, faculty and staff can access non-directory information only if they have a legitimate academic need to do so. Non-directory information may include:

- social security numbers
- student identification number

- race, ethnicity, and/or nationality

- gender

- transcripts; grade reports.

Transcripts are non-directory information and, therefore, are protected education records under FERPA. Students have a right to privacy regarding transcripts held by the school where third parties seek transcript copies. Institutions should require that students first submit a written request to have transcripts sent to any third party as the privilege of privacy of this information is held by the student under FERPA (Van Dusen, 2004).

What rights do parents have to review education records of their children by a participating agency?

"Education records" means the type of records covered under the definition of "education records" in 34 C.F.R. Part 99 (the regulations implementing the Family Educational Rights and Privacy Act of 1974) [20 U.S.C. 1232g; 34 C.F.R. 300.611].

"Participating agency" means any school district, agency or institution that collects, maintains, or uses personally identifiable information, or from which information is obtained, under Part B of the IDEA [34 C.F.R. 300.611].

The participating agency must permit parents to inspect and review any education records relating to their child that are collected, maintained, or used by their school district under Part B of IDEA. The participating agency must comply with a parental request to inspect and review any education records on the child without unnecessary delay and before any meeting regarding an IEP, or any impartial due process hearing (including a resolution meeting or a hearing regarding discipline), and in no case more than 45 calendar days after a request is made.

Parents' right to inspect and review education records includes the right to [34 C.F.R. 300.613; 20 U.S.C. 1412(a)(8); 1417(c)]:

- a response from the participating agency to their reasonable requests for explanations and interpretations of the records

- a request that the participating agency provide copies of the records if the parents cannot effectively inspect and review the records unless they receive those copies, and

- have the parents' representative inspect and review the records.

The participating agency may presume that parents have authority to inspect and review records relating to their child unless advised that they do not have the authority under applicable state law governing such matters as guardianship, or separation and divorce.

Do school districts have to maintain records of access?

Yes. Each participating agency must keep a record of parties obtaining access to education records collected, maintained, or used under Part B of IDEA (except access by parents and authorized employees of the participating agency), including the name of the party, the date access was given, and the purpose for which the party is authorized to use the records [34 C.F.R. 300.614; 20 U.S.C. 1412(a)(8); 1417(c)].

What if an education record includes information on more than one child?

If any education record includes information on more than one child, the parents of those children have the right to inspect and review only the information relating to their child or to be informed of that specific information [34 C.F.R. 300.615; 20 U.S.C. 1412(a)(8); 1417(c)].

Do school districts have to provide parents with a list of the types and locations of education records?

Yes. On request, each participating agency must provide parents with a list of the types and locations of education records collected, maintained, or used by the agency [34 C.F.R. 300.616; 20 U.S.C. 1412(a)(8); 1417(c)].

Can a school district charge a fee for copies of records?

Each participating agency may charge a fee for copies of records that are made for parents under Part B of IDEA, if the fee does not effectively prevent parents from exercising their right to inspect and review those records.

A participating agency may not charge a fee to search for or to retrieve information under Part B of IDEIA [34 C.F.R. 300.617; 20 U.S.C. 1412(a)(8); 1417(c)].

What if parents believe that the education records of their child are inaccurate or misleading, or violate the privacy or other rights of their child?

If parents believe that information in the education records regarding their child collected, maintained, or used under Part B of IDEA is inaccurate or misleading, or violates the privacy or other rights of their child, they may request the participating agency that maintains the information to change the information.

The participating agency must decide whether to change the information in accordance with a parental request within a reasonable period of time of receipt of their request [34 C.F.R. 300.618; 20 U.S.C. 1412(a)(8); 1417(c)].

Do parents have an opportunity for a hearing to challenge information in education records?

The participating agency must, on request, provide parents an opportunity for a hearing to challenge information in education records regarding their child to ensure that it is not inaccurate, misleading, or otherwise in violation of the privacy or other rights of their child [34 C.F.R. 300.619; 20 U.S.C. 1412(a)(8); 1417(c)].

What law dictates hearing procedures of education records?

A hearing to challenge information in education records must be conducted according to the procedures for such hearings under FERPA [34 C.F.R. 300.621].

What happens if a hearing finds the education records not to be inaccurate, misleading, or otherwise in violation of the privacy or other rights of the child?

If, as a result of the hearing, the participating agency decides that the information is *not* inaccurate, misleading, or otherwise in violation of the privacy or other rights of the child, it must inform the parents of their right to place in the records that it maintains on their child a statement commenting on the information or providing any reasons the parents disagree with the decision of the participating agency.

Such an explanation placed in the records of the child must [34 C.F.R. 300.620; 20 U.S.C. 1412(a)(8); 1417(c)]:

- be maintained by the participating agency as part of the records of the child as long as the record or contested portion is maintained by the participating agency, and

- if the participating agency discloses the records of the child or the challenged portion to any party, the explanation must also be disclosed to that party.

Is parental consent for disclosure of personally identifiable information required?

Yes. Unless the information is contained in education records, and the disclosure is authorized without parental consent under FERPA, parental consent must be obtained before personally identifiable information is disclosed to parties other than officials of participating agencies. Except under the circumstances specified below, parental consent is not required before personally identifiable information is released to officials of participating agencies for purposes of meeting a requirement of Part B of IDEIA [34 C.F.R. 300.622; 20 U.S.C. 1412(a)(8); 1417(c)].

Parental consent, or consent of an eligible child who has reached the age of majority under state law, must be obtained before personally identifiable information is released to officials of participating agencies providing or paying for transition services.

If a child is in, or is going to go to, a private school that is not located in the same school district the parents reside in, parental consent must be obtained before any personally identifiable information about the child is released between officials in the school district where the private school is located and officials in the school district where the parents reside.

What safeguards are in IDEIA to protect personally identifiable information?

Under IDEIA, safeguards regarding personally identifiable information include:

- Each participating agency must protect the confidentiality of personally identifiable information at collection, storage, disclosure, and destruction stages.

- One official at each participating agency must assume responsibility for ensuring the confidentiality of any personally identifiable information.

- All persons collecting or using personally identifiable information must receive training or instruction regarding the state's policies and procedures regarding confidentiality under Part B of IDEIA and the Family Educational Rights and Privacy Act (FERPA).

- Each participating agency must maintain, for public inspection, a current listing of the names and positions of those employees within the agency who may have access to personally identifiable information.

[34 C.F.R. 300.623; 20 U.S.C. 1412(a)(8); 1417(c)]

What does IDEIA require regarding destruction of information?

"Destruction" means physical destruction or removal of personal identifiers from information so that the information is no longer personally identifiable [34 C.F.R. 300.611].

A school district must inform parents when personally identifiable information collected, maintained, or used is no longer needed to provide educational services to a child [34 C.F.R. 300.624; 20 U.S.C. 1412(a)(8); 1417(c)].

The information must be destroyed at parent request. However, a permanent record of their child's name, address, and phone number, his/her grades, attendance record, classes attended, grade level completed, and year completed may be maintained without time limitation.

What are children's rights when they turn the age of majority?

The state education agency must have in effect policies and procedures regarding the extent to which children are afforded rights of privacy similar to those afforded to parents, taking into consideration the age of the child and type or severity of disability. Under the regulations for FERPA, the rights of parents regarding education records are transferred to the student at age 18.

If the rights accorded to parents are transferred to a student who reaches the age of majority, the rights regarding education records must also be transferred to the student. However, the public agency must provide notice to the student and the parents [34 C.F.R. 300.625; 20 U.S.C. 1412(a)(8); 1417(c)].

Early Intervention for Infants and Toddlers with Disabilities

NOTE TO READERS

At the time of this book's printing, the Office of Special Education and Rehabilitative Services (OSERS), U.S. Department of Education, had released an unofficial copy of the final Part C regulations (infants and toddlers program, 0–2 years) to implement the Individuals with Disabilities Education Improvement Act of 2004. The official copy of the final regulations was delivered to the Office of the Federal Register but had not yet been scheduled for publication. The official version of this document is the document that will be published in the Federal Register. The regulations become effective 30 days after it is published in the Federal Register.

What is the definition of early intervention (EI) under Part C of IDEIA?

Under Part C of IDEIA, states must provide services to any child "under 3 years of age who needs early intervention services" because the child [34 C.F.R. 303.16; 20 U.S.C. 1432(5)(A)]:

1. is experiencing developmental delays, as measured by appropriate diagnostic instruments and procedures in one or more of the areas of cognitive development, physical development, communication development, social or emotional development, and adaptive development, or

2. has a diagnosed physical or mental condition which has a high probability of resulting in developmental delay.

A state also may provide services, at its discretion, to at-risk infants and toddlers. An at-risk infant or toddler is defined under Part C as "an individual under 3 years of age who would be at risk of experiencing a substantial developmental delay if early intervention services were not provided to the individual" [20 U.S.C. 1432(1)].

Note: The full text of the Federal Regulations for the Early Intervention Program for Infants and Toddlers with Disabilities can be found in Part 303 rather than Part

300. For example, the purpose of the Early Intervention Program for Infants and Toddlers with Disabilities can be found in 34 C.F.R. 303.1. The contents for an IFSP can be found in 34 C.F.R. 303.344

What is the purpose of early intervention?

In 1986, Congress created a nationwide incentive for states to implement coordinated systems of early intervention services for infants and toddlers with disabilities and their families by adding Part C to the federal law. Today, this law is known as the Individuals with Disabilities Education Improvement Act (IDEIA).

Part C of the Individuals with Disabilities Education Improvement Act provides financial assistance to states for the purpose of providing services to infants and toddlers (age birth through two) with disabilities. The purpose of these services is to enhance the development of infants and toddlers with disabilities and to minimize their potential for developmental delay (Pierangelo and Giuliani, 2007).

Each year, since 1987, the state lead agency has received federal funds by submitting an application to the U.S. Department of Education which ensures that the state will implement the early intervention system in compliance with statutory and regulatory requirements.

Part C policies are based on the principles of family-centered and community-based service delivery and require that services to infants and toddlers with disabilities and their families be provided through a coordinated, interagency system rather than a single agency (Maryland State Department of Education, 2003).

Research shows that participation in family-centered early intervention services during the first years of life has substantial positive effects on the cognitive development, social adjustment, and overall development of children with developmental disabilities. These services to eligible children are federally mandated under Part C of IDEIA. Upon referral to an early intervention program, providers work with families to develop an individualized family service plan (IFSP), and each family is provided a service coordinator to advocate at their request.

Additionally, the American Academy of Pediatrics (AAP) has strongly advocated for a "medical home" for children with disabilities in which regular and specialized medical services are family-centered and well coordinated with other early intervention services. Coordinated care should attempt to maximize appropriate services and avoid duplication and gaps in services. The relationship between the child, parents, and primary care physician is very important in promoting the long-term health and development of the child, and should take the form of a partnership as much as possible. The family's culture, values, resources, priorities, and expectations may impact family-centered services.

Who is an infant or toddler with a disability?

An infant or toddler with a disability means an individual under three years of age who needs early intervention services because the individual [34 C.F.R. 300.25; 20 U.S.C. 1401(16) and 1432(5)]:

- is experiencing developmental delays, as measured by appropriate diagnostic instruments and procedures in one or more of the areas of cognitive development, physical development, communication development, social or emotional development

- has a diagnosed physical or mental condition that has a high probability of resulting in developmental delay, and

- may also include, at a state's discretion, "at-risk" infants and toddlers.

What are the eligibility criteria for early intervention services?

Referral to early intervention services can be based on objective criteria, screening tests, or clinical suspicion. Under IDEIA (Part C), individual states retain the right to determine eligibility criteria for early intervention services, and some require referral within a certain time period.

The following two eligibility criteria are typical of most states (Alabama State Department of Education, 2002):

- birth to three years of age, and

- developmental delay or deficit in one or more of these areas:

    a. cognitive development (e.g. limited interest in environment, play, and learning)

    b. physical and motor development, including vision and hearing (e.g. hypertonia, dystonia, asymmetry)

    c. communication development (e.g. limited sound use, limited response to speech)

    d. emotional-social development (e.g. impaired attachment, self-injurious behavior)

    e. adaptive development (e.g. feeding difficulties).

Although most states require children to demonstrate one or more of these types of deficits, some states permit children to be enrolled who are at risk for delays or disabilities due to environmental factors.

What is the process of evaluation of infants and toddlers for early intervention services?

IDEIA requires that a child receive a timely, comprehensive, multidisciplinary evaluation and assessment. The purposes of the evaluation and assessment are to find out:

- the nature of the child's strengths, delays, or difficulties

- whether or not the child is eligible for early intervention services

- how the child functions in five areas of development: cognitive development, physical development, communication, social-emotional development, and adaptive development.

When a child's needs are assessed and the child is found eligible for services, a service coordinator will be assigned to the family. This person should have a background in early childhood development and methods for helping young children who may have developmental delays. The service coordinator should know the policies for early intervention programs and services in the parents' state. This person can help parents locate other services in their community, such as recreation, child care, or family support groups. The service coordinator will work with the family as long as the baby is receiving early intervention services and, after the child is two years old, the service coordinator will help the family move on to programs for children ages three through five (National Dissemination Center for Children and Youth with Disabilities, 2005).

What types of early intervention services are available to infants and toddlers?

Early intervention services help meet the developmental needs of the infant or toddler and the family. Needed services are identified during evaluation and assessment and agreed upon at the IFSP meeting. The service coordinator helps the family coordinate the services from all agencies and providers of services and assists the family through transition.

Early intervention services include (California Department of Developmental Services, 2006):

- assistive technology

- audiology

- family training, counseling, and home visits

- health services

- medical services (only for diagnostic or evaluation purposes)

- nursing

- nutrition
- occupational therapy
- physical therapy
- psychological services
- service coordination
- social work services
- special instruction
- speech and language pathology
- transportation and related costs
- vision services.

For an explanation of many of these related services, see Chapter 7.

What is an individualized family service plan (IFSP)?

An individualized family service plan (IFSP) documents and guides the early intervention process for children with disabilities and their families. This written plan is developed with the family. The information gathered during the evaluation process is used to identify all of the services the child needs and services the family needs to enhance the development of their child. The IFSP identifies and describes the services that are going to be provided and who will provide the services. The IFSP also identifies the service coordinator who will assist families throughout the child's eligibility (Pierangelo and Giuliani, 2008).

What is the purpose of the initial IFSP process?

- To summarize all information known regarding the child's strengths and needs and the family's strengths, concerns, priorities, preferences, and current resources.
- To review the family's identified routines, daily activities, and natural environments.
- To develop and refine outcomes the family has chosen (includes outcomes for both the child and the family).
- To develop strategies for meeting the identified outcomes.
- To determine appropriate services and supports that link to meeting the identified outcomes.

- To develop a written document that will guide the family, the family service coordinator, and the other service providers.

- To determine the responsibilities of each team member.

- To determine how communication between the parent and other team members will be maintained.

- To determine where (natural environments), when, and how services and supports will be delivered to the child and family (Pierangelo and Giuliani, 2008; Pierangelo and Giuliani, 2007).

Is notice required to families for an IFSP meeting?

Yes. Under IDEIA, meeting arrangements must be made with, and written notice of the meeting provided to, the family and other participants early enough before the IFSP meeting date to ensure that they will be able to attend. It is strongly recommended that providers give the family and other participants a ten-calendar-day written notice of the IFSP meeting. Parents must be informed of their rights prior to the meeting, including the right to bring a family member or other individual who knows the child and family and can contribute to preparing the IFSP.

IFSP meetings must be conducted in settings and at times that are convenient to families and in the native language of the family or other mode of communication used by the family, unless it is clearly not feasible to do so.

If parents (or child advocate) are unable to attend the scheduled IFSP meeting, the team will not meet. The reason for the cancellation of the meeting must be documented in the child's records. The IFSP meeting must be rescheduled as soon as possible and at a time mutually agreed upon by the parents and other team members [34 C.F.R. 303.342(d)].

What is the timeline corresponding with an IFSP?

The first IFSP meeting is held after the initial evaluation (including any assessments of the child and family) and determination of eligibility. According to the law, the IFSP must be developed within 45 days of the time the initial referral is made to the state's early intervention program. This requirement necessitates a streamlined approach to responding to new referrals and determining eligibility so that the planning can begin for the IFSP, which is completed on or before the 45th day. The meeting is to be scheduled at a mutually convenient time and place for the family and other participants.

If the IFSP is not developed within the prescribed timeline, then the team must document the reasons the timelines were not met.

In the event of exceptional circumstances that make it impossible to complete the evaluation (including any assessments of the child and family) and assessment of service needs within 45 calendar days from receiving the referral for evaluation (e.g. if a child is ill), then the team must document the reasons the timelines were not met [34 C.F.R. 303.342(a)(b)(c)].

Are all children who are eligible for the state's early intervention service system entitled to an IFSP?

Yes. Each child who is eligible for the state's early intervention service system is entitled to an IFSP that addresses the needs of the child and family. This is a written plan that outlines the provision of early intervention services for the child and family. The plan must [34 C.F.R. 303.340]:

- be developed jointly by the family and appropriate qualified personnel be involved in the provision of early intervention services

- be based on the multidisciplinary evaluation and assessment of the child and the assessment of the family, and

- include services necessary to enhance the development of the child and the capacity of the family to meet the special needs of the child.

What are the contents of an IFSP?

According to IDEIA, the contents of the IFSP *must* include:

- a statement of the child's present levels of physical development (including vision, hearing, and health status), cognitive development, communication development, social or emotional development, and adaptive development, based on professionally acceptable objective criteria [34 C.F.R. 303.344(a)]

- a statement of the family's resources, priorities, and concerns related to enhancing the development of the child (with the concurrence of the family) [34 C.F.R. 303. 344(b)]

- a statement of the major outcomes expected to be achieved for the child and family [34 C.F.R. 303.344(c)]

- a statement of the criteria, procedures, and timelines used to determine the degree to which progress toward achieving the outcomes is being made [34 C.F.R. 303.344(c)(1)]

- a statement of the specific early intervention services necessary to meet the unique needs of the child and the family to achieve the outcomes identified, including the location of the services [34 C.F.R. 303.344(d)(1)]

- the frequency, intensity, and method of delivering each early intervention service [34 C.F.R. 303.344(d)(1)(i)]

- a statement of the specific early intervention services to be provided in the natural environments and a justification of the extent, if any, to which the services will not be provided in a natural environment [34 C.F.R. 303.344(d)(1)(ii)]

- the payment arrangements, if any [34 C.F.R. 303.344(d)(1)(iv)]

- a statement of whether modifications or revisions of the outcomes or services are necessary [34 C.F.R. 303.344(c)(2)]

- the projected dates for initiation of the services as soon as possible after the IFSP meetings [34 C.F.R. 303.344(f)(1)]

- the anticipated duration of those services [34 C.F.R. 303.344(f)(2)]

- parental consent for the early intervention services. If the parents do not provide consent with respect to a particular early intervention service or withdraw consent after first providing it, that service may not be provided [34 C.F.R. 303.342(e)]

- the steps to be taken to support the transition of the child to preschool services under Part B of IDEIA, or other services that may be available, if appropriate [34 C.F.R. 303.344(h)(1)]

- the name of the service coordinator from the profession most immediately relevant to the child's or family's needs (or who is otherwise qualified to carry out all applicable responsibilities), who will be responsible for the implementation of the IFSP and coordination with other agencies and persons [34 C.F.R. 303.344(g)(1)].

Who must be in attendance at an initial IFSP meeting?

Each initial IFSP meeting must include the following participants [34 C.F.R. 303.343]:

1. the parent or parents of the child

2. other family members, as requested by the parent(s), if feasible to do so

3. an advocate or person outside of the family, if the parent requests that the person participate

4. the intake coordinator who has been working with the family since the initial referral for evaluation

5. a person or persons directly involved in conducting the evaluations and assessments

6. as appropriate, service providers to the child and/or family.

If an ongoing service coordinator has been successfully identified by the family, that individual may also be invited and participate in the initial IFSP meeting.

Are periodic IFSP reviews required?

Yes. Periodic IFSP reviews for a child and his/her family must be conducted every six months or more frequently if conditions warrant, or if the family requests a review. Such reviews may be carried out at a face-to-face meeting or by another means that is acceptable to the parents and other participants. The intent of this review is to ensure that the constantly changing developmental needs of the child and priorities of the family are acknowledged and documented. The purposes of the periodic review are to (Georgia Department of Health, 2011):

- review and revise the IFSP, as appropriate
- determine the degree to which progress toward achieving the outcomes is occurring
- determine whether modification or revision of the outcomes or services is necessary
- discuss the family's satisfaction with services being received
- review the results of any new evaluations and ongoing assessments
- share any other new and relevant information related to the child and family
- outline plans for the next six months.

Who must be in attendance at an annual IFSP meeting?

Each annual IFSP meeting must include the following participants [34 C.F.R. 303.343]:

1. the parent or parents of the child
2. other family members, as requested by the parent(s) if feasible to do so
3. an advocate or person outside of the family, if the parent requests that the person participate
4. the ongoing service coordinator who has been designated responsible for the implementation of the IFSP
5. a person or persons directly involved in conducting the evaluations and assessments
6. as appropriate, service providers to the child and/or family.

If a person directly involved in conducting an evaluation and/or assessment is unable to attend the IFSP meeting, arrangements must be made for that person's involvement through other means, such as participation by telephone conference call or through pertinent records that are available at the meeting. A knowledgeable, authorized representative may also attend the meeting as a substitute for the person unable to attend [34 C.F.R. 303.343(2)]. This includes early intervention service providers who conduct ongoing assessments.

Can early intervention services for an eligible child and the child's family commence before the completion of the evaluation and assessment?

Yes. Early intervention services for an eligible child and the child's family may commence before the completion of the evaluation and assessment if the following conditions are met [34 C.F.R. 303.345]:

1. Informed, written parental consent is obtained.

2. An interim IFSP is developed that includes:

   a. the name of the service coordinator who will be responsible consistent with 303.344(g) for implementation of the interim IFSP and coordination with other agencies and persons, and

   b. the early intervention services that have been determined to be needed immediately by the child and the child's family.

3. The evaluation and assessment are completed within 45 calendar days of referral. The use of an interim IFSP does not release the public system from meeting the 45 calendar day timeline and is rarely used.

Is parental consent required prior to the provision of any early intervention services described in the IFSP?

Yes. The contents of the IFSP must be fully explained to the parents and informed written consent must be obtained prior to the provision of any early intervention services described in the IFSP. The early intervention services for which parental consent is obtained must be provided [20 U.S.C. 1436(e); 34 C.F.R. 303.342(e); 34 C.F.R. 303.403; 303.404; 34 C.F.R. 303.405].

The parent must be provided with prior written notice and a request for consent in his/her native language indicating that early intervention services will be provided for the child and the family and the reason for providing the early intervention services [34 C.F.R. 303.403].

The parent must provide informed written consent for the provision of early intervention services [34 C.F.R. 303.404].

The parent may determine whether the family will accept or decline any early intervention service written into the IFSP without jeopardizing the right to receive other early intervention services. If the parent does not provide consent for the services, or some part of the services, only the services to which consent has been obtained must be provided [34 C.F.R. 303.405].

Are there transition services for infants and toddlers?

Yes. Transition can occur at any time there is a change from one service delivery system to another. The purpose of transition services is to ensure that children continue to receive services and support as they move within and between service delivery systems.

The federal law for early intervention and special education supports a seamless system of services for children from birth up to age three. The law requires that this should be a smooth activity, that services should continue throughout the transition period, and that there should be no interruption in services for the child (U.S. Department of Education, 2011).

There are two types of transition that can be addressed by the IFSP:

1. There are transitions within the early intervention program. These can include transitions between service providers or service settings. For example, support and planning would be required to move smoothly from a program designed for infants to a program for toddlers. The physical environment in the toddler setting will differ significantly to support the developmental goals of toddlers who are more mobile and expected to explore their environment.

2. Another type of transition takes place when the child moves from early intervention services to a variety of preschool settings. When the child with disabilities nears the age of three, he/she must be considered for services beyond early intervention services. These services include, but are not limited to, special education preschool programs (under Part B of the IDEIA), Head Start programs, and public and private preschool programs.

Special education preschool programs are available to children with disabilities who are three to five years old. If the child is eligible for preschool special education services, he/she must have an individualized education program (IEP) in place by age three. All services provided under the IEP must be free to the parents. If a child is not eligible for special education preschool, then Head Start or public or private preschool programs should be considered.

Does IDEIA require that any agency or person be held accountable if an eligible child does not achieve the growth projected in the child's IFSP?

No. Each agency or person who has a direct role in the provision of early intervention services is responsible for making a good faith effort to assist each eligible child in achieving the outcomes in the child's IFSP. However, Part C of the Act does not require that any agency or person be held accountable if an eligible child does not achieve the growth projected in the child's IFSP [34 C.F.R. 303.346].

Section 504 and the Education of Children with Disabilities

What is Section 504 of the Rehabilitation Act?

Section 504 of the Vocational Rehabilitation Act of 1973 forbids discrimination on the basis of disability in any program or activity receiving federal money from the U.S. Department of Education. The purpose of the law is to provide equal access for people with disabilities.

Section 504 provides:

No otherwise qualified individual with a disability in the United States…shall, solely by reason of her or his disability, be excluded from the participation in, be denied the benefits of, or be subjected to discrimination under any program or activity receiving Federal financial assistance…

In education, Section 504 means that a student has an identified and documented disability, or a suspected disability, that substantially limits a major life activity (caring for oneself, performing manual tasks, walking, seeing, hearing, speaking, breathing, learning, and working). The person requires reasonable accommodations in order to access education (Portland Schools, 2011).

Section 504 is often referred to as the first civil rights act for individuals with disabilities.

The Section 504 regulations require a school district to provide a "free appropriate public education" to each qualified student with a disability who is in the school district's jurisdiction, regardless of the nature or severity of the disability (U.S. Department of Education, 2010).

Who enforces Section 504?

The Office for Civil Rights (OCR) enforces Section 504 in programs and activities that receive federal financial assistance from the U.S. Department of Education. Recipients of this federal financial assistance include public school districts, institutions of higher education, and other state and local education agencies. An important responsibility of the OCR is to eliminate discrimination on the basis of disability against students with disabilities.

The OCR receives numerous complaints and inquiries in the area of elementary and secondary education involving Section 504 from parents, students, or advocates. It conducts agency-initiated compliance reviews and provides technical assistance to school districts, parents, or advocates.

Whom does Section 504 protect?

Section 504 covers qualified students with disabilities who attend schools receiving federal financial assistance. To be protected under Section 504, a student must be determined to:

1. have a physical or mental impairment that substantially limits one or more major life activities, or

2. have a record of such an impairment, or

3. be regarded as having such an impairment.

Section 504 requires that school districts provide a free appropriate public education (FAPE) to qualified students in their jurisdictions who have a physical or mental impairment that substantially limits one or more major life activities (U.S. Department of Education, 2010).

On the average, approximately 1–2 percent of the student population in any school is deemed Section 504 eligible (Lewis, 2011).

What is a physical or mental impairment that substantially limits a major life activity?

The determination of whether a student has a physical or mental impairment that substantially limits a major life activity must be made on the basis of an individual inquiry. Section 504 defines a physical or mental impairment as:

> any physiological disorder or condition, cosmetic disfigurement, or anatomical loss affecting one or more of the following body systems: neurological; musculoskeletal; special sense organs; respiratory, including speech organs; cardiovascular; reproductive; digestive; genito-urinary; hemic and lymphatic; skin; and endocrine; or any mental or psychological disorder, such as mental retardation, organic brain syndrome, emotional or mental illness, and specific learning disabilities. [34 C.F.R. 104.3(j)(2)(i)]

Section 504 does not set forth an exhaustive list of specific diseases and conditions that may constitute physical or mental impairments because of the difficulty of ensuring the comprehensiveness of such a list (Menlo Park City School District, 2011).

What does "substantially limit" mean?

Determining whether an impairment is substantially limiting is critical to deciding Section 504 eligibility. Regulations fail to provide a definition for the term "substantial limits." According to the U.S. Supreme Court, "substantial" means the impairment must "prevent or severely restrict" the individual from performing the life function in question. The student must be severely restricted in his/her ability to, for example, read or write. The proper comparison in determining if a substantial limitation exists is not with the student's own theoretical potential, either now or at some point in the future, but instead with the average member of the general population (Mesa Public Schools, 2009).

The determination of substantial limitation must be made on a case-by-case basis with respect to each individual student. Section 504 requires that a group of knowledgeable persons draw upon information from a variety of sources in making this determination [34 C.F.R. 104.35(c)].

What are "major life activities"?

Major life activities include functions such as caring for oneself, performing manual tasks, walking, seeing, hearing, speaking, breathing, learning, and working. This list is not exhaustive. Other functions can be major life activities for purposes of Section 504. Congress provided additional examples of general activities that are major life activities, including eating, sleeping, standing, lifting, bending, reading, concentrating, thinking, and communicating. Congress also provided a non-exhaustive list of examples of "major bodily functions" that are major life activities, such as the functions of the immune system, normal cell growth, digestive, bowel, bladder, neurological, brain, respiratory, circulatory, endocrine, and reproductive functions [34 C.F.R. 104.3; Giordano, 2011).

Is a temporary impairment considered a disability under Section 504?

Maybe. A temporary impairment only constitutes a disability for purposes of Section 504 if its severity is such that it results in a substantial limitation of one or more major life activities for an extended period of time. The issue of whether a temporary impairment is substantial enough to be a disability must be resolved on a case-by-case basis, taking into consideration both the duration (or expected duration) of the impairment and the extent to which it actually limits a major life activity of the affected individual. In terms of temporary disabilities:

- The physical or mental impairment at issue must be permanent or anticipated to be very long term.

- Temporary, non-chronic impairments (i.e. broken arm, surgery, temporary at-home medical status) should generally not trigger Section 504 eligibility.

- Most temporary disabilities can be addressed via regular education services (i.e. homebound, make-up work, minor classroom/environment accommodations).

Note: Pregnancy is generally not a qualifying disability unless unexpected complications arise (Lewis, 2011).

Is an impairment that is episodic or in remission a disability under Section 504?

Maybe. Congress clarified that an impairment that is episodic or in remission is a disability if it would substantially limit a major life activity when active. A student with such an impairment is entitled to a free appropriate public education (FAPE) under Section 504 (San Mateo County Office of Education, 2011).

Is Section 504 used for "at-risk" students?

No. Section 504 eligibility is not for "at-risk" students. Since the phrase "substantially limits" is in present indicative verb form, the student must be presently, not potentially or hypothetically, substantially limited (Walsh and Gallegos, 2009).

Is a student who "has a record of disability" or is "regarded as disabled" automatically deemed Section 504 eligible?

No. In public elementary and secondary schools, unless a student actually has an impairment that substantially limits a major life activity, the mere fact that a student has a "record of" or is "regarded as" disabled is insufficient, in itself, to trigger those Section 504 protections that require the provision of a free appropriate public education (FAPE). Congress clarified that an individual who meets the definition of disability solely by virtue of being "regarded as" disabled is not entitled to reasonable accommodations or the reasonable modification of policies, practices, or procedures. The phrases "has a record of disability" and "is regarded as disabled" are meant to reach the situation in which a student either does not currently have or has never had a disability, but is treated by others as such (Weatherly, 2011).

What types of conditions deem students 504 eligible?

Although the list is not exhaustive, students who may be deemed eligible for Section 504 may have any of the following conditions (in alphabetical order) (Tucson Unified School District, 2010):

- attention deficit disorder with/without hyperactivity (ADD/ADHD)

- allergies
- arthritis
- asthma
- cancer
- cerebral palsy
- chronic fatigue
- conduct disorder
- diabetes
- epilepsy
- heart disease
- HIV/AIDS
- migraine headache
- multiple sclerosis
- obesity
- orthopedic impairments
- traumatic brain injury
- temporary disability
- tuberculosis.

What are the fundamental differences between IDEIA (special education) and Section 504?

A student who qualifies for special education services under the Individuals with Disabilities Education Improvement Act (IDEIA) is, in all cases, a qualified student with a disability under Section 504. The converse, however, is not true: a qualified student with a disability under Section 504 is not qualified in all cases to receive special education services and the protections of IDEIA. In other words, some students with disabilities may qualify for accommodations under Section 504 but do not qualify for special education services under IDEIA.

If a student with a disability is receiving special education services in accordance with IDEIA, then the student is adequately accommodated for the purposes of Section 504. For this reason, it is not necessary or appropriate to provide a student with a disability with Section 504 protections (i.e. notice, evaluation, and accommodation) if the student has already been determined eligible under IDEIA.

However, if a student is determined to be not eligible under IDEIA, the evaluation team may want to consider whether the student would, nevertheless, qualify for accommodations under Section 504 (Tucson Unified School District, 2010; U.S. Department of Education, 2010; Mesa Public Schools, 2009).

Other differences include those described below.

IDEIA

- IDEIA is a federal funding statute that ensures the provision of free appropriate public education (FAPE) to children with disabilities.

- IDEIA requires the student to have one of 13 specific disabilities. It covers infants and toddlers with disabilities birth–2 and children 3–21 who meet the definition of a preschool child with a disability or one of the 13 categories of disabilities applicable to school-age children.

- IDEIA is designed to provide specialized instruction to enable the student to achieve at a level commensurate with his/her own ability.

- IDEIA is limited to students with an educational need.

- Under IDEIA, any suspension of more than ten consecutive days or more is a significant change of placement triggering the procedural safeguards of IDEIA, including the right to remain in the current educational placement pending appeals. Cumulative suspensions of more than ten days within the school year may trigger the procedural safeguards under IDEIA. FAPE cannot be terminated as a disciplinary measure.

Section 504

- Section 504 is a civil rights statute protecting individuals with disabilities from discrimination in programs and activities receiving federal funds.

- Section 504 is not categorical, but covers any qualifying physical or mental impairments. It protects any person with a physical/mental impairment which substantially limits one or more major life activities (e.g. self-care, manual tasks, walking, seeing, hearing, breathing, learning, working), who has a record of such an impairment, or is regarded as having such an impairment.

- Section 504 is a non-discrimination statute designed to provide equal opportunity.

- Section 504 may cover students with no educational need, such as a wheelchair-bound student.

- Under Section 504, with respect to discipline, the district must reevaluate the child prior to any suspension of ten days or more. Is there a nexus between the child's disability and the behavior complained of? If yes, the child may not be suspended for more than ten days unless the behavior is drug sales or weapon(s) related. There is no automatic right to remain in the current educational placement.

What sources of information should be used to determine whether a student is eligible under Section 504?

In determining eligibility for accommodations under Section 504, the 504 team should utilize data from a variety of sources (Region XIII Education Service Center, 2011). These include:

- health records
- standardized test scores/class test scores
- informal checklists
- report cards
- parent/teacher reports and observations
- student work samples/student input
- disciplinary records
- prior special education testing results (if the student is not eligible for special education)
- cumulative records.

What is the difference between accommodations and modifications?

Accommodations are changes in course presentation, location, and timing of student responses that do not fundamentally alter or lower the standard or expectations. Modifications are changes that fundamentally alter or lower the standard or expectations of the learning activity (Portland Schools, 2011).

What are considered reasonable accommodations?

Reasonable accommodations are the steps teachers take to ensure that a student with a disability has access to classroom information and instruction. Examples of accommodations are (Portland Schools, 2011):

- presenting material in a different modality
- use of extended time on assignments or tests

- adaptive equipment
- alternative textbooks
- enlarged print or Braille materials
- a wheelchair ramp.

Examples of 504 accommodations include (New Mexico Public Education Department, 2011; Chambersburg School District, 2011; Campbell, 2011; School District of Reedsburg, 2008):

- ask frequent questions
- call student's name before asking a question
- enlarge or highlight key words on test items
- establish rules and review frequently
- give both oral and written directions
- group for cooperative learning
- have student repeat directions
- have student summarize at end of lesson
- highlight relevant words/features
- increase allocated time
- pause during speaking
- provide anticipated cues
- provide content/lecture summaries
- provide daily and weekly assignment sheets
- provide essential fact list
- provide pencil grips
- provide visual cues
- put desk close to blackboard
- reduce number of items on a task
- repeat major points
- seat child away from the doors/windows
- simplify or shorten directions
- tape paper to desk
- tape-record directions

- tape-record student responses

- use a study guide

- use computer for writing tasks

- use peer-mediated strategies ("buddy system")

- use self-teaching materials

- use timers to show allocated time.

Does the nature of services to which a student is entitled under Section 504 differ by educational level?

Yes. Public elementary and secondary schools are required to provide a free appropriate public education (FAPE) to qualified students with disabilities. Such an education consists of regular or special education and related aids and services designed to meet the individual educational needs of students with disabilities as adequately as the needs of students without disabilities are met.

At the postsecondary level, the institution is required to provide students with appropriate academic adjustments and auxiliary aids and services that are necessary to afford an individual with a disability an equal opportunity to participate in a school's program. Recipients are not required to make adjustments or provide aids or services that would result in a fundamental alteration of a recipient's program or impose an undue burden (U.S. Department of Education, 2010).

When should a 504 plan be considered?

There are four primary cases when a 504 plan should be considered (Wilmette Public Schools, 2011):

- When an IEP team determines that a child no longer requires an IEP and a 504 plan is needed to document the necessary general education accommodations or modifications to ensure ongoing student success.

- When an IEP team has conducted a case study and a student is found ineligible for special education under IDEA, the team will consider whether a disability under 504 is indicated.

- When there is an identified disability not covered by special education (remember, although there are literally hundreds of different types of disabilities, special education law only covers 13 specific types of disabilities).

- When a parent approaches a teacher with concerns that his/her child may have a disability that requires special instructional accommodations or program modifications.

Must a school district obtain parental consent prior to conducting an initial 504 evaluation?

Yes. Section 504 requires districts to obtain parental permission for initial evaluations. If a district suspects a student needs or is believed to need special instruction or related services and parental consent is withheld, IDEIA and Section 504 provide that districts may use due process hearing procedures to seek to override the parents' denial of consent for an initial evaluation (U.S. Department of Education, 2010).

What form of parental consent is required prior to conducting an initial 504 evaluation?

Section 504 is silent on the form of parental consent required. Written consent is accepted as compliance. IDEIA and many state laws also require written consent prior to initiating an evaluation (Menlo Park City School District, 2011).

What can a school district do if a parent withholds consent for a student to secure services under Section 504 after a student is determined eligible for services?

Section 504 neither prohibits nor requires a school district to initiate a due process hearing to override a parental refusal to consent with respect to the initial provision of special education and related services. Nonetheless, school districts should consider that IDEIA no longer permits school districts to initiate a due process hearing to override a parental refusal to consent to the initial provision of services (Mesa Public Schools, 2009).

What procedural safeguards are required under Section 504?

Recipient school districts are required to establish and implement procedural safeguards that include notice, an opportunity for parents to review relevant records, an impartial hearing with opportunity for participation by the student's parents or guardian, representation by counsel, and a review procedure (Watertown Public Schools, 2011).

What is a school district's responsibility under Section 504 to provide information to parents and students about its evaluation and placement process?

Section 504 requires districts to provide notice to parents explaining any evaluation and placement decisions affecting their children and explaining the parents' right to review education records and appeal any decision regarding evaluation and placement through an impartial hearing (U.S. Department of Education, 2010).

What is an appropriate evaluation under Section 504?

School districts must establish standards and procedures for initial evaluations and periodic reevaluations of students who need or are believed to need special education and/or related services because of disability. Section 504 regulations requires school districts to individually evaluate a student before classifying the student as having a disability or providing the student with special education [34 C.F.R. 104.35(b)]. Tests used for this purpose must be selected and administered so as best to ensure that the test results accurately reflect the student's aptitude or achievement or other factor being measured, rather than reflect the student's disability, except where those are the factors being measured. Section 504 also requires that tests and other evaluation materials include those tailored to evaluate the specific areas of educational need and not merely those designed to provide a single intelligence quotient. The tests and other evaluation materials must be validated for the specific purpose for which they are used and appropriately administered by trained personnel (New Mexico Public Education Department, 2011; U.S. Department of Education, 2010).

At the elementary and secondary education level, the amount of information required is determined by the multidisciplinary committee gathered to evaluate the student. The committee should include persons knowledgeable about the student, the meaning of the evaluation data, and the placement options. The committee members must determine if they have enough information to make a knowledgeable decision as to whether or not the student has a disability. Section 504 regulatory provision at 34 C.F.R. 104.35(c) requires that school districts draw from a variety of sources in the evaluation process so that the possibility of error is minimized [34 C.F.R. 104.35(c)]. The information obtained from all such sources must be documented and all significant factors related to the student's learning process must be considered. These sources and factors may include aptitude and achievement tests, teacher recommendations, physical condition, social and cultural background, and adaptive behavior. In evaluating a student suspected of having a disability, it is unacceptable to rely on presumptions and stereotypes regarding persons with disabilities or classes of such persons. Compliance with IDEIA regarding the group of persons present when an evaluation or placement decision is made is satisfactory under Section 504 (Nomura, 2011).

School districts may use the same process to evaluate the needs of students under Section 504 as they use to evaluate the needs of students under IDEIA. If school districts choose to adopt a separate process for evaluating the needs of students under Section 504, they must follow the requirements for evaluation specified in the Section 504 regulatory provision at 34 C.F.R. 104.35 (U.S. Department of Education, 2010).

May school districts consider "mitigating measures" used by a student in determining whether the student has a disability under Section 504?

No. As of January 1, 2009, school districts, in determining whether a student has a physical or mental impairment that substantially limits that student in a major life activity, must not consider the ameliorating effects of any mitigating measures that student is using. This is a change from prior law. Before January 1, 2009, school districts had to consider a student's use of mitigating measures in determining whether that student had a physical or mental impairment that substantially limited that student in a major life activity.

Congress did not define the term "mitigating measures," but rather provided a non-exhaustive list of "mitigating measures." Mitigating measures are devices or practices that a child uses to correct for or reduce the effects of his/her mental or physical impairment. Mitigating measures include (Northwest Area Education Agency, 2011):

- equipment or appliances

- hearing aids and cochlear implants or other implantable hearing devices

- learned behavioral or adaptive neurological modifications

- low-vision devices (which do not include ordinary eyeglasses or contact lenses)

- medical supplies

- medication

- mobility devices

- oxygen therapy equipment and supplies

- prosthetics (including limbs and devices)

- reasonable accommodations or auxiliary aids or services

- use of assistive technology.

Congress created one exception to the mitigating measures analysis. The ameliorative effects of the mitigating measures of ordinary eyeglasses or contact lenses shall be considered in determining if an impairment substantially limits a major life activity. "Ordinary eyeglasses or contact lenses" are lenses that are intended to fully correct visual acuity or eliminate refractive error, whereas "low-vision devices" (listed above) are devices that magnify, enhance, or otherwise augment a visual image.

School districts can no longer consider mitigation measures to determine whether an impairment substantially limits a major activity except for the use of ordinary eyeglasses or contact lenses. Congress stated that the determination whether an impairment substantially limits a major life activity shall be made without regard to ameliorative effects of mitigating measures such as medication, medical supplies, equipment, or other devices.

Is there any impairment that automatically determines a child to be eligible under Section 504?

No. An impairment in and of itself is not a disability. The impairment must substantially limit one or more major life activities in order to be considered a disability under Section 504 (Council Bluffs Community School District, 2011).

Can a medical diagnosis suffice as an evaluation for the purpose of providing FAPE?

No. A physician's medical diagnosis may be considered among other sources in evaluating a student with an impairment or believed to have an impairment that substantially limits a major life activity. Other sources to be considered, along with the medical diagnosis, include aptitude and achievement tests, teacher recommendations, physical condition, social and cultural background, and adaptive behavior. However, a physician's or psychologist's opinion as to a student's eligibility status is only one source of information the team should consider. Remember, the team is making an educational decision, not a medical decision. A physician or psychologist, though helpful in providing documentation of a physical or mental impairment, is not qualified to ultimately determine whether that impairment "substantially limits" a major life activity in a school setting. A mere medical diagnosis is not enough for eligibility (Menlo Park City School District, 2011).

Does a medical diagnosis of an illness automatically mean a student can receive services under Section 504?

No. A medical diagnosis of an illness does not automatically mean a student can receive services under Section 504. The illness must cause a substantial limitation on the student's ability to learn or another major life activity. For example, a student who has a physical or mental impairment would not be considered a student in need of services under Section 504 if the impairment does not in any way limit the student's ability to learn or other major life activity, or only results in some minor limitation in that regard (U.S. Department of Education, 2010).

Does a diagnosis of ADHD, depression, or diabetes mean a student should be identified as eligible for Section 504?

No. A student with one or more of these diagnoses may or may not meet the criteria for Section 504 accommodations. When compared to the average student, if the student is significantly restricted from performing the same activity as compared to the duration, condition, or manner under which the average person can perform that same activity, he/she may require a 504 plan. For example, if a student with ADHD is obtaining average grades in the same classes as other students, then it is likely he/she would not require 504 accommodations because the ADHD is not substantially limiting a major life activity (learning). Furthermore, a student with diabetes or a health-related disability could be placed on an individual health plan, not a 504 plan (Portland Schools, 2011).

How should a school district handle an outside independent evaluation?

The results of an outside independent evaluation may be one of many sources to consider. Multidisciplinary committees must draw from a variety of sources in the evaluation process so that the possibility of error is minimized. All significant factors related to the subject student's learning process must be considered. These sources and factors include aptitude and achievement tests, teacher recommendations, physical condition, social and cultural background, and adaptive behavior, among others. Information from all sources must be documented and considered by knowledgeable committee members. The weight of the information is determined by the committee given the student's individual circumstances (Campbell, 2011).

What should a school district do if a parent refuses to consent to an initial evaluation under IDEIA but demands a Section 504 plan for a student without further evaluation?

A school district must evaluate a student prior to providing services under Section 504. Section 504 requires parental consent for initial evaluations. If a parent refuses consent for an initial evaluation and a school district suspects a student has a disability, IDEIA and Section 504 provide that school districts may use due process hearing procedures to seek to override the parents' denial of consent (School District of Reedsburg, 2008).

Who makes the decision regarding a student's eligibility for services under Section 504?

Section 504 requires that school districts ensure that the determination that a student is eligible for special education and/or related aids and services be made by a group of persons, including persons knowledgeable about the meaning of the evaluation data and knowledgeable about the placement options. If a parent disagrees with the determination, he/she may request a due process hearing ([34 C.F.R.104.35(c)(3)]; Nomura, 2011).

Once a student is identified as eligible for services under Section 504, is that student always entitled to such services?

Yes, as long as the student remains eligible. The protections of Section 504 extend only to individuals who meet the regulatory definition of a person with a disability. If a recipient school district reevaluates a student and determines that the student's mental or physical impairment no longer substantially limits his/her ability to learn or any other major life activity, the student is no longer eligible for services under Section 504 (U.S. Department of Education, 2010).

Once a student is identified as eligible for services under Section 504, is there an annual or triennial review requirement?

Periodic reevaluation is required. This may be conducted in accordance with the IDEIA regulations, which require reevaluation at three-year intervals (unless the parent and public agency agree that reevaluation is unnecessary) or more frequently if conditions warrant, or if the child's parent or teacher requests a reevaluation, but not more than once a year (unless the parent and public agency agree otherwise) (Birthinjury.org, 2011).

What is a school district's responsibility under Section 504 toward a student with a Section 504 plan who transfers from another district?

If a student with a disability transfers to a district from another school district with a Section 504 plan, the receiving district should review the plan and supporting documentation. If a group of persons at the receiving school district, including persons knowledgeable about the meaning of the evaluation data and knowledgeable about the placement options, determines that the plan is appropriate, the district is required to implement the plan. If the district determines that the plan is inappropriate, the district must evaluate the student consistent with the Section 504 procedures [34 C.F.R. 104.35] and determine which educational program is appropriate for the student (Chambersburg School District, 2011).

What are the responsibilities of regular education teachers with respect to implementation of Section 504 plans?

Regular education teachers must implement the provisions of Section 504 plans when those plans govern the teachers' treatment of students for whom they are responsible. If the teachers fail to implement the plans, such failure can cause the school district to be in noncompliance with Section 504 (School District of Reedsburg, 2008).

Glossary of IDEIA Terms

34 C.F.R. 300.4 Act

Act means the Individuals with Disabilities Education Act, as amended.

[Authority: 20 U.S.C. 1400(a)]

34 C.F.R. 300.5 Assistive technology device

Assistive technology device means any item, piece of equipment, or product system, whether acquired commercially off the shelf, modified, or customized, that is used to increase, maintain, or improve the functional capabilities of a child with a disability. The term does not include a medical device that is surgically implanted, or the replacement of such device.

[Authority: 20 U.S.C. 1401(1)]

34 C.F.R. 300.6 Assistive technology service

Assistive technology service means any service that directly assists a child with a disability in the selection, acquisition, or use of an assistive technology device. The term includes—

(a) The evaluation of the needs of a child with a disability, including a functional evaluation of the child in the child's customary environment;

(b) Purchasing, leasing, or otherwise providing for the acquisition of assistive technology devices by children with disabilities;

(c) Selecting, designing, fitting, customizing, adapting, applying, maintaining, repairing, or replacing assistive technology devices;

(d) Coordinating and using other therapies, interventions, or services with assistive technology devices, such as those associated with existing education and rehabilitation plans and programs;

(e) Training or technical assistance for a child with a disability or, if appropriate, that child's family; and

(f) Training or technical assistance for professionals (including individuals providing education or rehabilitation services), employers, or other individuals who provide services to, employ, or are otherwise substantially involved in the major life functions of that child.

[Authority: 20 U.S.C. 1401(2)]

34 C.F.R. 300.7 Charter school

Charter school has the meaning given the term in section 5210(1) of the Elementary and Secondary Education Act of 1965, as amended, 20 U.S.C. 6301 *et seq.* (ESEA).

[Authority: 20 U.S.C. 7221i(1)]

34 C.F.R. 300.8 Child with a disability

(a) *General.* (1) *Child with a disability* means a child evaluated in accordance with 34 C.F.R. 300.304 through 300.311 as having mental retardation, a hearing impairment (including deafness), a speech or language impairment, a visual impairment (including blindness), a serious emotional disturbance (referred to in this part as "emotional disturbance"), an orthopedic impairment, autism, traumatic brain injury, an other health impairment, a specific learning disability, deaf-blindness, or multiple disabilities, and who, by reason thereof, needs special education and related services.

(2)(i) Subject to paragraph (a)(2)(ii) of this section, if it is determined, through an appropriate evaluation under 34 C.F.R. 34 C.F.R. 300.304 through 300.311, that a child has one of the disabilities identified in paragraph (a)(1) of this section, but only needs a related service and not special education, the child is not a child with a disability under this part.

(ii) If, consistent with 34 C.F.R. 300.39(a)(2), the related service required by the child is considered special education rather than a related service under State standards, the child would be determined to be a child with a disability under paragraph (a)(1) of this section.

(b) *Children aged three through nine experiencing developmental delays.* Child with a disability for children aged three through nine (or any subset of that age range, including ages three through five), may, subject to the conditions described in 34 C.F.R. 300.111(b), include a child—

(1) Who is experiencing developmental delays, as defined by the State and as measured by appropriate diagnostic instruments and procedures, in one or more of the following areas: Physical development, cognitive development, communication development, social or emotional development, or adaptive development; and

(2) Who, by reason thereof, needs special education and related services.

(c) *Definitions of disability terms.* The terms used in this definition of a child with a disability are defined as follows:

(1)(i) *Autism* means a developmental disability significantly affecting verbal and nonverbal communication and social interaction, generally evident before age three, that adversely affects a child's educational performance. Other characteristics often associated with autism are engagement in repetitive activities and stereotyped movements, resistance to environmental change or change in daily routines, and unusual responses to sensory experiences.

(ii) Autism does not apply if a child's educational performance is adversely affected primarily because the child has an emotional disturbance, as defined in paragraph (c)(4) of this section.

(iii) A child who manifests the characteristics of autism after age three could be identified as having autism if the criteria in paragraph (c)(1)(i) of this section are satisfied.

(2) *Deaf-blindness* means concomitant hearing and visual impairments, the combination of which causes such severe communication and other developmental and educational needs that they cannot be accommodated in special education programs solely for children with deafness or children with blindness.

(3) *Deafness* means a hearing impairment that is so severe that the child is impaired in processing linguistic information through hearing, with or without amplification, that adversely affects a child's educational performance.

(4)(i) *Emotional disturbance* means a condition exhibiting one or more of the following characteristics over a long period of time and to a marked degree that adversely affects a child's educational performance:

(A) An inability to learn that cannot be explained by intellectual, sensory, or health factors.

(B) An inability to build or maintain satisfactory interpersonal relationships with peers and teachers.

(C) Inappropriate types of behavior or feelings under normal circumstances.

(D) A general pervasive mood of unhappiness or depression.

(E) A tendency to develop physical symptoms or fears associated with personal or school problems.

(ii) Emotional disturbance includes schizophrenia. The term does not apply to children who are socially maladjusted, unless it is determined that they have an emotional disturbance under paragraph (c)(4)(i) of this section.

(5) *Hearing impairment* means an impairment in hearing, whether permanent or fluctuating, that adversely affects a child's educational performance but that is not included under the definition of deafness in this section.

(6) *Mental retardation* means significantly subaverage general intellectual functioning, existing concurrently with deficits in adaptive behavior and manifested during the developmental period, that adversely affects a child's educational performance.

(7) *Multiple disabilities* means concomitant impairments (such as mental retardation-blindness or mental retardation-orthopedic impairment), the combination of which causes such severe educational needs that they cannot be accommodated in special education programs solely for one of the impairments. Multiple disabilities does not include deaf-blindness.

(8) *Orthopedic impairment* means a severe orthopedic impairment that adversely affects a child's educational performance. The term includes impairments caused by a congenital anomaly, impairments caused by disease (e.g., poliomyelitis, bone tuberculosis), and impairments from other causes (e.g., cerebral palsy, amputations, and fractures or burns that cause contractures).

(9) *Other health impairment* means having limited strength, vitality, or alertness, including a heightened alertness to environmental stimuli, that results in limited alertness with respect to the educational environment, that—

(i) Is due to chronic or acute health problems such as asthma, attention deficit disorder or attention deficit hyperactivity disorder, diabetes, epilepsy, a heart condition, hemophilia, lead poisoning, leukemia, nephritis, rheumatic fever, sickle cell anemia, and Tourette syndrome; and

(ii) Adversely affects a child's educational performance.

(10) *Specific learning disability*—

(i) *General.* Specific learning disability means a disorder in one or more of the basic psychological processes involved in understanding or in using language, spoken or written, that may manifest itself in the imperfect ability to listen, think, speak, read, write, spell, or to do mathematical calculations, including conditions such as perceptual disabilities, brain injury, minimal brain dysfunction, dyslexia, and developmental aphasia.

(ii) *Disorders not included.* Specific learning disability does not include learning problems that are primarily the result of visual, hearing, or motor disabilities, of mental retardation, of emotional disturbance, or of environmental, cultural, or economic disadvantage.

(11) *Speech or language impairment* means a communication disorder, such as stuttering, impaired articulation, a language impairment, or a voice impairment, that adversely affects a child's educational performance.

(12) *Traumatic brain injury* means an acquired injury to the brain caused by an external physical force, resulting in total or partial functional disability or psychosocial impairment, or both, that adversely affects a child's educational performance.

Traumatic brain injury applies to open or closed head injuries resulting in impairments in one or more areas, such as cognition; language; memory; attention; reasoning; abstract thinking; judgment; problem-solving; sensory, perceptual, and motor abilities; psychosocial behavior; physical functions; information processing; and speech. Traumatic brain injury does not apply to brain injuries that are congenital or degenerative, or to brain injuries induced by birth trauma.

(13) *Visual impairment including blindness* means an impairment in vision that, even with correction, adversely affects a child's educational performance. The term includes both partial sight and blindness.

[Authority: 20 U.S.C. 1401(3); 1401(30)]

[71 FR 46753, Aug. 14, 2006, as amended at 72 FR 61306, Oct. 30, 2007]

34 C.F.R. 300.9 Consent

Consent means that—

(a) The parent has been fully informed of all information relevant to the activity for which consent is sought, in his or her native language, or through another mode of communication;

(b) The parent understands and agrees in writing to the carrying out of the activity for which his or her consent is sought, and the consent describes that activity and lists the records (if any) that will be released and to whom; and

(c)(1) The parent understands that the granting of consent is voluntary on the part of the parent and may be revoked at any time.

(2) If a parent revokes consent, that revocation is not retroactive (i.e., it does not negate an action that has occurred after the consent was given and before the consent was revoked).

(3) If the parent revokes consent in writing for their child's receipt of special education services after the child is initially provided special education and related services, the public agency is not required to amend the child's education records to remove any references to the child's receipt of special education and related services because of the revocation of consent.

[Authority: 20 U.S.C. 1414(a)(1)(D)]

[71 FR 46753, Aug. 14, 2006, as amended at 72 FR 61306, Oct. 30, 2007; 73 FR 73027, Dec. 1, 2008]

34 C.F.R. 300.10 Core academic subjects

Core academic subjects means English, reading or language arts, mathematics, science, foreign languages, civics and government, economics, arts, history, and geography.

[Authority: 20 U.S.C. 1401(4)]

34 C.F.R. 300.11 Day; business day; school day

(a) *Day* means calendar day unless otherwise indicated as business day or school day.

(b) *Business day* means Monday through Friday, except for Federal and State holidays (unless holidays are specifically included in the designation of business day, as in 34 C.F.R. 300.148(d)(1)(ii)).

(c)(1) *School day* means any day, including a partial day that children are in attendance at school for instructional purposes.

(2) *School day* has the same meaning for all children in school, including children with and without disabilities.

[Authority: 20 U.S.C. 1221e–3]

34 C.F.R. 300.12 Educational service agency

Educational service agency means—

(a) A regional public multiservice agency—

(1) Authorized by State law to develop, manage, and provide services or programs to LEAs;

(2) Recognized as an administrative agency for purposes of the provision of special education and related services provided within public elementary schools and secondary schools of the State;

(b) Includes any other public institution or agency having administrative control and direction over a public elementary school or secondary school; and

(c) Includes entities that meet the definition of intermediate educational unit in section 602(23) of the Act as in effect prior to June 4, 1997.

[Authority: 20 U.S.C. 1401(5)]

34 C.F.R. 300.13 Elementary school

Elementary school means a nonprofit institutional day or residential school, including a public elementary charter school, that provides elementary education, as determined under State law.

[Authority: 20 U.S.C. 1401(6)]

34 C.F.R. 300.14 Equipment

Equipment means—

(a) Machinery, utilities, and built-in equipment, and any necessary enclosures or structures to house the machinery, utilities, or equipment; and

(b) All other items necessary for the functioning of a particular facility as a facility for the provision of educational services, including items such as instructional equipment and necessary furniture; printed, published and audio-visual instructional materials; telecommunications, sensory, and other technological aids and devices; and books, periodicals, documents, and other related materials.

[Authority: 20 U.S.C. 1401(7)]

34 C.F.R. 300.15 Evaluation

Evaluation means procedures used in accordance with 34 C.F.R. 300.304 through 300.311 to determine whether a child has a disability and the nature and extent of the special education and related services that the child needs.

[Authority: 20 U.S.C. 1414(a) (c)

34 C.F.R. 300.16 Excess costs

Excess costs means those costs that are in excess of the average annual per-student expenditure in an LEA during the preceding school year for an elementary school or secondary school student, as may be appropriate, and that must be computed after deducting—

(a) Amounts received—

(1) Under Part B of the Act;

(2) Under Part A of title I of the ESEA; and

(3) Under Parts A and B of title III of the ESEA and;

(b) Any State or local funds expended for programs that would qualify for assistance under any of the parts described in paragraph (a) of this section, but excluding any amounts for capital outlay or debt service. (See Appendix A to part 300 for an example of how excess costs must be calculated.)

[Authority: 20 U.S.C. 1401(8)]

34 C.F.R. 300.17 Free appropriate public education

Free appropriate public education or *FAPE* means special education and related services that—

(a) Are provided at public expense, under public supervision and direction, and without charge;

(b) Meet the standards of the SEA, including the requirements of this part;

(c) Include an appropriate preschool, elementary school, or secondary school education in the State involved; and

(d) Are provided in conformity with an individualized education program (IEP) that meets the requirements of 34 C.F.R. 300.320 through 300.324.

[Authority: 20 U.S.C. 1401(9)]

34 C.F.R. 300.18 Highly qualified special education teachers

(a) *Requirements for special education teachers teaching core academic subjects.* For any public elementary or secondary school special education teacher teaching core academic subjects, the term highly qualified has the meaning given the term in section 9101 of the ESEA and 34 C.F.R. 200.56, except that the requirements for highly qualified also—

(1) Include the requirements described in paragraph (b) of this section; and

(2) Include the option for teachers to meet the requirements of section 9101 of the ESEA by meeting the requirements of paragraphs (c) and (d) of this section.

(b) *Requirements for special education teachers in general.* (1) When used with respect to any public elementary school or secondary school special education teacher teaching in a State, highly qualified requires that—

(i) The teacher has obtained full State certification as a special education teacher (including certification obtained through alternative routes to certification), or passed the State special education teacher licensing examination, and holds a license to teach in the State as a special education teacher, except that when used with respect to any teacher teaching in a public charter school, highly qualified means that the teacher meets the certification or licensing requirements, if any, set forth in the State's public charter school law;

(ii) The teacher has not had special education certification or licensure requirements waived on an emergency, temporary, or provisional basis; and

(iii) The teacher holds at least a bachelor's degree.

(2) A teacher will be considered to meet the standard in paragraph (b)(1)(i) of this section if that teacher is participating in an alternative route to special education certification program under which—

(i) The teacher—

(A) Receives high-quality professional development that is sustained, intensive, and classroom-focused in order to have a positive and lasting impact on classroom instruction, before and while teaching;

(B) Participates in a program of intensive supervision that consists of structured guidance and regular ongoing support for teachers or a teacher mentoring program;

(C) Assumes functions as a teacher only for a specified period of time not to exceed three years; and

(D) Demonstrates satisfactory progress toward full certification as prescribed by the State; and

(ii) The State ensures, through its certification and licensure process, that the provisions in paragraph (b)(2)(i) of this section are met.

(3) Any public elementary school or secondary school special education teacher teaching in a State, who is not teaching a core academic subject, is highly qualified if the teacher meets the requirements in paragraph (b)(1) or the requirements in (b)(1) (iii) and (b)(2) of this section.

(c) *Requirements for special education teachers teaching to alternate academic achievement standards.* When used with respect to a special education teacher who teaches core academic subjects exclusively to children who are assessed against alternate academic achievement standards established under 34 C.F.R. 200.1(d), highly qualified means the teacher, whether new or not new to the profession, may either—

(1) Meet the applicable requirements of section 9101 of the ESEA and 34 C.F.R. 200.56 for any elementary, middle, or secondary school teacher who is new or not new to the profession; or

(2) Meet the requirements of paragraph (B) or (C) of section 9101(23) of the ESEA as applied to an elementary school teacher, or, in the case of instruction above the elementary level, meet the requirements of paragraph (B) or (C) of section 9101(23) of the ESEA as applied to an elementary school teacher and have subject matter knowledge appropriate to the level of instruction being provided and needed to effectively teach to those alternate academic achievement standards, as determined by the State.

(d) *Requirements for special education teachers teaching multiple subjects.* Subject to paragraph (e) of this section, when used with respect to a special education teacher who teaches two or more core academic subjects exclusively to children with disabilities, highly qualified means that the teacher may either—

(1) Meet the applicable requirements of section 9101 of the ESEA and 34 C.F.R. 200.56(b) or (c);

(2) In the case of a teacher who is not new to the profession, demonstrate competence in all the core academic subjects in which the teacher teaches in the same manner as

is required for an elementary, middle, or secondary school teacher who is not new to the profession under 34 C.F.R. 200.56(c) which may include a single, high objective uniform State standard of evaluation (HOUSSE) covering multiple subjects; or

(3) In the case of a new special education teacher who teaches multiple subjects and who is highly qualified in mathematics, language arts, or science, demonstrate, not later than two years after the date of employment, competence in the other core academic subjects in which the teacher teaches in the same manner as is required for an elementary, middle, or secondary school teacher under 34 C.F.R. 200.56(c), which may include a single HOUSSE covering multiple subjects.

(e) Separate HOUSSE standards for special education teachers. Provided that any adaptations of the State's HOUSSE would not establish a lower standard for the content knowledge requirements for special education teachers and meet all the requirements for a HOUSSE for regular education teachers—

(1) A State may develop a separate HOUSSE for special education teachers; and

(2) The standards described in paragraph (e)(1) of this section may include single HOUSSE evaluations that cover multiple subjects.

(f) *Rule of construction.* Notwithstanding any other individual right of action that a parent or student may maintain under this part, nothing in this part shall be construed to create a right of action on behalf of an individual student or class of students for the failure of a particular SEA or LEA employee to be highly qualified, or to prevent a parent from filing a complaint under 34 C.F.R. 34 C.F.R. 300.151 through 300.153 about staff qualifications with the SEA as provided for under this part.

(g) *Applicability of definition to ESEA; and clarification of new special education teacher.* (1) A teacher who is highly qualified under this section is considered highly qualified for purposes of the ESEA.

(2) For purposes of 34 C.F.R. 300.18(d)(3), a fully certified regular education teacher who subsequently becomes fully certified or licensed as a special education teacher is a new special education teacher when first hired as a special education teacher.

(h) *Private school teachers not covered.* The requirements in this section do not apply to teachers hired by private elementary schools and secondary schools including private school teachers hired or contracted by LEAs to provide equitable services to parentally-placed private school children with disabilities under 34 C.F.R. 300.138.

[Authority: 20 U.S.C. 1401(10)]

[71 FR 46753, Aug. 14, 2006; 72 FR 61306, Oct. 30, 2007]

34 C.F.R. 300.19 Homeless children

Homeless children has the meaning given the term homeless children and youths in section 725 (42 U.S.C. 11434a) of the McKinney-Vento Homeless Assistance Act, as amended, 42 U.S.C. 11431 *et seq.*

[Authority: 20 U.S.C. 1401(11)]

34 C.F.R. 300.20 Include

Include means that the items named are not all of the possible items that are covered, whether like or unlike the ones named.

[Authority: 20 U.S.C. 1221e–3]

34 C.F.R. 300.21 Indian and Indian tribe

(a) *Indian* means an individual who is a member of an Indian tribe.

(b) *Indian tribe* means any Federal or State Indian tribe, band, rancheria, pueblo, colony, or community, including any Alaska Native village or regional village corporation (as defined in or established under the Alaska Native Claims Settlement Act, 43 U.S.C. 1601 *et seq.*).

(c) Nothing in this definition is intended to indicate that the Secretary of the Interior is required to provide services or funding to a State Indian tribe that is not listed in the Federal Register list of Indian entities recognized as eligible to receive services from the United States, published pursuant to Section 104 of the Federally Recognized Indian Tribe List Act of 1994, 25 U.S.C. 479a–1.

[Authority: 20 U.S.C. 1401(12) and (13)]

34 C.F.R. 300.22 Individualized education program

Individualized education program or *IEP* means a written statement for a child with a disability that is developed, reviewed, and revised in accordance with 34 C.F.R. 300.320 through 300.324.

[Authority: 20 U.S.C. 1401(14)]

34 C.F.R. 300.23 Individualized education program team

Individualized education program team or *IEP team* means a group of individuals described in 34 C.F.R. 300.321 that is responsible for developing, reviewing, or revising an IEP for a child with a disability.

[Authority: 20 U.S.C. 1414(d)(1)(B)]

34 C.F.R. 300.24 Individualized family service plan

Individualized family service plan or *IFSP* has the meaning given the term in section 636 of the Act.

[Authority: 20 U.S.C. 1401(15)]

34 C.F.R. 300.25 Infant or toddler with a disability

Infant or toddler with a disability—

(a) Means an individual under three years of age who needs early intervention services because the individual—

(1) Is experiencing developmental delays, as measured by appropriate diagnostic instruments and procedures in one or more of the areas of cognitive development, physical development, communication development, social or emotional development, and adaptive development; or

(2) Has a diagnosed physical or mental condition that has a high probability of resulting in developmental delay; and

(b) May also include, at a State's discretion—

(1) At-risk infants and toddlers; and

(2) Children with disabilities who are eligible for services under section 619 and who previously received services under Part C of the Act until such children enter, or are eligible under State law to enter, kindergarten or elementary school, as appropriate, provided that any programs under Part C of the Act serving such children shall include—

(i) An educational component that promotes school readiness and incorporates pre-literacy, language, and numeracy skills; and

(ii) A written notification to parents of their rights and responsibilities in determining whether their child will continue to receive services under Part C of the Act or participate in preschool programs under section 619.

[Authority: 20 U.S.C. 1401(16) and 1432(5)]

34 C.F.R. 300.26 Institution of higher education

Institution of higher education—

(a) Has the meaning given the term in section 101 of the Higher Education Act of 1965, as amended, 20 U.S.C. 1021 *et seq.* (HEA); and

(b) Also includes any community college receiving funds from the Secretary of the Interior under the Tribally Controlled Community College or University Assistance Act of 1978, 25 U.S.C. 1801 *et seq.*

[Authority: 20 U.S.C. 1401(17)]

34 C.F.R. 300.27 Limited English proficient

Limited English proficient has the meaning given the term in section 9101(25) of the ESEA.

[Authority: 20 U.S.C. 1401(18)]

34 C.F.R. 300.28 Local educational agency

(a) *General. Local educational agency* or *LEA* means a public board of education or other public authority legally constituted within a State for either administrative control or direction of, or to perform a service function for, public elementary or secondary schools in a city, county, township, school district, or other political subdivision of a State, or for a combination of school districts or counties as are recognized in a State as an administrative agency for its public elementary schools or secondary schools.

(b) *Educational service agencies and other public institutions or agencies.* The term includes—

(1) An educational service agency, as defined in 34 C.F.R. 300.12; and

(2) Any other public institution or agency having administrative control and direction of a public elementary school or secondary school, including a public nonprofit charter school that is established as an LEA under State law.

(c) *BIA funded schools.* The term includes an elementary school or secondary school funded by the Bureau of Indian Affairs, and not subject to the jurisdiction of any SEA other than the Bureau of Indian Affairs, but only to the extent that the inclusion makes the school eligible for programs for which specific eligibility is not provided to the school in another provision of law and the school does not have a student population that is smaller than the student population of the LEA receiving assistance under the Act with the smallest student population.

[Authority: 20 U.S.C. 1401(19)]

34 C.F.R. 300.29 Native language

(a) *Native language,* when used with respect to an individual who is limited English proficient, means the following:

(1) The language normally used by that individual, or, in the case of a child, the language normally used by the parents of the child, except as provided in paragraph (a)(2) of this section.

(2) In all direct contact with a child (including evaluation of the child), the language normally used by the child in the home or learning environment.

(b) For an individual with deafness or blindness, or for an individual with no written language, the mode of communication is that normally used by the individual (such as sign language, Braille, or oral communication).

[Authority: 20 U.S.C. 1401(20)]

34 C.F.R. 300.30 Parent

(a) *Parent* means—

(1) A biological or adoptive parent of a child;

(2) A foster parent, unless State law, regulations, or contractual obligations with a State or local entity prohibit a foster parent from acting as a parent;

(3) A guardian generally authorized to act as the child's parent, or authorized to make educational decisions for the child (but not the State if the child is a ward of the State);

(4) An individual acting in the place of a biological or adoptive parent (including a grandparent, stepparent, or other relative) with whom the child lives, or an individual who is legally responsible for the child's welfare; or

(5) A surrogate parent who has been appointed in accordance with 34 C.F.R. 300.519 or section 639(a)(5) of the Act.

(b)(1) Except as provided in paragraph (b)(2) of this section, the biological or adoptive parent, when attempting to act as the parent under this part and when more than one party is qualified under paragraph (a) of this section to act as a parent, must be presumed to be the parent for purposes of this section unless the biological or adoptive parent does not have legal authority to make educational decisions for the child.

(2) If a judicial decree or order identifies a specific person or persons under paragraphs (a)(1) through (4) of this section to act as the "parent" of a child or to make educational decisions on behalf of a child, then such person or persons shall be determined to be the "parent" for purposes of this section.

[Authority: 20 U.S.C. 1401(23)]

34 C.F.R. 300.31 Parent training and information center

Parent training and information center means a center assisted under sections 671 or 672 of the Act.

[Authority: 20 U.S.C. 1401(25)]

34 C.F.R. 300.32 Personally identifiable

Personally identifiable means information that contains—

(a) The name of the child, the child's parent, or other family member;

(b) The address of the child;

(c) A personal identifier, such as the child's social security number or student number; or

(d) A list of personal characteristics or other information that would make it possible to identify the child with reasonable certainty.

[Authority: 20 U.S.C. 1415(a)]

34 C.F.R. 300.33 Public agency

Public agency includes the SEA, LEAs, ESAs, nonprofit public charter schools that are not otherwise included as LEAs or ESAs and are not a school of an LEA or ESA, and any other political subdivisions of the State that are responsible for providing education to children with disabilities.

[Authority: 20 U.S.C. 1412(a)(11)]

34 C.F.R. 300.34 Related services

(a) *General. Related services* means transportation and such developmental, corrective, and other supportive services as are required to assist a child with a disability to benefit from special education, and includes speech-language pathology and audiology services, interpreting services, psychological services, physical and occupational therapy, recreation, including therapeutic recreation, early identification and assessment of disabilities in children, counseling services, including rehabilitation counseling, orientation and mobility services, and medical services for diagnostic or evaluation purposes. Related services also include school health services and school nurse services, social work services in schools, and parent counseling and training.

(b) *Exception*; services that apply to children with surgically implanted devices, including cochlear implants.

(1) Related services do not include a medical device that is surgically implanted, the optimization of that device's functioning (e.g., mapping), maintenance of that device, or the replacement of that device.

(2) Nothing in paragraph (b)(1) of this section—

(i) Limits the right of a child with a surgically implanted device (e.g., cochlear implant) to receive related services (as listed in paragraph (a) of this section) that are determined by the IEP Team to be necessary for the child to receive FAPE.

(ii) Limits the responsibility of a public agency to appropriately monitor and maintain medical devices that are needed to maintain the health and safety of the child, including breathing, nutrition, or operation of other bodily functions, while the child is transported to and from school or is at school; or

(iii) Prevents the routine checking of an external component of a surgically implanted device to make sure it is functioning properly, as required in 34 C.F.R. 300.113(b).

(c) *Individual related services terms defined.* The terms used in this definition are defined as follows:

(1) *Audiology* includes—

(i) Identification of children with hearing loss;

(ii) Determination of the range, nature, and degree of hearing loss, including referral for medical or other professional attention for the habilitation of hearing;

(iii) Provision of habilitative activities, such as language habilitation, auditory training, speech reading (lip-reading), hearing evaluation, and speech conservation;

(iv) Creation and administration of programs for prevention of hearing loss;

(v) Counseling and guidance of children, parents, and teachers regarding hearing loss; and

(vi) Determination of children's needs for group and individual amplification, selecting and fitting an appropriate aid, and evaluating the effectiveness of amplification.

(2) *Counseling services* means services provided by qualified social workers, psychologists, guidance counselors, or other qualified personnel.

(3) *Early identification and assessment of disabilities in children* means the implementation of a formal plan for identifying a disability as early as possible in a child's life.

(4) *Interpreting services* includes—

(i) The following, when used with respect to children who are deaf or hard of hearing: Oral transliteration services, cued language transliteration services, sign language transliteration and interpreting services, and transcription services, such as communication access real-time translation (CART), C-Print, and TypeWell; and

(ii) Special interpreting services for children who are deaf-blind.

(5) *Medical services* means services provided by a licensed physician to determine a child's medically related disability that results in the child's need for special education and related services.

(6) *Occupational therapy*—

(i) Means services provided by a qualified occupational therapist; and

(ii) Includes—

(A) Improving, developing, or restoring functions impaired or lost through illness, injury, or deprivation;

(B) Improving ability to perform tasks for independent functioning if functions are impaired or lost; and

(C) Preventing, through early intervention, initial or further impairment or loss of function.

(7) *Orientation and mobility services*—

(i) Means services provided to blind or visually impaired children by qualified personnel to enable those students to attain systematic orientation to and safe movement within their environments in school, home, and community; and

(ii) Includes teaching children the following, as appropriate:

(A) Spatial and environmental concepts and use of information received by the senses (such as sound, temperature and vibrations) to establish, maintain, or regain orientation and line of travel (e.g., using sound at a traffic light to cross the street);

(B) To use the long cane or a service animal to supplement visual travel skills or as a tool for safely negotiating the environment for children with no available travel vision;

(C) To understand and use remaining vision and distance low vision aids; and

(D) Other concepts, techniques, and tools.

(8)(i) *Parent counseling and training* means assisting parents in understanding the special needs of their child;

(ii) Providing parents with information about child development; and

(iii) Helping parents to acquire the necessary skills that will allow them to support the implementation of their child's IEP or IFSP.

(9) *Physical therapy* means services provided by a qualified physical therapist.

(10) *Psychological services* includes—

(i) Administering psychological and educational tests, and other assessment procedures;

(ii) Interpreting assessment results;

(iii) Obtaining, integrating, and interpreting information about child behavior and conditions relating to learning;

(iv) Consulting with other staff members in planning school programs to meet the special educational needs of children as indicated by psychological tests, interviews, direct observation, and behavioral evaluations;

(v) Planning and managing a program of psychological services, including psychological counseling for children and parents; and

(vi) Assisting in developing positive behavioral intervention strategies.

(11) *Recreation* includes—

(i) Assessment of leisure function;

(ii) Therapeutic recreation services;

(iii) Recreation programs in schools and community agencies; and

(iv) Leisure education.

(12) *Rehabilitation counseling services* means services provided by qualified personnel in individual or group sessions that focus specifically on career development, employment preparation, achieving independence, and integration in the workplace and community of a student with a disability. The term also includes vocational rehabilitation services provided to a student with a disability by vocational rehabilitation programs funded under the Rehabilitation Act of 1973, as amended, 29 U.S.C. 701 *et seq.*

(13) *School health services and school nurse services* means health services that are designed to enable a child with a disability to receive FAPE as described in the child's IEP. School nurse services are services provided by a qualified school nurse. School health services are services that may be provided by either a qualified school nurse or other qualified person.

(14) *Social work services in schools* includes—

(i) Preparing a social or developmental history on a child with a disability;

(ii) Group and individual counseling with the child and family;

(iii) Working in partnership with parents and others on those problems in a child's living situation (home, school, and community) that affect the child's adjustment in school;

(iv) Mobilizing school and community resources to enable the child to learn as effectively as possible in his or her educational program; and

(v) Assisting in developing positive behavioral intervention strategies.

(15) *Speech-language pathology services* includes—

(i) Identification of children with speech or language impairments;

(ii) Diagnosis and appraisal of specific speech or language impairments;

(iii) Referral for medical or other professional attention necessary for the habilitation of speech or language impairments;

(iv) Provision of speech and language services for the habilitation or prevention of communicative impairments; and

(v) Counseling and guidance of parents, children, and teachers regarding speech and language impairments.

(16) *Transportation* includes—

(i) Travel to and from school and between schools;

(ii) Travel in and around school buildings; and

(iii) Specialized equipment (such as special or adapted buses, lifts, and ramps), if required to provide special transportation for a child with a disability.

[Authority: 20 U.S.C. 1401(26)]

34 C.F.R. 300.35 Scientifically based research

Scientifically based research has the meaning given the term in section 9101(37) of the ESEA.

[Authority: 20 U.S.C. 1411(e)(2)(C)(xi)]

34 C.F.R. 300.36 Secondary school

Secondary school means a nonprofit institutional day or residential school, including a public secondary charter school that provides secondary education, as determined under State law, except that it does not include any education beyond grade 12.

[Authority: 20 U.S.C. 1401(27)]

34 C.F.R. 300.37 Services plan

Services plan means a written statement that describes the special education and related services the LEA will provide to a parentally-placed child with a disability enrolled in a private school who has been designated to receive services, including the location of the services and any transportation necessary, consistent with 34 C.F.R. 300.132, and is developed and implemented in accordance with 34 C.F.R. 300.137 through 300.139.

[Authority: 20 U.S.C. 1412(a)(10)(A)]

34 C.F.R. 300.38 Secretary

Secretary means the Secretary of Education.

[Authority: 20 U.S.C. 1401(28)]

34 C.F.R. 300.39 Special education

(a) *General.* (1) *Special education* means specially designed instruction, at no cost to the parents, to meet the unique needs of a child with a disability, including—

(i) Instruction conducted in the classroom, in the home, in hospitals and institutions, and in other settings; and

(ii) Instruction in physical education.

(2) Special education includes each of the following, if the services otherwise meet the requirements of paragraph (a)(1) of this section—

(i) Speech-language pathology services, or any other related service, if the service is considered special education rather than a related service under State standards;

(ii) Travel training; and

(iii) Vocational education.

(b) *Individual special education terms defined.* The terms in this definition are defined as follows:

(1) *At no cost* means that all specially-designed instruction is provided without charge, but does not preclude incidental fees that are normally charged to nondisabled students or their parents as a part of the regular education program.

(2) *Physical education* means—

(i) The development of—

(A) Physical and motor fitness;

(B) Fundamental motor skills and patterns; and

(C) Skills in aquatics, dance, and individual and group games and sports (including intramural and lifetime sports); and

(ii) Includes special physical education, adapted physical education, movement education, and motor development.

(3) *Specially designed instruction* means adapting, as appropriate to the needs of an eligible child under this part, the content, methodology, or delivery of instruction—

(i) To address the unique needs of the child that result from the child's disability; and

(ii) To ensure access of the child to the general curriculum, so that the child can meet the educational standards within the jurisdiction of the public agency that apply to all children.

(4) *Travel training* means providing instruction, as appropriate, to children with significant cognitive disabilities, and any other children with disabilities who require this instruction, to enable them to—

(i) Develop an awareness of the environment in which they live; and

(ii) Learn the skills necessary to move effectively and safely from place to place within that environment (e.g., in school, in the home, at work, and in the community).

(5) *Vocational education* means organized educational programs that are directly related to the preparation of individuals for paid or unpaid employment, or for additional preparation for a career not requiring a baccalaureate or advanced degree.

[Authority: 20 U.S.C. 1401(29)]

34 C.F.R. 300.40 State

State means each of the 50 States, the District of Columbia, the Commonwealth of Puerto Rico, and each of the outlying areas.

[Authority: 20 U.S.C. 1401(31)]

34 C.F.R. 300.41 State educational agency

State educational agency or *SEA* means the State board of education or other agency or officer primarily responsible for the State supervision of public elementary schools and secondary schools, or, if there is no such officer or agency, an officer or agency designated by the Governor or by State law.

[Authority: 20 U.S.C. 1401(32)]

34 C.F.R. 300.42 Supplementary aids and services

Supplementary aids and services means aids, services, and other supports that are provided in regular education classes, other education-related settings, and in extracurricular and nonacademic settings, to enable children with disabilities to be educated with nondisabled children to the maximum extent appropriate in accordance with 34 C.F.R. 34 C.F.R. 300.114 through 300.116.

[Authority: 20 U.S.C. 1401(33)]

34 C.F.R. 300.43 Transition services

(a) *Transition services* means a coordinated set of activities for a child with a disability that—

(1) Is designed to be within a results-oriented process, that is focused on improving the academic and functional achievement of the child with a disability to facilitate the child's movement from school to post-school activities, including postsecondary education, vocational education, integrated employment (including supported employment), continuing and adult education, adult services, independent living, or community participation;

(2) Is based on the individual child's needs, taking into account the child's strengths, preferences, and interests; and includes—

(i) Instruction;

(ii) Related services;

(iii) Community experiences;

(iv) The development of employment and other post-school adult living objectives; and

(v) If appropriate, acquisition of daily living skills and provision of a functional vocational evaluation.

(b) Transition services for children with disabilities may be special education, if provided as specially designed instruction, or a related service, if required to assist a child with a disability to benefit from special education.

[Authority: 20 U.S.C. 1401(34)]

34 C.F.R. 300.44 Universal design

Universal design has the meaning given the term in section 3 of the Assistive Technology Act of 1998, as amended, 29 U.S.C. 3002.

[Authority: 20 U.S.C. 1401(35)]

34 C.F.R. 300.45 Ward of the State

(a) *General.* Subject to paragraph (b) of this section, *ward of the State* means a child who, as determined by the State where the child resides, is—

(1) A foster child;

(2) A ward of the State; or

(3) In the custody of a public child welfare agency.

(b) *Exception.* Ward of the State does not include a foster child who has a foster parent who meets the definition of a parent in 34 C.F.R. 300.30.

[Authority: 20 U.S.C. 1401(36)]

References

The CFR material in the references can be accessed online at http://ecfr.gpoaccess.gov.

Chapter 1

20 U.S.C. 1400

20 U.S.C. 1401

20 U.S.C. 1412

34 C.F.R. 300.1

34 C.F.R. 300.8

34 C.F.R. 300.17

34 C.F.R. 300.39

34 C.F.R. 300.117

34 C.F.R. 300.320

117 Cong. Rec. 45, 974 (1971).

Brown v. Board of Education of Topeka, 347 U.S. 483 (1954).

Council for Exceptional Children (2002) *Understanding the Differences Between IDEIA and Section 504*. Available at www.ldonline.org/article/6086, accessed on May 12, 2011.

Diagnostic Center of Northern California (2010) *What is Section 504?* Available at www.dcn-cde. ca.gov/504/Units/UnitIII.htm, accessed on May 12, 2011.

LDOnline (2010) *IDEA 2004*. Available at www.ldonline.org/features/idea2004, accessed on June 2, 2011.

Mills v. Board of Education of District of Columbia, 348 Supp. 866, C.D. DC (1972).

National Dissemination Center for Children with Disabilities (2010) *Special Education*. Available at http://nichcy.org/schoolage/iep/iepcontents/specialeducation, accessed on June 1, 2011.

Office of Special Education and Rehabilitative Services (2000) *A Guide to the Individualized Education Program*. Available at www2.ed.gov/parents/needs/speced/iepguide/index.html, accessed on May 12, 2011.

PARC v. Commonwealth of Pennsylvania, 343 F. Supp. 279, E.D. PA (1972).

Pierangelo, R. and Giuliani, G. (2008) *Assessment in Special Education: A Practical Approach* (3rd edition). Boston, MA: Allyn and Bacon.

Plessy v. Ferguson, 163 U.S. 537 (1896).

President's Panel on Mental Retardation (1962) *A Proposed Program for National Action to Combat Mental Retardation*. Washington, DC: Superintendent of Documents.

Pulsifer, L. (2010) *The Four Major Parts of the Individuals with Disabilities Education Act*. Available at www.ehow.com/list_6577548_four-individuals-disabilities-education-act.html, accessed on June 2, 2011.

The Rehabilitation Act of 1973 (RA), 29 U.S.C. 701 *et seq.*

U.S. Department of Education (2011) *Digest of Education Statistics: 2009* (Table 50). Washington, DC: Author.

Chapter 2

20 U.S.C. 1401

20 U.S.C. 1415

42 U.S.C. 11434

34 C.F.R. 300.20

34 C.F.R. 300.30

34 C.F.R 300.45

34 C.F.R. 300.519

34 C.F.R. 300.520

Adoption Media LLC (2011a) *Adoption.* Available at http://glossary.adoption.com/adoption.html, accessed on June 1, 2011.

Adoption Media LLC (2011b) *Foster Parents.* Available at http://glossary.adoption.com/foster-parents.html, accessed on July 3, 2011.

Education Law Center (2007) *Who Can Make Special Education Decisions for a Child with a Disability in Out-of-Home Care in Pennsylvania?* Available at www.drnpa.org/File/publications/who-can-make-special-education-decisions-for-a-child-with-a-disability-in-out-of-home-care-in-pennsylvania-.pdf, accessed on May 11, 2011.

Judicial Council of California (1995) *Probate Guardianship Pamphlet.* Available at www.markwelch.com/law/gc205.htm, accessed on June 22, 2011.

Legal Services of Missouri (2006) *Who Can Represent the Interests of a Special Education Student?* Available at www.lsmo.org/Home/PublicWeb/Library/Documents/1083697149.72/Who%20Has%20Rights(2.8).htm?topic_id=1111300&library=PublicWeb#FosterParents, accessed on June 18, 2011.

National Center on Secondary Education and Transition (2002) *Age of Majority: Preparing Your Child to Make Their Own Choices.* Minneapolis, MN: Author.

Ohio Legal Rights Service (2005) *Surrogate Parents for Children with Disabilities.* Available at www.olrs.ohio.gov/faq-surrogate#cannot, accessed on June 22, 2011.

Taylor v. Vermont Department of Education, 313 F.3d768, 777 (2d Cir., 2002).

Chapter 3

20 U.S.C. 1401

20 U.S.C. 1412

34 C.F.R. 300.17

34 C.F.R. 300.39

34 C.F.R. 300.101

34 C.F.R. 300.102

34 C.F.R. 300.154

Arkansas Department of Education (2011) *Frequently Asked Questions Related to Billing for the School-Based Medicaid Program.* Available at http://arksped.k12.ar.us/documents/faqs/MedicaidBillingFaq.pdf, accessed on July 17, 2011.

Guersney, T.F. and Klare, K. (2008) *Special Education Law* (3rd edition). Durham, NC: Carolina Academic Press.

Hendrick Hudson District Board of Education v. Rowley. 458 U.S. 176 (1982).

Johnson, S.F. (2003) "Reexamining Rowley: A new focus in special education law." *Brigham Young University Education and Law Journal 2,* 561.

Letter to Greer (1992) 19 IDELR 348, OSEP.

MedStat (n.d.) *Medicaid Billings for IDEA Services: Analysis and Policy Implications of Site Visit Results.* Available at http://aspe.hhs.gov/health/reports/99/IDEA/report.pdf, accessed on July 7, 2011.

PACER Center: Families and Advocates Partnership for Education (2011) *Facts on Hand: Third Party Payments.* Available at www.fape.org/pubs/fape-31.pdf, accessed on July 7, 2011.

Sen. Rep. No. 168, 94th Congress, 1st Session (1975).

St Cyr, T.S. (2011) *The Anatomy of a Special Education Due Process Claim.* Available at www.edlawsoup.com/journal/2011/6/3/the-anatomy-of-a-special-education-due-process-claim.html, accessed on July 12, 2011.

U.S. Department of Education (2010) *Free Appropriate Public Education for Students with Disabilities: Requirements under Section 504 of the Rehabilitation Act of 1973. Available at* www2.ed.gov/about/offices/list/ocr/docs/edlite-FAPE504.html, accessed on July 3, 2011.

Chapter 4

20 U.S.C. 1401

20 U.S.C. 1414

20 U.S.C. 1415

34 C.F.R. 300.9

34 C.F.R. 300.30

34 C.F.R. 300.12

34 C.F.R. 300.121

34 C.F.R. 300.300

34 C.F.R. 300.321

34 C.F.R. 300.503

34 C.F.R. 300.504

34 C.F.R. 300.505

34 C.F.R. 300.622

Arkansas Department of Education (2011) *Special Education: Your Rights under the IDEA.* Available at http://arksped.k12.ar.us/documents/policy/rulesandregulations/A4.pdf, accessed on August 3, 2011.

Hamilton County Educational Service Center (2011) *Providing Special Education Documents to Parents Who Do Not Speak English: Required Practices and Culturally Responsive Practices.* Available at www.hcesc.org/resources/Culturally%20Responsive%20Practice/CulturallyRespons.pdf, accessed on August 5, 2011.

Indiana Department of Education (2011) *Notice of Procedural Safeguards and Parent Rights in Special Education.* Available at www.deafhoosiers.com/Outreach/document/NoticeofProceduralSafeguardswAddendum_000.pdf, accessed on August 10, 2011.

National Association of Special Education Teachers (2011) *Week in Review—June 3, 2011*, 7(20). Available at www.naset.org/3294.0.html, accessed on June 19, 2011.

National Dissemination for Children with Disabilities (2009) *Questions and Answers about IDEA: Parent Participation.* Available at http://nichcy.org/schoolage/qa-series-on-idea/qa2#ref28, accessed on August 15, 2011.

Pierangelo, R. and Giuliani, G. (2012) *Assessment in Special Education: A Practical Approach* (4th edition). Boston, MA: Allyn and Bacon.

Texas Education Agency, Division of IDEA Coordination (2006) *Notice of Procedural Safeguards: Rights of Parents of Students with Disabilities.* Available at www.hitchcockisd.org/pages/uploaded_files/Procedural%20Safeguards-English.pdf, accessed on August 3, 2011.

U.S. Department of Education (2010) *Questions and Answers on Individualized Education Programs (IEP's), Evaluations and Reevaluations.* Available at http://idea.ed.gov/explore/view/p/,root,dynamic,QaCorner,3, accessed on August 12, 2011.

Chapter 5

20 U.S.C.1401

20 U.S.C. 1412

20 U.S.C. 1414

34 C.F.R. 300.111

34 C.F.R 300.300

34 C.F.R. 300.301

34 C.F.R. 300.302

34 C.F.R. 300.303

34 C.F.R. 300.304

34 C.F.R. 300.305

34 C.F.R. 300.306

34 C.F.R. 300.315

34 C.F.R. 300.502

Alaska State Department of Education (2007) *Alaska State Special Education Handbook.* Available at www.eed.state.ak.us/tls/sped/handbook/Part_II_Identification.doc, accessed on June 11, 2011.

Guersney, T.F. and Klare, K. (2008) *Special Education Law* (3rd edition). Durham, NC: Carolina Academic Press.

Imber, S.C. and Cortiella, C. (2010) *Independent Educational Evaluations: It's a Testy Business!* Available at www.specialeducationadvisor.com/independent-educational-evaluations-iee, accessed on November 4, 2011.

Pierangelo, R. and Giuliani, G. (2008) *Understanding Assessment in the Special Education Process: A Step-by-Step Guide for Educators.* Thousand Oaks, CA: Corwin Press.

Pierangelo, R. and Giuliani, G. (2012) *Assessment in Special Education: A Practical Approach* (4th edition). Boston: Allyn and Bacon.

Chapter 6

20 U.S.C. 1221

20 U.S.C. 1401

20 U.S.C. 1414

34 C.F.R. 300.306

34 C.F.R. 300.307

34 C.F.R. 300.310

34 C.F.R. 300.311

Minnesota Department of Education (2004) *Special Education Evaluation and Services for Students with Traumatic Brain Injury: A Manual for Minnesota Educators.* Minneapolis, MN: Author. Available at http://specialed.spps.org/uploads/TraumaticBrainInjuryMnl.pdf, accessed on February 27 2012.

Pierangelo, R. and Giuliani, G. (2007a) *Special Education Eligibility: A Step-by-Step Guide for Educators.* Thousand Oaks, CA: Corwin Press.

Pierangelo, R. and Giuliani, G. (2007b) *EDM: The Educator's Diagnostic Manual of Disabilities and Disorders.* San Francisco, CA: Jossey Bass/John Wiley and Sons.

Pierangelo, R. and Giuliani, G. (2012) *Assessment in Special Education: A Practical Approach* (4th edition). Boston, MA: Allyn and Bacon.

Chapter 7

20 U.S.C. 1401

29 U.S.C. 701

34 C.F.R. 300.17

34 C.F.R. 300.24

34 C.F.R. 300.34

34 C.F.R. 300.39

34 C.F.R. 300.101

34 C.F.R. 300.107

34 C.F.R. 300.114

34 C.F.R. 300.117

34 C.F.R. 300.123

34 C.F.R. 300.320

34 C.F.R. 300.324

Adoption Media (2011) *Travel Training for Youth with Disabilities*. Available at http://special-needs.adoption.com/children/travel-training-for-youth-with-disabilities.html, accessed on July 3, 2011.

Cedar Rapids Community School District v. Garret F., 526 U.S. 66 (1999).

Classroom Interpreting.org (2011) *Classroom interpreting: Parents—What Does Special Education Law Say about Educational Interpreters?* Available at http://classroominterpreting.org/Parents/Law.asp, accessed on August 2, 2011.

Community Alliance for Special Education (2005) *Special Education Rights and Responsibilities*. Available at www.dredf.org/special_education/trainings-11-17-11/Update-SERR-cover-page.pdf, accessed on 20 February 2012.

Families and Advocates Partnership for Education (2011) *Facts on Hand: Related Services*. Available at www.fape.org/pubs/fape-33.pdf, accessed on August 18, 2011.

Guersney, T.F. and Klare, K. (2008) *Special Education Law* (3rd edition). Durham, NC: Carolina Academic Press.

Hendrick Hudson District Board of Education v. Rowley, 458 U.S. 176 (1982).

Los Angeles Unified School District (2011a) *Occupational Therapy and Physical Therapy*. Available at www.teachinla.com/cert/ot_pt.html, accessed on July 30, 2011.

Los Angeles Unified School District (2011b) *Speech and Language Therapy*. Available at www.teachinla.com/cert/language_speech.html, accessed on July 30, 2011.

Misericordia Community Hospital and Health Centre (2011) *What is Audiology?* Available at www.caritas.ab.ca/ther_new/audiology/whatis.html, accessed on August 1, 2011.

National Dissemination Center for Children with Disabilities (2010) *Related Services*. Available at http://nichcy.org/schoolage/iep/iepcontents/relatedservices, accessed on July 30, 2011.

National Information Center for Children and Youth with Disabilities (1996) *Travel Training for Youth with Disabilities*. Available at http://nichcy.org/wp-content/uploads/docs/ts9.pdf, accessed on July 4, 2011.

New York City Department of Education (2011a) *Occupational Therapy (OT)*. Available at http://schools.nyc.gov/Offices/District75/Departments/RelatedServices/OT/default.htm, accessed on July 31, 2011.

New York City Department of Education (2011b) *Physical Therapy (PT)*. Available at http://schools.nyc.gov/Offices/District75/Departments/RelatedServices/PT/default, accessed on July 29, 2011.

New York City Department of Education (2011d) *Special Education Services*. Available at http://schools.nyc.gov/NR/rdonlyres/C7A58626-6637-42E7-AD00-70440820661D/0/ContinuumofServices.pdf, accessed on July 2, 2011.

North Carolina Recreational Therapy (2011) *How Can Recreation Be Included as a "Related Service" in My Child's IEP?* Available at www.ncrta.org/consumer/related.htm, accessed on July 14, 2011.

Pierangelo, R. and Giuliani, G. (2012) *Assessment in Special Education: A Practical Approach* (4th edition). Boston, MA: Allyn and Bacon.

Texas Education Agency: Division of IDEA Coordination (2008) *Related Services for Students with Disabilities—Questions and Answers*. Available at http://ritter.tea.state.tx.us/special.ed/resources/relservqna.pdf, accessed on August 14, 2011.

Chapter 8

20 U.S.C. 1401

20 U.S.C. 1412

20 U.S.C. 1414

34 C.F.R. 99.31

34 C.F.R. 300.5

34 C.F.R. 300.6

34 C.F.R. 300.22

34 C.F.R. 300.23

34 C.F.R. 300.43

34 C.F.R. 300.101

34 C.F.R. 300.102

34 C.F.R. 300.116

34 C.F.R. 300.320

34 C.F.R. 300.321

34 C.F.R. 300.322

34 C.F.R. 300.323

34 C.F.R. 300.324

34 C.F.R. 300.325

34 C.F.R. 300.328

34 C.F.R. 303.106

Advocacy Institute (2007) *Transition Planning: Five Themes Addressed in Administrative and Judicial Decisions.* Available at www.advocacyinstitute.org/advocacyinaction/TransitionPlanning.shtml, accessed on August 11, 2011.

Assistive Technology Partnership (2008) *Assistive Technology in Education.* Available at www.atp.ne.gov/techassist/recycle-etc.html, accessed on July 16, 2011.

California Department of Education (2011) *Assistive Technology.* Available at www.cde.ca.gov/sp/se/sr/astvtech.asp, accessed on July 16, 2011.

Concord Special Education Parent Advisory Committee (2011) *Extended School Year (ESY) Services.* Available at www.concordspedpac.org/ESY.html, accessed on June 3, 2011.

Educational Service Unit 2 (2008) *Present Level of Educational Performance (PLEP).* Available at www.esu2.org/pages/ILCD/PLEPandGoalsHandout.pdf, accessed on July 2, 2011.

Florida Department of Education (2001) *Present Levels of Educational Performance: Technical Assistance Document.* Available at www.fldoe.org/ese/pdf/ieplevel.pdf, accessed on July 2, 2011.

Island Tress Union Free School District (2010) *Transition Plan: Transition from School to Post-School for Students with Disabilities.* Island Trees, NY: Nassau BOCES.

Maryland State Department of Education (1999) *Resource Information on Extended School Year Services.* Available at www.montgomeryschoolsmd.org/departments/specialed/resources/tab/FY03ESY.pdf, accessed on June 3, 2011.

National Association of Special Education Teachers (2011) *How to Determine Measurable Annual Goals in an IEP*. Available at www.naset.org/760.0.html, accessed on July 2, 2011.

National Center on Secondary Education and Transition (2002) *Age of Majority: Preparing Your Child for Making Good Choices*. Minneapolis, MN: University of Minnesota.

National Dissemination Center for Children with Disabilities (2010) *Special Education*. Available at http://nichcy.org/schoolage/iep/iepcontents/specialeducation, accessed on June 25, 2011.

National Transition Network (1996) *Transition Planning for Success in Adult Life*. Minneapolis, MN: PACER Center.

New York City Department of Education (2004) *Creating a Quality IEP*. New York, NY: Division of Teaching and Learning Office of Special Education Initiatives.

New York City Department of Education, Office of Special Education Initiatives (2011) *Special Education Services*. Available at http://schools.nyc.gov/NR/rdonlyres/C7A58626-6637-42E7-AD00-70440820661D/0/ContinuumofServices.pdf, accessed on July 1, 2011.

PAVE (2011) *Technology and the IEP*. Available at www.wapave.org/RES/packets/23pt.pdf, accessed on July 16, 2011.

Pierangelo, R. and Giuliani, G. (2007) *Understanding, Developing, and Writing Effective IEPs: A Step-by-Step Guide for Educators*. Thousand Oaks, CA: Corwin Press.

Pierangelo, R. and Giuliani, G.A. (2009) "The importance of individualized education programs in family law." *New York State Bar Association Family Law Review 41*, 3, 16–26.

Pierangelo, R. and Giuliani, G. (2012) *Assessment in Special Education: A Practical Approach* (4th edition). Boston, MA: Allyn and Bacon.

Reusch v. Fountain, 872 F.Supp. 1421 (D. MD 1994).

Chapter 9

20 U.S.C. 1401

20 U.S.C. 1412

34 C.F.R. 300.38

34 C.F.R. 300.42

34 C.F.R. 300.104

34 C.F.R. 300.106

34 C.F.R. 300.114

34 C.F.R. 300.115

34 C.F.R. 300.116

34 C.F.R. 300.117

34 C.F.R. 300.137

34 C.F.R. 300.146

Alaska State Department of Education (2007) *Alaska State Special Education Handbook*. Available at www.eed.state.ak.us/tls/sped/handbook/Part_V_Placement.doc, accessed on June 11, 2011.

Georgia Department of Education (2011) *Frequently Asked Questions Regarding LRE*. Available at www.doe.k12.ga.us/DMGetDocument.aspx/Frequently_Asked_Questions_Regarding_LRE. pdf?p=6CC6799F8C1371F6A4793945CC17E723333AA630EAB1186A8B437735B37 FC12C&Type=D, accessed on July 2, 2011.

Guersney, T.F. and Klare, K. (2008) *Special Education Law* (3rd edition). Durham, NC: Carolina Academic Press.

Illinois State Board of Education (2011) *Educational Rights and Responsibilities: Understanding Special Education in Illinois*. Available at www.isbe.state.il.us/SPEC-ED/pdfs/parent_guide/ch7-lre. pdf, accessed on July 12, 2011.

New York City Department of Education, Office of Special Education Initiatives (2011) *Special Education Services*. Available at http://schools.nyc.gov/NR/rdonlyres/C7A58626-6637-42E7-AD00-70440820661D/0/ContinuumofServices.pdf, accessed on July 1, 2011.

Pawlisch, J.S. (2000) *The Least Restrictive Environment: Information Bulletin Update 00.04*. Available at www.dpi.state.wi.us/sped/bul00-04.html, accessed on July 12, 2011.

Pierangelo, R. and Giuliani, G. (2012) *Assessment in Special Education: A Practical Approach* (4th edition). Boston, MA: Allyn and Bacon.

State of New Mexico Department of Education (2003) *Frequently Asked Questions about Least Restrictive Environment (LRE), Placement, and Inclusion under the IDEA*. Available at www. parentsreachingout.org/resources/publications/nmped/lrefacts_nmped.pdf, accessed on July 13, 2011.

Texas Education Agency (2009) *The Least Restrictive Environment (LRE): Question and Answer Document*. Available at http://ritter.tea.state.tx.us/special.ed/stplan/9496/pdf/chap07.pdf, accessed on February 20, 2012.

Chapter 10

20 U.S.C. 1401

20 U.S.C. 1415

34 C.F.R. 300.28

34 C.F.R. 300.30

34 C.F.R. 300.41

34 C.F.R. 300.151

34 C.F.R. 300.152

34 C.F.R. 300.153

34 C.F.R. 300.307

34 C.F.R. 300.324

34 C.F.R. 300.506

34 C.F.R. 300.507

34 C.F.R. 300.508

34 C.F.R. 300.509

34 C.F.R. 300.510

34 C.F.R. 300.511

34 C.F.R. 300.512

34 C.F.R. 300.513

34 C.F.R. 300.514

34 C.F.R. 300.515

34 C.F.R. 300.516

34 C.F.R. 300.517

34 C.F.R. 300.518

34 C.F.R. 300.520

71 Fed. Reg. 46,606 (Aug. 1, 2006).

Assistance to States for the Education of Children with Disabilities and Preschool Grants for Children with Disabilities (2006) *Final Rule, 71 Fed. Reg. 46540* (codified at 34 C.F.R. pt.300). Available at http://idea.ed.gov, accessed on February 27, 2012.

CADRE (2007) *From Regulation to Resolution: Emerging Practices in Special Education Dispute Resolution. A Presentation at the OSEP Regional Implementation Meetings in Washington, DC; Los Angeles, CA; and Kansas City, MO.* Available at www.directionservice.org/cadre/rim.cfm, accessed on August 11, 2011.

Conflict Resolution Program (2011) *IEP Meeting Facilitation Services.* Available at www.ipa.udel.edu/crp/IEPfacilservices.pdf, accessed on June 15, 2011.

Consortium for Appropriate Dispute Resolution in Special Education (2011) *Facilitated IEP Meetings: An Emerging Practice.* Available at www.parentcenternetwork.org/assets/files/national/Facilitated%20IEP.pdf, accessed on June 18, 2011.

Consortium for Appropriate Dispute Resolution in Special Education and Technical Assistance: ALLIANCE for Parent Centers (2008) *Resolution Meetings: A Guide for Parents.* Available at www.directionservice.org/cadre/pdf/Resolution%20Meetings%20-%20A%20Guide%20for%20Parents%20-%20Rev%20June%202008.pdf, accessed on February 20, 2012.

Disability Rights Education and Defense Fund (2008) *A Guide for California Parents: Special Education Due Process and the Resolution Meeting.* Available at www.dredf.org/special_education/dueprocess.pdf, accessed on June 3, 2011.

Maryland State Department of Education, Division of Special Education/Early Intervention Services (2011) *A Parent's Guide to Frequently Asked Questions about Special Education* State Complaints. Available at www.marylandpublicschools.org/MSDE/divisions/earlyinterv/complaint_investigation, accessed on February 20, 2012.

Maryland State Department of Education, Division of Special Education/Early Intervention Services (2007) *Facilitated IEP Team Meetings in Maryland.* Available at www.marylandpublicschools.org/NR/rdonlyres/5F4F5041-02EE-4F3A-B495-5E4B3C850D3E/13899/FacilitatedIEPMeetingFAQ.pdf, accessed on June 18, 2011.

Minnesota Special Education Mediation Service (2011) Questions and Answers about a Facilitated Individual Education Plan (IEP)/Independent Interagency Intervention Plan (IIIP)/Individual Family Service Plan (IFSP). Available at http://education.state.mn.us/MDE/SchSup/SpecEdComp/ComplMonitor/AltDispRes/index.html, accessed on February 20, 2012.

National Dissemination Center for Children with Disabilities (2010a) *Informal Approaches to Resolving Disputes.* Available at http://nichcy.org/schoolage/disputes/informal, accessed on June 11, 2011.

National Dissemination Center for Children with Disabilities (2010b) *Filing a State Complaint.* Available at http://nichcy.org/schoolage/disputes/statecomplaint, accessed on June 3, 2011.

National Dissemination Center for Children with Disabilities (2010c) *Mediation.* Available at http://nichcy.org/schoolage/disputes/mediation, accessed on June 3, 2011.

New Mexico Public Education Department, Special Education Bureau (2006) *The Facilitated IEP Meeting: Fact Sheet.* Available at www.ped.state.nm.us/seo/dispute/FIEP%20HANDOUT.pdf, accessed on June 22, 2011.

North Dakota Department of Instruction (2011) *Due Process Hearing and Resolution Meeting.* Available at www.dpi.state.nd.us/speced/resource/conflict/dueprocess.pdf, accessed on June 5, 2011.

Partners Resources Network, Inc. (2011) *Resolution Meetings: A Guide for Parents.* Available at www.partnerstx.org/PDF/Resolution_Meetings_Guide_for_Parents.pdf, accessed on June 12, 2011.

Schaffer v. Weast, 546 U.S. (2005).

State Education Department of New York Office of Vocational and Educational Services for Individuals with Disabilities (2001) *Special Education Mediation: Real Solutions Where Everyone Wins.* Albany, NY: University of the State of New York.

U.S. Department of Education (2009) *Questions and Answers on Procedural Safeguards and Due Process Procedures for Parents and Children with Disabilities (Revised June 2009).* Washington, DC: Author. Available at http://idea.ed.gov/explore/view/p/,root,dynamic,QaCorner,6 accessed on February 27, 2012.

U.S. House of Representatives Committee on Education and the Workforce (2005) *Individuals with Disabilities Education Act (IDEA): Guide to Frequently Asked Questions.* Available at www.doe.in.gov/exceptional/speced/docs/idea_faq.pdf, accessed on August 11, 2011.

Utah Department of Education (2011) *Frequently Asked Questions about Special Education Formal IDEA State Complaints.* Available at www.schools.utah.gov/sars/DOCS/law/faqfideascomplaints.aspx, accessed on August 12, 2011.

Wisconsin Special Education Mediation System (2011) *The Resolution Meeting: A Guide for Parents and Educators.* Available at www.wsems.us/resmeeeting/resmeet.html, accessed on June 1, 2011.

Chapter 11

18 U.S.C. 930

20 U.S.C. 1412

20 U.S.C. 1415

21 U.S.C. 812

34 C.F.R. 300.101

34 C.F.R. 300.153

34 C.F.R. 300.300

34 C.F.R. 300.502

34 C.F.R. 300.503

34 C.F.R 300.504

34 C.F.R. 300.506

34 C.F.R. 300.511

34 C.F.R. 300.530

34 C.F.R. 300.531

34 C.F.R. 300.532

34 C.F.R. 300.534

34 C.F.R. 300.535

34 C.F.R. 300.536

Gindis, B. (2006) *Know Your Rights: Disability Manifestation Determination for Your Child.* Available at www.adoptionarticlesdirectory.com/Article/Know-Your-Rights--Disability-Manifestation-Determination-for-Your-Child/416, accessed on June 16, 2011.

Mills v. Board of Education of District of Columbia, 348 Supp. 866, C.D. DC (1972).

Office of Special Education and Rehabilitative Services (1999) *Discipline for Children with Disabilities: Questions and Answers from OSEP.* Available at http://wrightslaw.com/advoc/articles/discipline_faqs_osep.htm, accessed on May 28, 2011.

Pierangelo, R. and Giuliani, G. (2008) *Assessment in Special Education: A Practical Approach* (3rd edition). Boston: Allyn and Bacon.

Chapter 12

20 U.S.C. 1232

20 U.S.C. 1412

20 U.S.C. 1415

20 U.S.C. 1417

34 C.F.R. 99.31

34 C.F.R. 300.32

34 C.F.R. 300.611

34 C.F.R. 300.612

34 C.F.R. 300.613

34 C.F.R. 300.614

34 C.F.R. 300.615

34 C.F.R. 300.616

34 C.F.R. 300.617

34 C.F.R. 300.618

34 C.F.R. 300.619

34 C.F.R. 300.620

34 C.F.R. 300.621

34 C.F.R 300.622

34 C.F.R. 300.623

34 C.F.R. 300.624

34 C.F.R. 300.625

U.S. Department of Education (2011) *Family Education Rights and Privacy Act.* Available at www2. ed.gov/policy/gen/guid/fpco/ferpa/index.html, accessed on August 2, 2011.

Van Dusen, W.R., Jr. (2004) *FERPA: Basic Guidelines for Faculty and Staff: A Simple Step-by-Step Approach for Compliance.* Available from the *NACADA Clearinghouse of Academic Advising Resources* website: hwww.nacada.ksu.edu/Resources/FERPA-Overview.htm, accessed on July 2, 2011.

Chapter 13

20 U.S.C. 1401

20 U.S.C. 1432

20 U.S.C. 1436

34 C.F.R. 300.25

34 C.F.R. 303.16

34 C.F.R. 303.340

34 C.F.R. 303.342

34 C.F.R. 303.343

34 C.F.R. 303.344

34 C.F.R. 303.345

34 C.F.R. 303.346

34 C.F.R. 303.403

34 C.F.R. 303.404

34 C.F.R. 303.405

Alabama State Department of Education (2002) *Services for Alabama's Children with Disabilities: Ages Birth through 5.* Available at ftp://ftp.alsde.edu/documents/65/HANDBOOK.pdf, accessed on January 12, 2012.

California Department of Developmental Services (2006) *What is Early Start?* Available at www. disabilityrightsca.org/pubs/F01601.pdf, accessed on February 27, 2012.

Georgia Department of Health (2011). *Individualized Family Service Plan.* Available at http:// health.state.ga.us/pdfs/bcw/IFSP%20policy%20draft.pdf, accessed on June 10, 2011.

Maryland State Department of Education (2003) *Program Overview.* Available at www. marylandpublicschools.org/MSDE/programs/esea/, accessed on June 15, 2011.

National Dissemination Center for Children and Youth with Disabilities (2005) *Finding Help for Young Children with Disabilities (Birth–5).* Available at www.nichcy.org/pubs/parent/pa2txt. htm, accessed on June 15, 2011.

Pierangelo, R. and Giuliani, G. (2007) *EDM: The Educator's Diagnostic Manual of Disabilities and Disorders.* San Francisco, CA: Jossey Bass.

Pierangelo, R. and Giuliani, G. (2008) *Assessment in Special Education: A Practical Approach* (3rd edition). Boston, MA: Allyn and Bacon.

U.S. Department of Education (2011) *Supporting Individuals with Disabilities.* Available at www2. ed.gov/about/overview/budget/budget12/crosscuttingissues/indivdisabilities.pdf, accessed on June 18, 2011.

Chapter 14

34 C.F.R. 104.3

34 C.F.R. 104.35

Birthinjury.org (2011) *Section 504 Plans*. Available at www.birthinjury.org/government-services-section504-plans.html, accessed on July 20, 2011.

Campbell, G. (2011) *Section 504*. Available at www.gwencampbelladvocate.com/section-504.html, accessed on July 18, 2011.

Chambersburg School District (2011) *Section 504: Frequently Asked Questions and Answers*. Available at http://chambersburg.k12.pa.us/education/components/faq/faq.php?sectiondetailid=25909&&PHPSESSID=252ecf9f9e18bb5858edce1679be750a, accessed on August 1, 2011.

Council Bluffs Community School District (2011) *Section 504 Eligibility*. Available at www.council-bluffs.k12.ia.us/stu_serv/Section%20504-Eligibility.pdf, accessed on July 3, 2011.

Giordano, K. (2011) *504 Plan Eligibility: Fact Sheet*. Available at www.tsa-usa.org/bnewmedia/TSAEducatCommitteeJan2010/lib/playback.html, accessed on February 20, 2012.

Lewis, R. (2011) *Overview of Section 504 of the Rehabilitation Act of 1973*. Available at www.docstoc.com/docs/69968448/Eef-Employment-Guide, accessed on August 2, 2011.

Menlo Park City School District (2011) *Section 504: Frequently Asked Questions*. Available at http://504-plans.district.mpcsd.org/modules/locker/files/get_group_file.phtml?fid=10312866&gid=2251945&sessionid=12dbbe86c4b0c785b94c454c6351cb79, accessed on August 2, 2011.

Mesa Public Schools (2009) *Section 504 of the Rehabilitation Act of 1973*. Available at www.mpsaz.org/ssc/504/files/504_manual_2010_rev_7-1-2010.pdf, accessed on August 2, 2011.

New Mexico Public Education Department (2011) *New Mexico Section 504 Training*. Available at www.ped.state.nm.us/rti/dl10/504%20Tip%20Sheet.Evaluation.pdf, accessed on July 1, 2011.

Nomura, J. (2011) *Section 504*. Available at http://johnnomura.com/Resources-%7C-Mental-Health-%7C-Special-Education/about-504/Evaluation.html, accessed on July 10, 2011.

Northwest Area Education Agency (2011) *Section 504: Protecting Students with Disabilities*. Available at www.nwaea.k12.ia.us/index.cfm?nodeID=26589&articleid=1543&action=dspDetail, accessed on July 9, 2011.

Portland Schools (2011) *Section 504: Frequently Asked Questions*. Available at www.portlandschools.org/pages/SpecServ/documents/FAQ504staffAugust%2008.pdf, accessed on July 18, 2011.

Region XIII Education Service Center (2011) *Section 504: Introduction*. Available at www5.esc13.net/section504/faq.html, accessed on June 30, 2011.

San Mateo County Office of Education (2011) *Section 504 Guidance*. Available at www.smcoe.k12.ca.us/StudentServicesDivision/SELPA/Documents/SELPA_Forms/localplan.pdf, accessed on February 20, 2012.

School District of Reedsburg (2008) *Section 504 of the Rehabilitation Act of 1973: Handbook*. Available at www.rsd.k12.wi.us/pupilservices/Reedsburg_504_Handbook_08_04_2008.pdf, accessed on July 20, 2011.

Tucson Unified School District (2010) *Section 504 Handbook*. Tucson, AZ: Government Programs and Community Outreach Office.

U.S. Department of Education (2010) *Free Appropriate Public Education for Students with Disabilities: Requirements under Section 504 of The Rehabilitation Act of 1973.* Available at www2.ed.gov/about/offices/list/ocr/docs/edlite-FAPE504.html, accessed on July 8, 2011.

Walsh, J. and Gallegos, E. (2009) *Congress Amends the ADA and Section 504: The Impact on Student Services.* Available at http://special-programs.tisd.org/modules/locker/files/get_group_file. phtml?gid=1292421&fid=4471476&sessionid=1c1dda852042fd506195a636f8a301d2, accessed on August 16, 2011.

Watertown Public Schools (2011) *Civil Rights: Section 504 of the Rehabilitation Act of 1973.* Available at www.watertown.k12.ma.us/dept/personnel/504.html, accessed on July 6, 2011.

Weatherly, J.J. (2011) *Section 504 Eligibility: Keeping Current with Cases, Trends and the ADAAA.* Available at www.schools.utah.gov/sars/DOCS/disability/504elig.aspx, accessed on July 23, 2011.

Wilmette Public Schools (2011) *Understanding Section 504 Plans.* Available at www.wilmette39. org/index.php?option=com_content&view=article&id=765:understanding-section-504-plans&catid=440&Itemid=861, accessed on July 1, 2011.

Index